T0386745

The OCEAN

THE ULTIMATE HANDBOOK OF NAUTICAL KNOWLEDGE

CHRIS DIXON & JEREMY K. SPENCER

CHRONICLE BOOKS
SAN FRANCISCO

The Sun came up upon the left,

Out of the sea came he!

And he shone bright, and on the right

Went down into the sea.

—Samuel Taylor Coleridge, "The Rime of the Ancient Mariner"

Library of Congress Cataloging-in-Publication Data

Names: Dixon, Chris, 1966- author. | Spencer, Jeremy K., author.

Title: The ocean : the ultimate handbook of nautical knowledge / Chris Dixon and Jeremy K. Spencer.

Description: San Francisco : Chronicle Books, [2021].

Identifiers: LCCN 2020048131 | ISBN 9781452158662 (hardcover)

Subjects: LCSH: Aquatic sports. | Boats and boating. | Diving. | Surfing. | Swimming.

Classification: LCC GV775 .D58 2021 | DDC 797—dc23

LC record available at https://lccn.loc.gov/2020048131

Manufactured in Thailand.

Design: Jon Glick.

10 9 8 7 6 5 4 3 2

Chronicle Books LLC
680 Second Street
San Francisco, California 94107
www.chroniclebooks.com

Chronicle books and gift products are available at special quantity discounts to corporations, professional associations, literacy programs, and other organizations. For details and discount information, please contact our premiums department at corporatesales@chroniclebooks.com or at 1-800-759-0190.

BOATING 1

SURFING 87

SCIENCE 141

SURVIVAL 191

SCUBA AND SNORKELING 259

FISHING 297

INTRODUCTION

A few years back, on a bluebird day in Folly Beach, South Carolina, we walked into local favorite the Lost Dog Café and, notebooks in hand, ordered a couple of beers. It was early spring, the best days of the year were ahead of us, and we were intent on laying the groundwork for a new project. We wanted to create something we'd gone looking for but had never found: one of those books that might be considered *the one*. You know the kind. It's the first book that comes to mind when you need a gift for a friend with a particular passion. Think Julia Child's *Mastering the Art of French Cooking* for ambitious home chefs. Or Dale Carnegie's *How to Win Friends & Influence People* for determined business types.

Our subject? The ocean, of course. So we got to talking about all the maritime lessons passed along by family and friends, all the insights gleaned from natural experts we'd met on our respective watery adventures and journalistic endeavors around the world. We also recognized, as we discussed how much we'd learned about the all-important ocean over the years, that there was so much more that we didn't know. As fathers with children who joined us on the waves and on deck, that was kind of a problem. When one of your kids asks you a question or wants to learn how to do something, it feels great to share the answer with them in a way that cracks the world's mysteries open, even if just a little bit.

We decided that whatever we didn't know, we'd learn from the best. And then we'd pass all that knowledge along to our loved ones—and you. But we had to go even further, confirming what we did know (or thought we knew). As we drew up a skeletal plan of attack and hashed out our approach and dream collaborators, Chris relayed a recent conversation with his surfing buddy Jimmy Buffett, the famously salty bard of the sun-soaked life. One day, after a long morning among the swells, they'd sat right at that very bar and caught up. Between spoonfuls of steaming shrimp and grits, Chris brought up the idea we'd been kicking around.

"We're thinking of it as Poseidon's bible," he said, "a guide to all things ocean that'll be fun to read in a hammock strung between two palm trees—but will also help save your ass in a pinch."

Jimmy gave a chuckle, nodded sagely, and said, "The stuff you only really learn from time on the water." He then unspooled a veritable who's who of fishing guides, sailors, and surfers he'd learned from over the years (several of whom you'll find in these pages). "When I was a kid," he added, "I learned so much from this book called *The Sea Scout Handbook*." He described a manual packed with instruction on knots, navigating, fishing, and more. And sure enough, a timeworn 1962 edition of that book ended up being one of our many inspirations.

Since that first day at Folly Beach, we've spent thousands of hours researching and reporting the book you now hold in your hands, an unrivaled compendium of timeless oceanic knowledge—covering everything from ancient skills to cutting-edge science. Within these pages you'll learn how to catch a wave, spot and rescue a drowning person, cast a fly rod and a net, properly treat jellyfish stings, deal with heavy surf, recognize and reverse hypothermia, sail a boat, rig an emergency fishhook, clear a diving mask, and on and on. In short, we've tapped the greatest maritime minds to provide smart and concise master classes for every sea-besotted soul.

Here at the end of our voyage, yours begins: *The Ocean* has exceeded our vision, and we're thrilled to see it in your hands. It's a treasure chest of skills, scholarship, science, and seamanship given to all of us by a bunch of amazing people all the watery world over. We hope it will empower you with hard-won wisdom, introduce you to a crew of remarkable minds, crack open a few mysteries, and maybe even save your life.

Because, as legendary marine archaeologist Robert Ballard told us, "The ocean is the answer. Without it, we're toast."

—Chris Dixon & Jeremy K. Spencer

BOATING

THINGS A COAST GUARD RESCUE SWIMMER HAS ALWAYS WANTED TO SAY

AS TOLD BY SHANNON SCAFF,
a veteran United States Coast Guard (USCG) rescue swimmer and recipient of the distinguished flying cross.

I enlisted in the Coast Guard in 1993—specifically for the position of aviation survival man or helicopter rescue swimmer. I've always had a love of aviation and the ocean. What better way to combine those than to find yourself in the doorway of a helicopter during an air-sea rescue?

Three years into that, I was involved in a search-and-rescue case at the small boat station in Chestertown, Maryland. Two boats were in distress, foundering in nasty weather. The call came in at 2 a.m., as they normally do, and I was shimmying down a ladder. Just like that, my finger got caught in the ladder's handrail and tore right off. So I learned—literally firsthand—how quickly things in the maritime environment go from bad to worse to life-threatening.

My first day as a helicopter rescue swimmer, I was on a Greek container ship rescuing the wife of the chief engineer, who'd suffered a miscarriage. She was six flights up in the superstructure, and I had to get her down those stairs. She was bleeding to death. Ash gray. I remember thinking, *Wow, they didn't train me for this.* It just shows why rescue swimmer is one of the most challenging training programs in the US military arsenal. You have to be ready for a high-stress environment. You have to adapt and overcome. After that experience, it became the running joke: Well, Scaff's on duty, I guess the shit's gonna hit the fan.

The reality is that anytime you're out on the water, it's inherently dangerous. First, it sounds simple, but make a solid plan and stick to it. Say you're just going out fishing. Have a plan and voice your plan, so that somebody who cares about you knows your plan. That alone is of tremendous value, because if something bad happens, the first person who is going to call us is that person.

Other simple stuff. The radio. We understand that we're going to get calls from the newest of the new to the saltiest of the salty. We don't get wrapped around the axle about technical stuff. We're more interested in you passing along the information we need because time is of the essence. What should you pass along? Location and number of souls. Click. Done.

What have you just done? One: You've narrowed our search range from 50 square miles—the transmitting range of your radio—to a single square mile. And two: You've told us how big a rescue we need to launch. Basically, you've taken the search out of search-and-rescue.

Communication. Have multiple kinds. If you don't have flares, if you don't have a radio, a cell phone, a strobe light, a life raft—what have you done? You've stacked the deck against yourself. Every maritime store sells personal locator beacons. Put one on. It's a couple hundred bucks, but it sure beats drifting in the ocean for three days holding on to a cooler.

If you use a flare, use common sense. Don't blow them off all at once, and please do not shoot them directly at our helicopter. Our night-vision goggles are very sensitive. We'll see a flare from a country mile. But any light source—a lighter, a flashlight—is going to help.

Check the weather before you go out. You're the captain; that's your responsibility. Wear your life jackets, and don't drink and boat. What if you break down? It sounds cliché, it's not rocket science, but this stuff matters.

Of course, go out and have a good time. But know the rules of the road, and have respect for the environment you're in.

MAU PIAILUG: THE MAN WHO RESTORED WAYFINDING

AS TOLD BY BRUCE BLANKENFELD,
master navigator and captain of the Polynesian voyaging canoe *Hōkūleʻa*.

The Polynesian voyaging vessel *Hōkūleʻa*'s first epic journey to Tahiti happened in 1976. Pius "Mau" Piailug was the navigator, and he sailed 2,500 miles using only ancient navigation. At the time, it was such a radical idea, beyond comprehension. It proved Ben Finney's hypothesis that Polynesia was settled not by luck, sailing only downwind or being blown off course, but by skilled navigators.

MAU PIAILUG: THE NAVIGATOR

Mau was the last of the true Pacific Island navigators. He was born in the Caroline Islands in Micronesia on a tiny atoll called Satawal in a society that was pretty much unchanged for over a thousand years. He lived in an ocean world where people relied on themselves and their own culture—until World War II when the Japanese overran the islands, and then American missionaries came. After that, their world changed forever.

The Pacific Islanders—their way of learning was different. They were such keen observers of their environment. Whatever part of cultural life you were part of—shipbuilder, fisherman, craftsman, whatever—that was taught by master to apprentice. That knowledge was steeped in spirituality—science and spirituality were completely intertwined—and this wisdom was a thousand years old. Navigators like Mau started learning at two, three, four—usually from a father, grandfather, or uncle. Every day was a lesson.

When Mau was young, the men headed out in boats to fish every day. The women took care of things on the land. Mau was among the last of this long lineage, bearing a terrifically unique connection to ancient oceanic wisdom, navigation, and subsistence.

Mau's people passed their knowledge down through recitation and chanting of all these star lines and voyaging paths—ancient stuff, all the things you had to remember. Navigating—it's knowing where you came from and having an idea of where you're going.

Instead of a chart, you have this reference course—a line you're going to sail. You mainly use the sun and swell patterns to keep your course by day, and the stars to hold your course at night. If you deviate from that course, you have to track how far you've deviated, but you don't have an instrument to mark your position on a chart. The whole thing is so organic. Your mind is the instrument.

That's where seabirds and ocean swells and currents come in—a concept called expanded landfall. Polynesia has low-lying, small islands all over the place. The refraction and bending of the waves is part of that roadmap that shows where the islands are. You can't necessarily see an island, especially a low one, but you see a sign—a change in the sea, a seabird flying toward land. It's unbelievable.

THE POLYNESIAN VOYAGING SOCIETY

In 1973, anthropologist Ben Finney and Herb Kāne, an artist and sailor, cofounded the Polynesian Voyaging Society (PVS). The goal was to build a traditional open-water Polynesian voyaging vessel and prove the awe-inspiring precision of Polynesian navigation and seafaring. I was in high school when the *Hōkūle'a* project began. The crew included Nainoa Thompson, who today is our lead navigator and the PVS president, and Buffalo Keaulana, a famous Hawaiian lifeguard.

Hōkūle'a's first epic journey to Tahiti happened in 1976. The first time I sailed on *Hōkūle'a* was after she returned home in 1977. Nainoa was part of our local canoe club, and we'd gone down with him to work on her—sanding, varnishing, that sort of thing. Nainoa says, "Hey, you guys want to go sailing?" It was just awesome. A beautiful day.

In 1978, I was aboard the second voyage to Tahiti when *Hōkūle'a* capsized off Lanai, and one of our crew, famous big-wave surfer Eddie Aikau, disappeared after attempting to paddle a surfboard for help. We were attempting that journey without a master sailor—without all of Mau's knowledge—and the accident was the result. Afterward, Nainoa traveled to Satawal to convince Mau to come back to Hawaii. Mau had gotten word of the accident. He told Nainoa, "Maybe I'll come back so we don't lose any more people at sea."

You have to understand the importance of Mau's decision. The nature of his knowledge—it's sacred. For him to go off the island to teach a group of people entirely unrelated to him—everybody on Satawal was kind of gasping, like, "Really?" He caught a lot of grief, but he told them, "You guys are blind. Don't you see our knowledge base is dying on the vine? Nobody is learning navigation anymore, and these Hawaiians are hungry to learn. They're going to sail."

So Mau came back to Hawaii to help with the navigation apprenticeships. We'd ask questions, of course, but until you sail that first day, you really know nothing. Mau's awareness was so keen on every little thing that was going on. The wind, the swells, the squalls coming from miles away, the texture of the ocean's surface. Then his response—"Okay, close the sails, change course." It's a sixth sense.

In 1992, I was serving as an apprentice on a voyage that took us to Rarotonga. I had studied for two years with Nainoa, but on that voyage, I remember going to sleep under the stars one night and waking up an hour later with a feeling of déjà vu. The sky was as I had seen it in a dream. It was on that journey that I finally looked at the sea and sky and saw the pathway home.

RENAISSANCE OF POLYNESIAN CULTURE

When we sailed *Hōkūle'a* to New Zealand and back in 1985, the native Maori just couldn't believe it. They have an ancient voyaging history—and still know the name of the canoes, the navigators, the chiefs who first reached New Zealand. We made such a cultural connection, and today, they have their own canoes and a tremendous traditional voyaging community.

We sailed to Rapa Nui—Easter Island—in 1999 and planted seeds. In two weeks, we have four people coming from Easter Island to Hawaii to train and learn. Nainoa has this vision of navigational schools all across the Pacific Islands.

When I sailed to Satawal in 2007, five of us were honored by Mau and other islanders and pronounced *pwo*, navigators. Mau was set free to teach us. Today, Mau's youngest son, Sesario, is a captain and teaches navigation with the university on Palau.

We've been in this wonderful renaissance of Pacific Island and Hawaiian culture since the 1970s, and we're only scratching the surface. The idea with *Hōkūle'a* is to learn our culture by practicing it, then to get out of the realm of practice and into the realm of living it.

If we hadn't found Mau, all those generations of wisdom would have been lost. Had our crew only sailed to Tahiti and back, had Mau not agreed to teach us, how much would we really have learned? None of this would be taught in schools today. How can you measure Mau's gift? You can't.

PUEO: horn for tricing lines and halyards

KIA MUA: forward mast

KAULA PA'A: stays and shrouds (lines holding the mast up)

PALE WAI OR PALE KAI: splashguard

MANU IHU: bow endpiece

ĀKEA: starboard hull

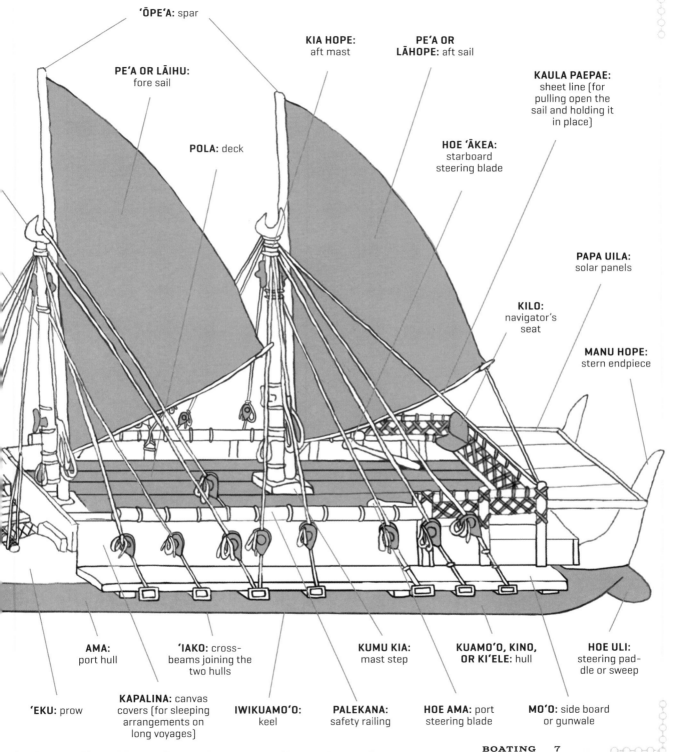

'ŌPE'A: spar

PE'A OR LĀIHU: fore sail

KIA HOPE: aft mast

PE'A OR LĀHOPE: aft sail

KAULA PAEPAE: sheet line (for pulling open the sail and holding it in place)

POLA: deck

HOE 'ĀKEA: starboard steering blade

PAPA UILA: solar panels

KILO: navigator's seat

MANU HOPE: stern endpiece

AMA: port hull

'IAKO: cross-beams joining the two hulls

KUMU KIA: mast step

KUAMO'O, KINO, OR KI'ELE: hull

HOE ULI: steering paddle or sweep

'EKU: prow

KAPALINA: canvas covers (for sleeping arrangements on long voyages)

IWIKUAMO'O: keel

PALEKANA: safety railing

HOE AMA: port steering blade

MO'O: side board or gunwale

START (AND STOP) A MUTINY

Frivolous floggings, meager rations, one too many maggot-ridden suppers doled out by a hoggish, draconian captain—the reasons are many for why a crew might mutiny. Here's what you need to succeed:

STARTING A MUTINY

- Have more crew, or at least more arms, on your side. You must outnumber the ship's officers.

- Get as many superiors as possible on your side—engineers, tacticians, and anyone who could hinder the mutiny.

- Cordon off or imprison non-mutinous officers.

- Be willing to fight to the death. If your mutiny doesn't succeed, and you don't die, you'll end up wishing you had.

STOPPING A MUTINY

Prevent a mutiny by demonstrating kindness, fairness, and generosity to your crew—keep them fat, drunk, and happy. Allow companions aboard and keep morale high; loneliness and frustration foment unrest. Also, keep your ship's location and course a secret. That way, potential mutineers might think twice, knowing they mightn't get back to port. That is, unless they have GPS.

What if you're bound and chained in your quarters as your mutinous crew ravages the ship's stores and hollers *jibe-o*, which means they've turned the vessel back toward the tropics, where desertion and bacchanalian debauchery will commence? By then, you can't beat them, so there's nothing left to do but join them.

FUN FACT: The term *strike*, as in the refusal to work as a means of protest, apparently derived from the call to "strike" (or lower) the ship's sails when the crew wasn't cooperating. This kept the ship from going anywhere until the dispute was settled.

NAUTICAL SUPERSTITIONS

Our salty forebears devised all manner of superstitions to make sense of the perils they faced. Most are considered little more than briny lore, but a few may yet hold water.

If you spot a rat abandoning a docked ship, mayhap that rat has the gift of prophecy.

Cast thine bananas overboard.
This is rooted in some historical fact. Banana bunches harbored biting spiders, and ships hauling them tended to hurry to avoid spoilage. Their captains might thus take prodigious risks to reach the market on time.

Never harm a swallow, seagull, or albatross, for they bear the souls of lost fishermen and bring luck.
Squawks and shrieks have long warned mariners of land looming from the fog. Hovering hunts above schools of fish have long pointed fishermen toward bountiful harvests.

Sunday sail, never fail. Friday sail, ill luck and gale.
Friday was widely assumed to be the day of Jesus's crucifixion. A Thursday (Thor's Day) departure would put you in the sights of the God of Thunder. Being the Sabbath, Sunday was considered a good day to set sail, even if the captain was a godless heathen.

What a ship is christened, so let her stay.
Once a ship is named, she develops her own personality, and according to nautical lore, she won't cotton to having her name changed.

Pass salt, pass sorrow.
When referring to salt at the galley table, call it "the white stuff." And never pass it by hand; set it upon the table for your crewmate to pick up. Throwing salt on a fisherman, however, is said to bring them luck.

Women were once considered bad luck at sea, unless unclad.
Hence the nearly naked female figureheads on the bow of sailing ships. There, they could "shame the seas to calm."

Don't "whistle up a storm."
If you whistle at sea, be sure not to do it into the wind.

Never call a line a "rope."
You'll summon the spirits of those hanged at sea.

Avoid the luck o' the Irish.
Redheads at sea are considered bad luck. Yet this can be allayed if you greet the redhead before they greet you.

Stir with a knife, stir up strife.
Stir your coffee or tea with a spoon, never a knife or fork.

Don't cry out or wave to your love as they set off for the ship.
A wave might wash them overboard.

Saint Christopher protect us.
This saint is said to have carried Jesus across a dangerous river, earning him renown as the patron saint of mariners. Many still wear his pendant today.

Red sky in the morning, sailors take warning. Red sky at night, sailor's delight.
If sunrise brings a red sky to the west, the rising sun is shining on the dust and clouds of an approaching front (weather generally moves eastward). If the sky is red to the east at sunset, high pressure and fine weather are chasing the clouds away.

Put the right foot forward.
Stepping onto a boat left foot first is a bad omen.

Never say "drown."
Lest ye bring it on.

Dolphins swimming with your ship bode good luck.
Sharks, not so much.

Ne'er count the miles ye've sailed till ye reach port.
You're not there yet.

"WONDERFULLY, ESSENTIALLY HUMAN"
A CHAT WITH CHRISTIAN BEAMISH

In 2009, fisherman, big-wave surfer, mariner, and father Christian Beamish sailed down the coast of Baja in an 18-foot hand-built wooden sailing skiff. His 2012 book *Voyage of the Cormorant* describes that epic journey.

ON OCEAN TIME

Ocean time is a different kind of time. You won't make your scheduled appointment traveling by water—unless your craft is so big and imposing that you lose any sense of being on the water—particularly traveling by sail. Of course, the feeling of arriving somewhere—like a beautiful island or an inaccessible coast—by sail and oar is incomparable and connects to the long lineage of human experience.

ON THE OCEAN AS WILDERNESS

The ocean is absolutely a wilderness, but there are few places where the waste stream of humanity does not reach. I think we are just realizing that, as a species, we have thoroughly inundated the world. Industrialization is a bitch, culturally and environmentally. However, in the same way that indigenous cultures have taken such abuse yet still exist, the natural world remains.

ON THE VALUE OF LIFE AS A SEAFARER

As the people of the Pacific traveled to and fro across the island chains, other people also made great sea voyages—the Basques, the Norsemen, the sailing monks of Ireland in their skin-and-frame boats. The sailors of Africa and Arabia traveled and traded widely. It's wonderfully and essentially human to travel by the sea. We are born to it, created for it.

The opportunity to reconnect with regional cultures is reason enough to continue traditional ocean travel. I would like to see communities come together to sponsor their youth in building traditional craft and learning to sail, then sending them on voyages as emissaries of good will and cultural exchange.

I have such great admiration for the Polynesian Voyaging Society for showing the world that the traditions of wayfinding are not only viable but essential to who we are as people on this extraordinary planet.

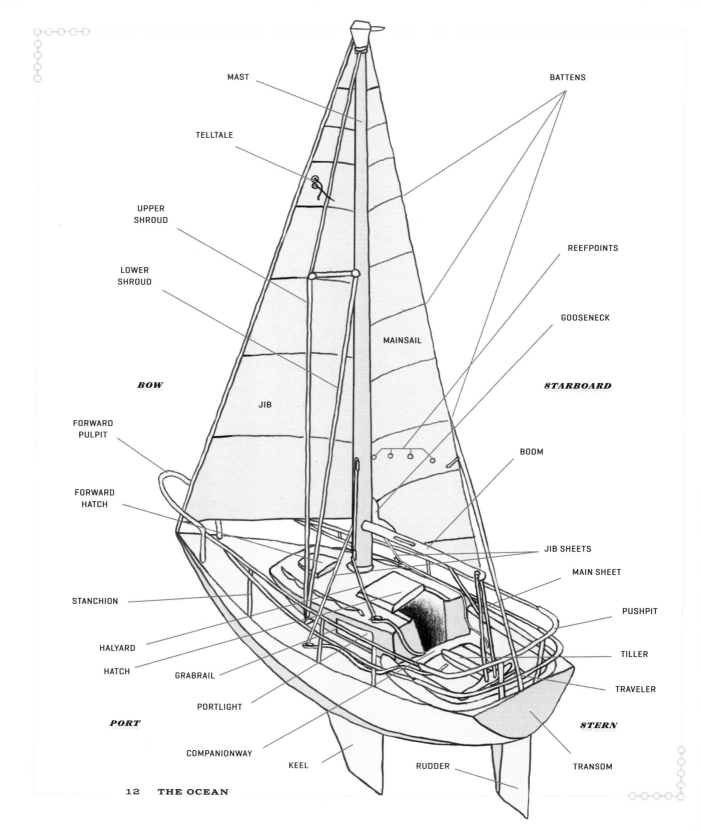

MAST

BATTENS

TELLTALE

UPPER
SHROUD

REEFPOINTS

LOWER
SHROUD

GOOSENECK

MAINSAIL

BOW

STARBOARD

JIB

FORWARD
PULPIT

BOOM

FORWARD
HATCH

JIB SHEETS

MAIN SHEET

STANCHION

PUSHPIT

HALYARD

TILLER

HATCH

GRABRAIL

TRAVELER

PORTLIGHT

PORT

STERN

COMPANIONWAY

KEEL

RUDDER

TRANSOM

You can't learn to sail from a book. But a book *can* describe how sailboats and sailing work. These are the basics. The rest is up to you.

ANATOMY OF A SAILBOAT

The four quadrants on the deck of any boat are the bow, the stern, starboard (right), and port (left). However, a sailing vessel in motion is always described in reference to the wind: windward, or the side facing the wind; leeward, or the side facing away from the wind; ahead, or in front of the bow; and astern, or behind the stern.

On the modern sloop—by far the most popular recreational sailing design—there are usually two sails, which can also be called sheets: a mainsail, which hangs between the mast and the boom, and a foresail (a large genoa or smaller jib), which hangs from the forestay.

HOW SAILING WORKS:
POINTS OF SAIL AND TRIM

Awareness of wind direction is the single most important piece of knowledge aboard a sailboat. "Point of sail" refers to the point where the wind makes contact with the boat and the sails. Which way does the wind blow? Read the surface patterns on the water or hold up a wet finger—the cold side is windward.

A sail's "trim" refers to the alignment of the sail with the imaginary centerline of the boat. This is determined by the vessel's point of sail, and each trim position has its own name. A close haul, also known as being "hard on the wind," trims the sails as far in as possible, pointing the boat's bow upwind without letting the sails luff (depower and flap). A close reach has the vessel still "reaching" upwind, but the trim of the sails is relaxed, and nearly halfway out.

When the wind is behind the boat and coming over the transom, the sails are let entirely out and the vessel is *running*, or headed directly downwind. If a main and a foresail are both out, the vessel will generally have one sail brought to port and the other to starboard, opening as much sail area to the wind and generating as much speed as possible; this is called going "wing et wing" (wing and wing).

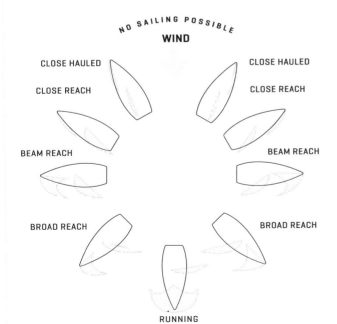

NO SAILING POSSIBLE

WIND

CLOSE HAULED   CLOSE HAULED

CLOSE REACH   CLOSE REACH

BEAM REACH   BEAM REACH

BROAD REACH   BROAD REACH

RUNNING

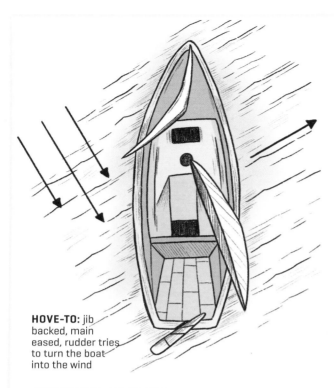

HOVE-TO: jib backed, main eased, rudder tries to turn the boat into the wind

SLOWING DOWN OR "HEAVING TO"

This important move is as old as sailing itself. If you need to slow down or bide some time in open water—say, to plot a course or use the head—a "heave to" allows a sailboat to fend for itself, more or less, by "idling" at a roughly 45-degree angle to wind and waves.

1. With the sail on a close haul, perform a tack, keeping the jib cleated.

2. As the boat tacks and the wind comes across the bow, release the mainsheet, and the boat will slow to about a quarter of its normal speed.

3. Push the tiller or helm all the way to windward and lash down.

ESSENTIAL HARDWARE AND TACKLE

Attached to each sail is a line called a halyard, which raises and trims the sails, and sheets—lines which control the moveable corners of a sail. On small sailboats, the halyard and sheet operate on a simple system of blocks (pulleys) and cleats (locks). Because of heavier loads, sails on larger boats operate through more elaborate blocks, winches, and sometimes clutches. The blocks function the same, but while on a small dinghy a mainsheet might be operated using bare hands and a cleat, a larger sail underway is too heavy for this.

If the wind is too heavy for the sails to be fully deployed to the top of the mast, they can often be reefed, or shortened.

The traveler, which is found on most larger sailboats, controls the mainsheet and the boom. It's usually located within close reach of the helm and the skipper, making single-handed sailing possible.

PRO TIP: The moment a rope is employed aboard a vessel (i.e., not coiled or otherwise idle), it is no longer called a rope; it's a *line*.

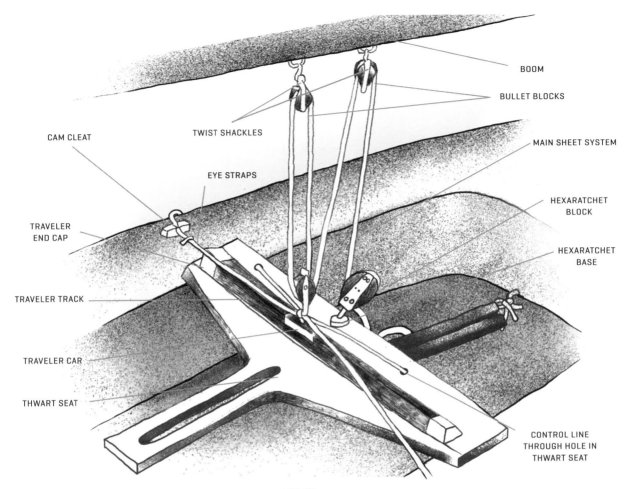

BOOM

BULLET BLOCKS

TWIST SHACKLES

CAM CLEAT

MAIN SHEET SYSTEM

EYE STRAPS

HEXARATCHET
BLOCK

TRAVELER
END CAP

HEXARATCHET
BASE

TRAVELER TRACK

TRAVELER CAR

THWART SEAT

CONTROL LINE
THROUGH HOLE IN
THWART SEAT

THE TRAVELER

SHACKLES, THIMBLES, AND OTHER BOAT HARDWARE

- Shackles are U-shaped connectors with pins used to attach sails to sheets and anchors to chains.

- Thimbles are teardrop-shaped pieces of metal that prevent chafing; placed on the ends of lines or wires.

- Turnbuckles are metal contraptions that adjust tension in rigging. The "hauling part" is the end of the line in use that bears the weight of the load.

- Mounted blocks contain one or more scored wheels (called sheaves or pulleys) that adjust the tension applied to an object (e.g., a sail sheet to the deck) and make hauling easier.

- Tackle is the term applied to blocks when combined with a line.

TAKE CARE OF YOUR BOAT

Whether you own a yacht or a dory, this wisdom will serve you in between those annual checkups with your mechanic.

- Unless your boat has a radiator-based cooling system, flush your boat's motor with freshwater after every saltwater run.

- Use ethanol-free gasoline boosted with a fuel additive called StaBil that makes gas last in your tank. If you use ethanol-blended gas, use an additive that neutralizes its effects.

- If your boat will be idle for several months, disconnect the fuel line and run the motor until it's completely out of gas to prevent old gas from damaging your fuel system.

- Protect electrical leads with a layer of grease or petroleum jelly and ensure wires are well-connected, not corroded or frayed, and insulation is solid. Main battery cables might need replacing if they become anything above "warm" after several seconds of engine cranking.

- Battery voltage should be around 12.5 with the engine off, 14 with the engine running. Batteries off-gas explosive hydrogen, so keep the battery in a ventilated spot. Maintain it by using a computer-controlled plug-in, or solar, trickle charger.

- Keep your motor's trim, tilt, and steering mechanism and all linkages well-lubricated; check hydraulic fluid annually.

- If you find oil in your bilge, wash the bilge with soapy water and pump the water out. Discharging oil into waterways is illegal, so if you're leaking oil, get it fixed.

- A clear-bottomed water-separation fuel filter lets you see if your fuel system has water and dirt in it.

- If hoses collapse easily or have soft spots, replace.

- Prevent galvanic corrosion (which occurs between dissimilar metals) by ensuring a motor's "sacrificial" zinc plugs are in good shape.

- Barnacles are the mariner's bane; they increase drag and can clog the engine and other intakes. Always trailer the boat and immediately scrape them off. Among hull-cleaning products, EZ-ON EZ-OFF Hull & Bottom Cleaner is far less toxic.

- Kill "dead fish smell" with copious amounts of 10 percent water-diluted bleach, then clean with freshwater. Keep bleach out of waterways!

Before leaving the dock, be ready should the guano hit the propeller. See also "Make a Float Plan" (page 22).

NAVIGATION AND COMMUNICATION DEVICES

Do you have the essential means for finding your way and communicating with shore? Charge batteries and ensure the following are functional and onboard:

- Up-to-date navigation charts and/or GPS software
- A mechanical compass
- A cell phone (or two) in a waterproof case
- Depthfinder
- An emergency horn and whistle
- A VHF radio and a backup VHF radio
- An emergency position-indicating radio beacon (EPIRB)

NAVIGATION LIGHTS AND VISUAL DEVICES

Just expecting a three-hour pleasure cruise? So was Gilligan. Ensure you have signal flares and/or signaling mirrors and a flashlight or lantern, and that navigation lights are working. Here are the basic navigation rules for smaller recreational craft (shorter than 39 feet).

- Lights must be on from sunset to sunrise and in low-visibility conditions (storm or fog).
- A masthead light, on the bow, must be at least 3 feet above the sidelights and visible for 2 miles.
- Sidelights must be red on the port side, green on the starboard side (to indicate boat orientation). Some boats have different light configurations; just ensure they work.
- For sailboats shorter than 21 feet, a flashlight waved or shined into the sail can suffice. Rowboats and kayaks should also have a light source.

PERSONAL FLOTATION DEVICES

In 2015, among people who drowned while boating in the United States, 85 percent were not wearing a personal flotation device (PFD). Legally, you must have a PFD on board for all passengers, and kids must wear one. Have a few throwable cushions, too.

There are six types of PFDs, but only types I though IV are USCG-approved. Make sure each person's PFD fits, especially on children. Ill-fitting PFDs can increase the chances of drowning (by sliding over your head).

Inflatables: Inflatable PFDs are among the most important aquatic safety innovations ever. They are unobtrusive and wearable all the time because they don't inflate till you need them. However, they provide far less insulation from cold water and must be tested annually.

Manual inflatables are easy to operate. To inflate, yank down on a lever to puncture a CO_2 cartridge or blow into a tube. The danger of a manual PFD is that if you're knocked unconscious, or suffer from cold shock, you may be unable to deploy.

Automatic inflatables rely on a sensor that triggers when wet or submerged. However, sometimes sensors will inflate accidentally.

Type I: Offshore life jacket. Bulky but very heavy duty, they turn most victims faceup; and float them in very rough water. Some include a spray hood to prevent the wearer from inhaling water.

Type II: Nearshore buoyant vest. The classic orange vest. Make sure to connect all straps to hold the buoyant section in place above your chest. They're adequate for calmer waters and, depending on body size, will turn some swimmers face up.

Type III: Marine buoyant device. These vests are commonly used by waterskiers and wakesurfers. Like type IIs, they are designed for calm water, comfort, and mobility, but they will not turn unconscious wearers faceup.

Type IV: Ring life buoys, buoyant cushions, and horseshoe buoys. These are USCG-approved throwable devices that do not count as life jackets. Ring buoys should have around 60 feet of line attached. Because they can be rigid, be careful throwing them—they can knock a victim out.

Type V: Special-use devices. Lots of "hybrid" devices (e.g., work vests, deck suits, kayak vests, and some inflatables) don't necessarily meet USCG specs, but they work.

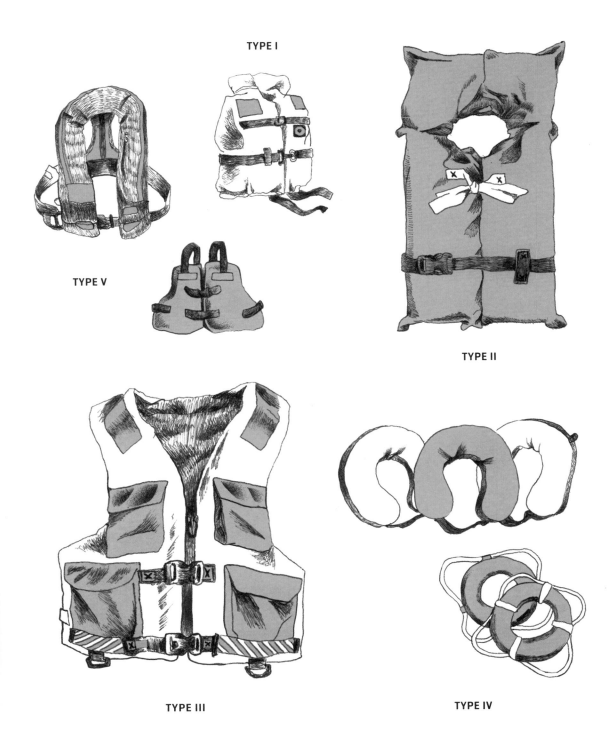

TYPE I

TYPE V

TYPE II

TYPE III

TYPE IV

FOOD AND SUPPLIES

Last but not least, make sure you have food, water, and the ability to repair damage—to people, equipment, and the boat.

- A first-aid kit (see "Ultimate Maritime First-Aid Kit," page 222)

- A toolbox and spare parts (see "Boater's Toolbox," page 21)

- Enough food and water for each person for a full day

- Sunscreen

- Foul-weather gear or rain jacket

- Sinking prevention devices: leak plugs, hand pump, bailing bucket, working bilge pump

- Smoke, carbon monoxide, and bilge-flooding detectors

- A fire extinguisher

- Oars or paddles for low-riding boats

- A full gas tank

- Anchors with nonchafed lines and nonrusty shackles (an anchor's only as strong as its weakest link)

- Plug/bung and live-well plugs installed, trailer straps off

She has no wrath to vent. Nor does she have a hand of kindness to extend. She is merely there, immense, powerful and indifferent. I do not resent her indifference, or my comparative insignificance. Indeed, it is one of the main reasons I like to sail: the sea makes the insignificance of my own small self and all of humanity so poignant.

—from *Adrift*, John Callahan

BOATER'S TOOLBOX
AKA THE "LEARN FROM OUR MISTAKES" CHECKLIST

Almost any boating website provides a solid rundown of necessary tools. Here are some space-saving options and gear we've learned we needed the hard way: after breaking down at sea.

SPACE-SAVING OPTIONS AND NECESSITIES

- Waterproof toolbox and plastic baggies for small gear
- Interchangeable magnetic screwdrivers
- Oversized flathead screwdriver for chiseling, levering, and releasing stuck parts
- Vise grip, channel lock, and needle-nose pliers
- A quality "Leatherman"-style multitool
- Electrical tape and wire-cutter/stripper

GEAR WE LEARNED TO CARRY THE HARD WAY

- Angled/bent needle-nose pliers (for tough-to-access holding jobs)
- An extension magnet (to fetch fallen screws and overboard items)
- A circuit tester/multimeter with "alligator clip" attachment wires (for hands-free electrical testing)
- Spare wire, 8-, 10-, and 14-gauge (handy in myriad ways)
- Spare kill-switch lanyard (accessible in emergencies)
- A headlamp (for hands-free working)
- A can of lithium grease or other water-resistant spray lube (for sticky trim or steering)

- Solar quick-cure fiberglass resin and quick-set epoxy (saves your hull)
- A bottle of auto transmission fluid and a mini-pump (to refill hydraulic steering and trim)
- Simple, spring-fed thumb-lock straps and zip ties (only 10 million uses)
- Wax-coated waterproof "strike anywhere" matches and a windproof lighter
- Wetsuit gloves (prevent cuts and frozen fingers)
- Duct tape and super glue (as useful on a boat as on land)
- Self-fusing silicone tape (to seal busted hoses, temporarily replace a snapped belt)
- A sheet of 100-grit sandpaper (to clean fouled spark plugs)
- Cone-shaped rubber leak plugs
- Heavy monofilament, 100 pound or higher test (to clean out a clogged engine cooling water intake)
- Spare parts for everything you think won't break (but will): engine belt, fuel hose, anchor shackle, spark plug, fuel pump bulb, propeller, shaft nut, cotter pin, fuses, hose clamps, and on and on . . .

MAKE A FLOAT PLAN

Every time you go boating, make two float plans: one for the boat and one to leave with someone on shore.

On the boat, define roles. Who's the captain? Who's second in command? Most of all, who's on watch and will keep an eye out for other boats, shellfish pots, marine creatures, and reefs? Who else can drive the boat? Does everyone know how to radio for help in an emergency? Does anyone have medical issues? Oh, and who is in command of the car keys?

Then, leave a written plan or message with a trusted friend, family member, or even a marina staff member—someone you trust to contact the Coast Guard if you fail to return. At minimum, specify where you were headed, the type of boat, and the names and contacts for all aboard. It's wise (and might be life-saving) to specify how your boat is equipped. This information can be vital to rescuers.

FLOAT PLAN

1. Phone Numbers

Coast Guard: _____

Marine Police: _____

BoatUS 24-Hour Dispatch: 800-391-4869

2. Owner/Skipper Information

Owner/Skipper [Filing Report]: _____

Phone: _____ Age: _____

Address: _____

Marina [Home Port]: _____ Phone: _____

Auto Parked At: _____

Model/color: _____ Lic. #: _____

Trailer Lic. #: _____

3. Boat Description

Boat Name: _____ Hailing Port: _____

Type: _____ Model Year: _____

Make: _____ Length: _____ Beam: _____ Draft: _____

Color, Hull: _____ Cabin: _____ Deck: _____ Trim: _____ Dodger: _____

Other Colors: _____ # of Masts: _____

Distinguishing Features: _____

Registration No: _____ Sail No: _____

Engine[s] Type: _____ Horsepower: _____ Cruising Speed: _____

Fuel Capacity, Gallons: _____ Cruising Range: _____

Electronics/Safety Equipment Aboard

VHF Radio: _____ Cell Phone: _____ CB: _____ SSB: _____

Frequency Monitored: _____

Depth Sounder: _____ Radar: _____ GPS: _____

Raft: _____ Dinghy: _____ EPIRB: _____

4. Trip Details

Additional Persons Aboard, Total: _____

Name: _____ Age: _____

Address: _____ Phone: _____

Boating Experience: _____

BATTEN DOWN THE HATCHES: WHEN CAUGHT IN BAD WEATHER

Marine weather conditions can change rapidly and unpredictably, and ocean storms can be incredibly violent. To recognize an approaching storm, see "Reading the Weather" (page 178). Ideally, if you have time, seek safe harbor, but if the storm reaches you first . . .

WHAT TO DO IF CAUGHT OUT IN A BOAT

- Put on your dang PFD.

- If fog or heavy rain disrupts visibility, slow down, get a bearing on your location, get clear of channels and shipping lanes, and lower anchor if you fear running aground.

- Lightning can strike better than a mile ahead of an approaching thundercloud. Don't assume you're safe just because the storm isn't directly over you.

- During a lightning storm, seek shelter under a bridge, if you can, but watch out for overhead storm drains!

- Lower radio antenna and other exposed metal points; lowering the motor will increase conductivity, so lightning passes to the water.

- Secure loose gear and straps.

- Wet, salty lines conduct electricity. Drop them in the water.

- Aim your bow into the wind; expect strong gusts. If under power, approach waves at a 45-degree angle, heave to (page 14), or deploy a sea anchor (page 30).

- Have everyone stay in the cabin or crouch as low in the boat as possible. Stay clear of any metal; wear rubber gloves when holding the tiller.

- If a tornado or waterspout appears to be standing still, it's heading directly toward you. Move at a right angle to get out of the way.

WHAT TO DO IF CAUGHT ON THE BEACH

If you're on the beach while the boat is anchored, consider staying on the beach and riding out the storm. You're safer on land than at sea.

- Secure your boat with an extra anchor line off the beach before the squall.

- Lower umbrellas, tents, and any loose objects.

- Seek the lowest spot on the beach, and use any sort of cover, like a tarp. Don't shelter under metal objects or trees.

- Shelter in a deep cave, but not under cliffside overhangs or even a porch. Lightning can channel along a shelter's edges.

- Avoid standing directly on the ground (by crouching atop a surfboard, boat cushion, and so on), or make sure only feet touch ground, not hands, and keep feet close together.

- If someone is struck, initiate CPR (page 200). A person is not charged with electricity after being struck.

HEAVE A LINE AND TIE OFF TO A CLEAT

These essential skills are both easy to learn and to screw up. Remember, everyone on the dock is watching.

HEAVE A LINE

1. Ensure your line is a lot longer than the throwing distance. A weight secured at the thrown end can help (use a monkey fist knot, page 74).

2. If throwing right-handed, coil the line in your left hand, and vice versa.

3. Loop the line clockwise, starting with coils of about 15 inches. Make each successive coil slightly smaller, and layer in the direction of the throw, to allow the coils to unfurl smoothly.

4. Once coiled, shift between half or more of the line to your throwing hand, with enough line between hands for the swing. Point your nonthrowing hand outward, so coils can unspool.

5. Use an underhand, softball-style swing to heave the line. Practice a few swings with your arm nearly straight, then release the line at the top of your swing, allowing the line in your nonthrowing hand to unspool.

TIE OFF TO A CLEAT

It's important that your entering line (step 1) come in on the opposite side of the cleat, or else the line can become stuck under the cleat under tension. Also make sure you do a complete turn around the cleat (step 2); otherwise, the knot will not develop enough friction to hold and your boat might float away.

1. Bring the line to opposite side of the cleat from where the line is coming in. This is your "entering line."

2. Take the line one complete round turn around base of the cleat.

3. Cross over the top of the cleat and bring line around the horn where you started.

4. Come back across, crossing back over the top line, and wrap around the opposite horn in a figure eight.

5. Make a "locking hitch" by flipping the line over and forming a loop around the horn that sends the line away, in the opposite direction from the entering line.

6. Tighten loop.

Think Manhattan traffic is bad? Try a busy harbor or tourist cove. Unlike driving terrestrial highways, the ocean has no lanes, lines, traffic lights, or curbs. Unseen hazards lurk below, and no guardrail prevents oncoming boats from running right over you. In short, boating demands intense situational awareness.

SHIPPING LANES ARE DANGEROUS!

- Commercial boats always have right of way.

- Shipping lanes are marked on nautical charts. Stay clear if possible.

- Big ships take thousands of feet to stop or take evasive action. Stay out of the way.

- If you're too close to a ship, the bridge may not see you, and the captain may not be monitoring VHF.

- Cross shipping lanes quickly and at a 90-degree angle to traffic.

- If traveling the same speed as a big ship, follow from well behind.

- Don't get beheaded! Tug boats may be towing boats or barges with hard-to-see cables.

PASSING BOATS AND AVOIDING WAKES

Boat wake accidents are responsible for swampings, broken teeth, back and neck injuries, enormous financial settlements, and fights. BoatUS says to slow and come completely off plane, or wave-pushing speeds, "anywhere your wake could compromise the safety of other boats."

The USCG definition of *no wake* is "a speed whereby there is no white water in the track or path of the vessel or in created waves immediate to the vessel." Slow down well before reaching a slow-speed zone, and if running slowly, shift passengers forward to minimize your wake. When dealing with another boat's wake, slow down but keep moving, approaching at a slight angle (which is more stable than stopping). Warn passengers to brace themselves.

DIVER DOWN FLAGS

Give diver down flags a wide berth. Divers should ensure these flags are large and visible.

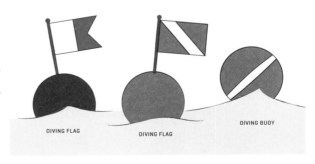

DIVING FLAG   DIVING FLAG   DIVING BUOY

BOATING IN BIG WAVES AND HEAVY SEAS

Whether in a sailboat or a motorboat, here's how to deal with big waves or heavy seas that threaten to flip you over.

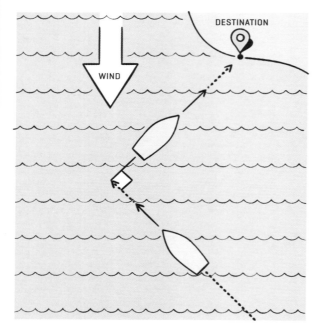

RUNNING "INTO THE SEA"

Don't run your boat straight into waves or swells. It will beat you and your boat severely as the bow plows into waves rather than lifting over them. Then, if the propeller leaves the water—either as you go airborne or your stern rises over a wave crest— you can over-rev and damage your motor.

Slow down and meet the waves at a roughly 45-degree angle. The boat will pitch and roll, but that's better than a straight-on pounding.

BEAM SEAS

"Beam seas" means your boat is broadside to the waves, which can cause roll-induced capsizing. Unless absolutely necessary, turn into the seas and follow the aforementioned 45-degree rule. If you have no choice, zigzag forward: Turn your boat 45 degrees into incoming waves on your forward quarter (broad on your bow); then turn 90 degrees and take the seas on your stern quarter (broad on your stern).

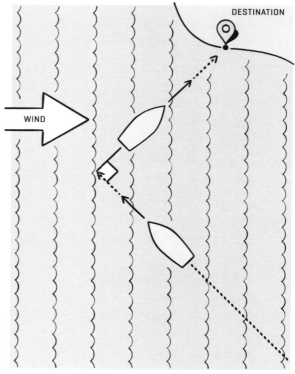

Pitchpoling (left) and being broadside to the seas (right) are easy ways to flip your boat.

RUNNING "BEFORE THE SEA"

You're said to be running before the sea when waves and wind are moving in the same direction as you. In deep water, with low swells, this is not typically a problem.

But if waves grow big and steepen, or if you're in shallower water with breaking waves, your boat can be forced to yaw from side to side. If a wave overtakes you from astern, the propeller can lift clear of the water, causing a loss of control, throwing the boat into a broadside turn, and potentially capsizing it—a condition called broaching. If you fail to stay behind a wave's crest, your boat can slide forward down a wave and be driven nose-first into the trough, while the next wave flips it end over end—a condition called pitchpoling.

Prevent this by working the throttle to stay behind the crest in front of you and in front of the crest behind you. If your boat can't outrun the waves, slow down but don't stop as the incoming wave passes under you. Then speed up and follow that wave until the next one comes.

NEGOTIATING AN INLET

Inlets can be subjected to major tidal currents, rapidly shifting sandbars, and all manner of waves. Plus, every inlet is different. Indeed, a chart or GPS map can be nearly useless. Don't try to run a sketchy inlet without a knowledgeable local or prior advice. When an outgoing tide runs out of an inlet channel into incoming waves, the waves will steepen and become more dangerous. Rather than plodding through the middle of an inlet, consider running closer to the sides, where wave and current action appears lightest. The water may be deeper near a side because the sand has been scoured out by the current. Regardless, know before you go.

DEPLOYING AN EMERGENCY SEA ANCHOR

If you find yourself in an emergency offshore situation with a loss of power and broadside seas, deploy a makeshift sea anchor to keep your bow pointed into wind and waves. You can improvise a sea anchor by streaming out PFDs, a bucket, planks of wood tied in the middle, a dry bag nearly full of water, even a used car tire—anything that's semi-buoyant to produce drag.

1. To deploy, point the boat into the waves and wind if possible. If sailing, lower sails. Attach sea anchor to the bow stanchion or bow eye (which avoids line chafe and keeps the bow higher into oncoming waves).

2. Drop the sea anchor and its floating retrieval buoy and line, if so equipped, into the water on the windward side of the boat, and slowly let out the rode (anchor line).

3. When there's tension on the line, pay out the rode at least one more "wavelength"—or the distance between two wave crests to maintain more steady pressure on the anchor. Very rough seas might require multiple wavelengths. Keep tiller/rudder straight ahead or motor lowered and pointed straight to prevent side-to-side drift.

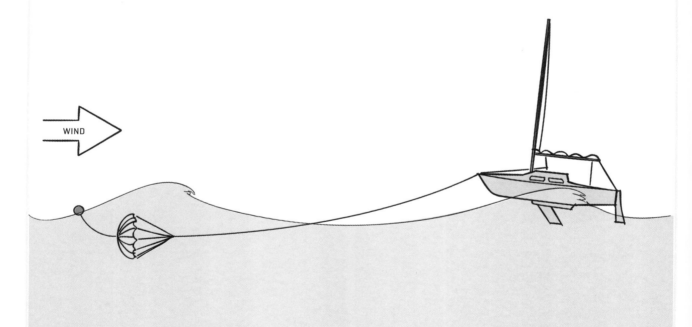

WIND

HOW TO RIGHT A SMALL SAILBOAT

Small sailboats are known to flip, becoming "keeled over" (on its side) or "turtled" (upside-down). Whether righting a monohulled boat or a multihulled catamaran, first, obviously, make sure everyone is safe and not caught in the rigging. Next, uncleat the sheets or lines so the sails will drain.

RIGHTING A MONOHULL

For a monohull, point the bow upwind. As the sails rise, you want them slack and into the wind, so the boat won't take off.

If the boat is keeled over, climb onto the daggerboard, centerboard, or keel and grab the deck rail at the highest point. If the boat is turtled, climb onto the hull, grab the keel, and pull, leaning back, keeping your weight on the edge, or "chine," of the hull, until the boat rotates into a keeled-over position.

Then, while standing on the keel, lean backward, pulling on the deck rail. Stay clear as the boat rights itself. If you have help, someone can push up from either the base or top of the mast.

RIGHTING A MULTIHULL OR CATAMARAN

Position multihulls so the trampoline faces the wind, which helps right the vessel. Most catamarans have "righting lines" that are used for leverage. Some have "righting poles," which dramatically increase leverage, or water-filled "righting bags," which are tied to the upright pontoon to add rolling weight.

First, loosen the main halyard. If you're halfway keeled over, fasten the "righting line" to the shroud (the mast-support wire) on the hull that is not in the water. Then, from the boat's underside, stand on the middle of the pontoon that is in the water and pull the righting line. If you're turtled, attach the righting line to one pontoon, stand on the other, and lean back, pulling until righted.

BE SHALLOW-MINDED

Any boat owner who says they've never been stuck is probably lying. It's how you deal with the shallows and get unstuck that shows your salty mettle. Then again, it also takes skill to safely beach your boat when you want to.

First, know the draft of your boat and learn to recognize shoal (or shallow) waters. Use a chart and/or depthfinder and stay in the center of channels. Polarized sunglasses cut through surface glare, allowing a much better view of the seafloor.

If there are no channel markers, know the following:

- Shorebirds only walk in very shallow water.

- Very shallow water is often slightly calmer than surrounding deeper water.

- Deeper water is generally darker, unless you're above a dark reef or eel grass.

- Along the edges of shoal water, tidal currents visibly swirl, and wind-driven waves or boat wakes will break.

HOW TO AVOID GETTING STUCK

- A flatter hull reduces draft. In a V-hull boat, carefully move as much weight as reasonable to list the boat to one side.

- Trim your motor up, but be aware that this reduces steerage and stopping control.

- If the water is just deep enough, running on a plane reduces your draft considerably, but note: Striking shallow bottom at planing speed can end badly.

- In a shallow channel, rev the motor as a wave sweeps beneath you, then throttle back as the wave recedes.

HOW TO GET UNSTUCK

- On a hard bottom, reverse with the engine trimmed up enough so it doesn't touch bottom. If you don't budge quickly, abort to avoid damage to the engine and seafloor.

- In sand only, off-load crew and rock the boat side to side to reduce its draft while pushing it to deeper water.

- In deep mud, remain onboard and rock the boat side to side while carefully reversing throttle. Since the motor will be sucking up mud, don't do this for long!

- In mud or sand, lever a heavy oar or flats pushpole against the hull, just like a prybar—stick it down and wedge forward.

- Forgot to join a boat-towing service? Wait for the return of high tide, enjoying all the food and water you remembered to pack.

HOW TO PULL ONTO A BEACH

In some places, like the sandy US East Coast, beaching a boat is a vital skill. The general rule is to proceed very slowly and beach your boat stern-first, with the bow facing the ocean. This makes the boat easier to push out as the tide drops, keeps the bow into incoming waves, and ensures you won't swamp at the stern on a rising tide.

- Use a pole or paddle to assess the seafloor for rocks or shellfish and scan for ecologically sensitive seagrass. Don't beach if either are present.

- Deploy a bow anchor in deeper water and back the boat up close to the beach with the engine trimmed up. Once you're close enough, secure the bow anchor.

- Have a lookout go ashore with a stern anchor and dig it firmly into beach sand to keep the boat secure at both ends.

- As the tide drops, keep pushing the boat into deeper water unless you plan to stay ashore through an entire tide cycle.

PRO TIP: A longboard or standup paddleboard makes great transit from boat to beach.

A JET SKI IS A BOAT,
NOT A TOY

Personal watercraft (PWC)—known commercially as Jet Skis, Waverunners, and Sea-Doos—are fun, maneuverable, powerful, and extremely fast (some reach 70 miles per hour [mph]). In other words, when careless drivers forget they're piloting an actual boat, they're highly dangerous. Don't be that driver.

PWCs come in two basic types: standup and sit-down models. Boating rules, laws, guidelines, and cautions are essentially the same—and if someone else drives your PWC, you're likely liable for injuries and damage. PWCs drive differently from every other powerboat. They ride very high in the water, and most have no brakes. Further, because PWCs are controlled by a jet of water, releasing the throttle loses steering control. Release the throttle at high speed, and you might plane for a hundred yards, unable to turn—so always maintain some throttle.

Before driving, check the stern sticker indicating the proper direction to "reroll" the PWC when it flips, and always lift the seat and check for loose wires, compromised hoses or through-hull fittings, and gasoline odors. Deadly explosions can result when trapped vapors are sparked by ignition; always allow the PWC hull to thoroughly ventilate before cranking.

Obviously, always wear a PFD. Since wind chill is an issue, bring backup clothing and consider a wetsuit or neoprene shorts for warmth and impact protection. Sunglasses and reef shoes are a good idea, as is a floating marine radio (attached to you) and a whistle.

PWCs are dramatically affected by wind and waves, and a heavily laden PWC will handle unpredictably, so obey the capacity placard. Before driving, ensure everything is clear of both the jet intake and the exhaust, and always keep the emergency cutoff lanyard attached to your wrist. While driving, lean into turns (like on a motorcycle), though turning too sharply can cause a PWC to flip, ejecting you violently. If this happens, reroll the PWC quickly to prevent water from getting into the engine—and destroying it.

Oh, and have fun!

1. **No fuel:** Check gas level or for a kinked fuel hose or a poorly pumped fuel bulb. If the fuel bulb doesn't become firm when pumped, you may have air intrusion in the line.

2. **Trim:** Some engines, particularly older ones, don't like to start when trimmed up.

3. **No juice:** Is the battery master switch or console master power switch turned off— or the battery low (below 11 volts)?

4. The engine is not shifted into neutral.

5. Your lanyard/kill switch is not installed.

6. **Blown fuse:** Outboard motors often have a 20+ amp automotive-type forked plug fuse underneath a cover under the engine cowling. If it's burned, replace it (but know why it burned before heading out!). Some inboard motors have a circuit breaker in the engine compartment that runs to the starter wire. Reset by pushing the button.

7. **Oxidation:** Many engines have a big, round, red power plug under the cowling. If the plug leads are oxidized, sand them and scrape the inside of the plugs with a screwdriver.

8. If the engine turns over but doesn't stay running, you may have fouled plugs— very common on two-stroke (oil-burning) engines. Remove plugs, keeping track of associated ignition wires, and scrape or sand deposits of burned carbon or oil.

9. **Filthy, watery fuel:** Clean your fuel filters of water and contaminants. Your boat may have two. A small, glass unit on the engine screws off with a wrench. Clean by blowing it out or swishing in gasoline. Another, bigger unit is a can-size cylinder mounted to the boat's stern; it screws off by hand or with an oil-filter wrench. If your filter has a small "petcock" valve at the bottom, you can see water and contaminants below the gasoline. Unscrew the valve to drain the gunk until only gas remains. Or, unscrew the filter, dump its contents into a bucket, and follow primer instructions to refill the filter with fuel.

10. **Clogged exhaust:** This can happen if your outboard's propeller has been sitting in mud. Remove the propeller to check.

ANCHORS AWEIGH

Few skills are as important as anchoring, especially if your boat becomes disabled, and few skills are as easy to overlook.

TYPES OF ANCHORS

- **Fluke-style or Danforth anchor:** This is the most commonly used anchor by recreational boaters. Its lightweight and excellent holding strength make it the best all-around. It has flukes that flap open to engage and "self-bury" into the seafloor. Not great in vegetation.

- **Plow-style or delta anchor:** Very common. Good at "plowing" into soft seafloor, but fairly heavy. Does not grip as strongly as a fluke anchor, but better in vegetation.

- **Yachtsman's anchor, aka kedge:** This classically shaped anchor has good penetration in vegetation and holding within rocks, but it's big and ungainly.

- **Mushroom anchor:** This is for small boats only—like canoes, kayaks, and small skiffs—in mild weather. Little holding power.

PREPARING THE ANCHORS

- "Ground tackle" refers to everything that attaches the anchor to the boat: a metal chain attached to the anchor, a nylon line attached to the chain (using a U-shaped shackle), and a "mooring bitt," a bow cleat that holds the line. Together, the chain/line combo is called the "rode."

- The anchor chain should be 7 to 8 feet long. The anchor won't set well without downforce provided by the chain.

- Ensure the line is strong enough. For boats up to 25 feet, a $7/16$-inch nylon line is good.

- Always have two, preferably three, anchors: main anchor at the bow, ready to deploy in an emergency. Store a second at the bow with the line ready to unspool. Keep a third, storm anchor stowed astern just in case.

- Only set an anchor from the bow, and never from your boat's sides or stern (unless the boat is beached), which may allow currents, wind, or waves to swamp it.

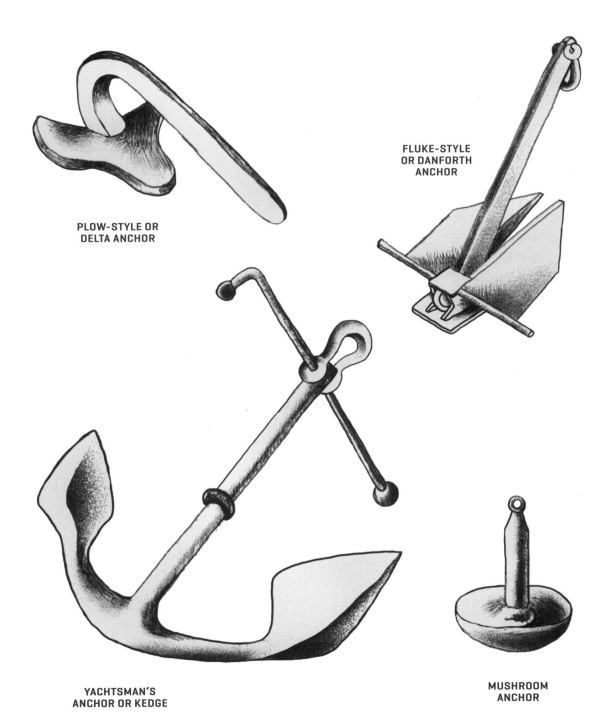

PLOW-STYLE OR DELTA ANCHOR

FLUKE-STYLE OR DANFORTH ANCHOR

YACHTSMAN'S ANCHOR OR KEDGE

MUSHROOM ANCHOR

ANCHOR, MAN: SET THE HOOK

- Locate a stretch of water with room for the boat to drift. Determine wind and current direction: Where will they push the idle boat, and where do you want to end up?

- The more horizontal the rode, the better the anchor will dig in. Determine the "scope": That is, how long does the rode need to be so the anchor will set properly in current weather conditions? Stormy conditions require more rode. First, determine the water depth, and add to that the height of the mooring bitt on the bow; thus, if the water is 10 feet deep, and the bitt 3 feet above the waterline, it would be 13 feet. Multiply this by the necessary scope: 7 is usually the minimum in clear weather, and 10 if stormy. Here's our sample equation: 7 x 13 = 91 feet of rode.

PRO TIP: It's easiest to measure the anchor line if you attach small zip ties at "boat lengths"—or better still, attach numbered plastic cable markers.

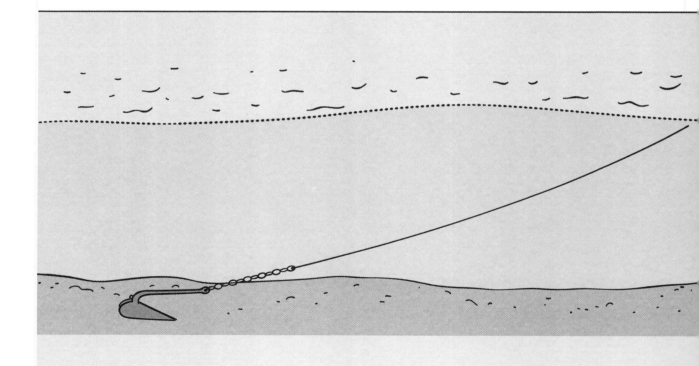

When you're ready to drop anchor, shift the motor into neutral and wait until the boat stops or begins to drift backward. Then slowly lower the anchor while ensuring you're clear of the line!

As the boat drifts back, maintain some tension on the rode.

Once you've reached the proper rode length, tie off the line to the mooring bitt or bow cleat, ensuring the line won't chafe. Pull the rode hard to ensure the anchor is set—preferably by reversing the engine. Regularly check surroundings (triangulating with onshore landmarks) to ensure the anchor's not dragging.

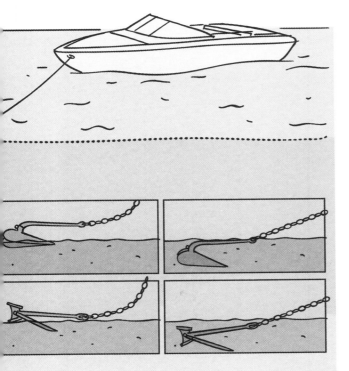

FREE THE HOOK

Pull in the line slowly and steadily until the boat is directly above anchor; this should break it free. If it doesn't, drive to an opposite angle of the holding angle (avoiding the propeller!) to free it.

Raise anchor steadily. If it's caked with mud and grass, shake it vigorously in the water to clear, then coil the line.

ANCHORING TECHNIQUES AND TIPS

Best anchorages will generally be marked on a nautical chart, as will "bottom characteristics": clay, mud, gravel, oyster, rock, sand, and so on. The best bottom is firm sand. Rocks and oysters are problematic because an anchor often won't bite till it snags. Don't anchor on coral or seagrass! Both are vital habitats.

You can sometimes tell if your anchor is sliding on the bottom because the line vibrates. Lengthen the rode for more scope and try to reset. If needed, ease tension on the line by motoring into the wind or current and then lengthening scope.

If your boat "yaws" back and forth at anchor, lower the motor to stabilize the boat or set two anchors off the bow at 45-degree angles.

If the anchor is missing a shackle, employ an anchor bowline knot (page 68) to attach the line. Finally, always ensure your anchor line is secured to the boat at the line's far end, so you don't lose the anchor.

SO YOU WANT TO **BUY A BOAT**

It's always sad to hear someone say, "I paid all this money for that damn boat, I gotta use it." That's the wrong reason to buy—or use—a boat. Indeed, yachties often say that the best kind of boat is an OPB. That is, an "other person's boat." They're not wrong.

- Still want one? Check out a marina boat show. You'll learn things you'd never thought of and manage a test drive.

- Really think about how, and how often, you'll use the boat. What size and function suits your needs? Consider weather protection and sleeping arrangements, stowage areas, and your family (will kids need shade?). Consider the waters you'll frequent: shallow tidal waters and beaches (think skiff or bay hull), or offshore waters (think V-hull). Can you pilot and trailer the boat by yourself?

- Saltwater and UV light take an unseen toll. If buying used, have the boat thoroughly checked by a reputable mechanic. Considering a boat over 25 feet? Hire a proper surveyor.

- A musty cabin indicates possible mildew. Water in the bilge can mean a leak from a through-hull fitting or an engine cooling hose. Oil in the bilge can indicate an oil leak.

- The Coast Guard will also perform a free "vessel safety check," and they keep track of boat recalls and maintenance issues by make.

- It's impossible to measure corrosion inside an inboard engine, so consider an outboard motor for saltwater use. For this reason, too, if you buy used, consider buying from a freshwater area.

- With sailboats, consider how comfortable the boat will be heeled over at uncomfortable angles.

- Before buying a used boat, ensure it's free of liens with a clear title both in the state it's currently registered and in your state.

- Join Seatow, TowBoat US, or a similar towing service. A single "unprotected" tow can cost over a thousand bucks.

WHATEVER FLOATS YOUR BOAT: **SEA KAYAKS**

Sea kayaks come in two basic flavors: sit-on-top and sit-inside. The former are best for short jaunts in calmer weather; the latter for touring and rougher conditions.

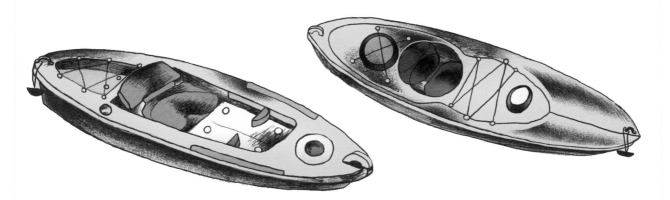

SIT-ON-TOP KAYAKS

For basic fishing and kayaking, "sit-on-top" kayaks in the 10- to 14-foot range are affordable, fun, functional, short, wide, stable, and easy to use—with no need for gear like spray skirts or bilge pumps. They're also great in hot weather, enabling easy cool-off splashing and jumps in the water. Designated "fishing kayaks" include rod and gear holders.

Their main limitations? Sit-on-tops don't often offer much storage space; they're slow, wet rides; and they can be a handful in current and wind. Some feature cool pedal-driven propulsion systems, but pedalers should never leave shore without a paddle.

SIT-INSIDE KAYAKS

"Sit-inside" kayaks come in "recreational" and "touring" versions. All have a cockpit and an optional, protective "spray skirt." Recreational styles range from 10 to 12 feet long. Some have inner-hull foam for buoyancy or sealed bulkheads. A nonbuoyant capsized "rec boat" might fill with water and be impossible to refloat. So consider adding kayak airbags fore and aft to displace water and allow a pump-out when you reboard.

Touring kayaks range from 12 to 17 feet long. They have increased storage capacity for longer treks, sealed bulkheads, usually perimeter lines to assist with reboarding, more advanced construction, and better handling in waves and seas. But seaworthy does not necessarily mean stable. These kayaks are narrow and "tippy," so get plenty of experience before your first long trip.

OCEAN KAYAKING: TOUR PLANNING AND SUPPLIES

Kayaking is a terrific way to explore between remote islands and along shore-lines. Sleek and efficient, kayaks can travel far with little effort. But be prepared: Changing weather and difficult currents can turn an easy outing into a critical situation. Until you gain experience, keep your first forays short and close to shore. As with all boating, make a float plan (page 22). Special thanks to kayak master Joshua Hall for the in-person demos and dunkings.

- Check the weather forecast and tides. Thanks to daytime heating, calm mornings often become breezy, even stormy, afternoons.

- Know tidal current directions. Currents can reach several knots—or as fast as you can paddle. If doing an "out and back," always head out against the current and wind, so coming back is easier.

- Wear appropriate, layered clothing. The rule of thumb is to add water and air temperature together. If the combined number is less than 120 degrees, wear a wet or drysuit or a paddling jacket with wrist and neck seals. To avoid overheating in the sun, wear a sweat-wicking undergarment or an easily removable wet suit. Separately, in a dry bag, bring a neoprene or wool beanie and spare clothes (no cotton).

- Always bring double the food and water you'll need. For a two-hour paddle, bring four hours of supplies.

KAYAK GEAR YOU DIDN'T KNOW YOU NEEDED

- A kayak-specific PFD (page 18; no inflatables) offers more freedom of movement for arms. Loop a whistle to the strap.

- A plastic laminated chart of your route (don't rely on cell phones!).

- Trauma shears attached to your PFD (to cut lines with one hand).

- An orienteering compass (to get home).

- A first-aid kit with sling, for shoulder injuries (in a pinch, a big safety pin can attach a jacket wrist to a PFD).

- Adhesive window flashing (for quick "slap-on" repairs).

- Some kayak ponchos can double as "human tents" for shelter; others fit over the cockpit like a spray skirt.

- A bailing pump.

- A deflated beach ball (when inflated, replaces lost hatch cover).

- A waterproof VHF attached to your PFD (reachable if you capsize).

PADDLING A KAYAK: GOING THROUGH THE MOTIONS

Get in, get out, make yourself go, handle waves, beach your craft, signal your status, and right a wrong: Yup, it's all here.

SQUEEZING ABOARD A SIT-IN KAYAK

It's simple: In shallow water, straddle the boat with one leg on either side, grasp the lip of the cockpit for stability, and lower yourself down. While sitting, bring one leg inside at a time, then affix the skirt.

Many people use the paddle to brace and stabilize the kayak when entering, but don't do this. A slip can result in shoulder injuries.

DRAW
STROKE

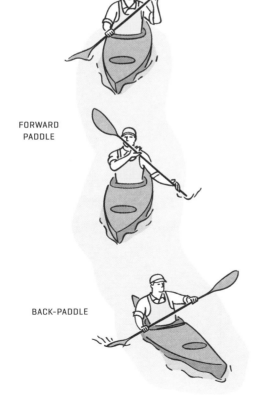

FORWARD
PADDLE

BACK-PADDLE

DIFFERENT STROKES

Your paddle is your engine, your rudder, your friend.

- **Draw stroke:** To bring yourself to starboard or port, reach paddle out to the side and draw paddle toward you, feathering the blade.

- **Forward paddle:** Keep elbows and shoulders down to prevent strain on rotator cuff. Dig into the water and pull paddle toward you with bottom hand, while top hand pushes out and keeps fingers pointed to the sky.

- **Back-paddle:** Reverse a forward paddle.

- **Stop:** Push hard against paddle in opposite direction of travel.

- **Spin the boat:** On one side, sweep paddle in an arc, reaching as far out as possible.

- **Brace or recovery:** If you feel yourself capsizing, sweep paddle sideways and push down into the water hard (pushing yourself upright).

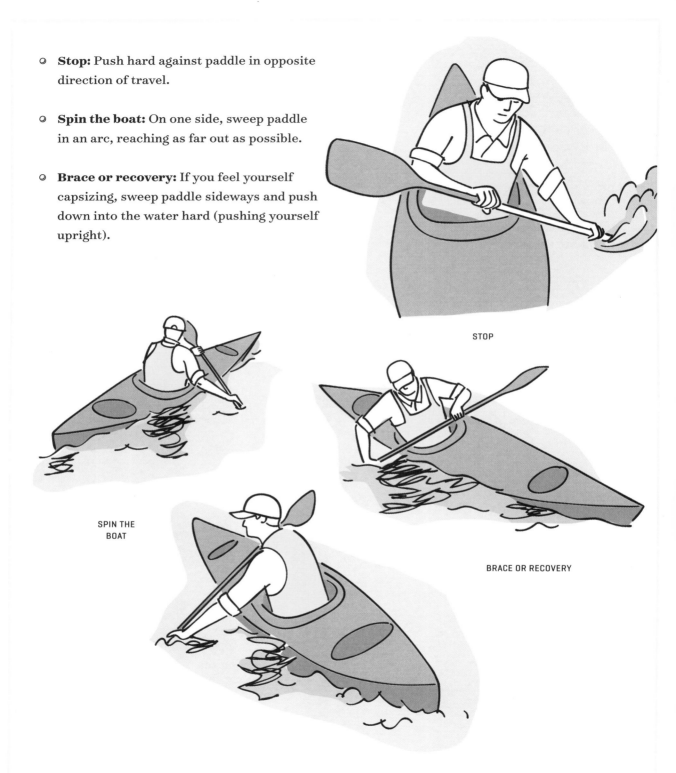

STOP

SPIN THE
BOAT

BRACE OR RECOVERY

RIGHTING A WRONG, PART I: WITH HELP

A kayaker is always "in between swims." If your kayaking companion flips, use the "T rescue" procedure to help them get righted and back onboard.

1. Confirm the capsized kayaker is okay.

2. If so, the person should flip their boat upright while you paddle alongside.

3. Hold or stabilize their boat as the person swims to your boat and holds the bow (to stabilize your boat and stay out of the way).

4. Position their boat at a 90-degree angle to your boat, pulling it partway onto your boat.

5. Flip their kayak upside down to drain water from the cockpit, then flip the kayak upright in the water. Most sit-in kayaks have a watertight bulkhead astern and one inside the bow (so water won't collect at the stern).

6. When drained, flip their kayak upright.

7. Position both kayaks side by side. Take the paddle from the capsized kayaker.

4. Pull partway onto your boat positioned at a 90-degree angle

5. Flip the kayak upside down to drain and then flip

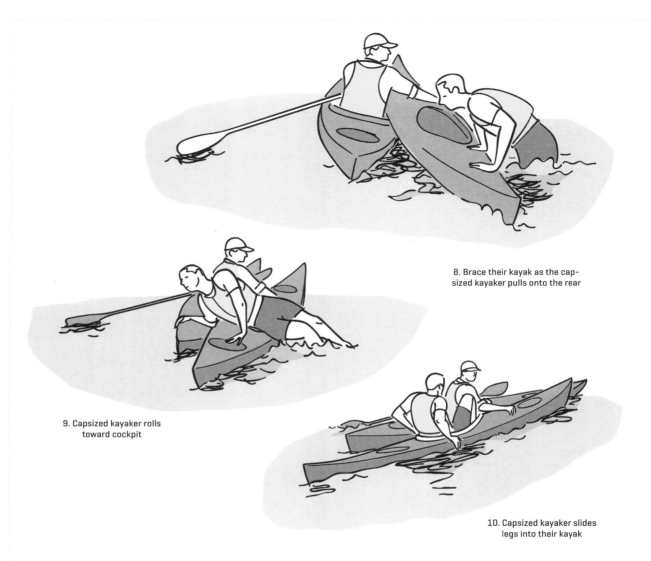

8. Brace their kayak as the capsized kayaker pulls onto the rear

9. Capsized kayaker rolls toward cockpit

10. Capsized kayaker slides legs into their kayak

8. As you brace their kayak, the person pulls onto and across the rear deck of their kayak.

9. The person rolls toward their boat's cockpit sideways until their butt is in the cockpit.

10. The person rotates around to face forward while bracing with their arms.

11. As you both continue to brace the kayaks, the person slides their legs into the kayak.

12. If some water remains, pump it out and reattach skirt.

RIGHTING A WRONG, PART II: ON YOUR OWN

If it's windy, don't let go of your boat. It can blow away faster than you can swim.

1. Flip your kayak upright.

2. Hold the paddle perpendicular to the hull and flat against the water to provide stability. Grasp the stern quarter—preferably at the lip of the storage compartment.

3. Give a powerful kick and pull yourself onto and across the stern.

4. Straddle the stern of the kayak as if sitting on a surfboard.

5. Inch forward while straddling the kayak, until your butt is over the cockpit.

6. Take a seat; slide in your legs.

7. Pump out water.

3. Pull yourself onto the stern

4. Straddle the kayak

6. Take a seat

HANDLING ROUGH WATER, WAVES, AND CURRENTS

First, if conditions seem beyond your abilities, don't paddle out. If you're out and conditions deteriorate dangerously, abandon your intended destination and seek the safest shore.

A kayak is least stable, most easily capsized, and most difficult to control when wind or waves push from astern or abeam (from the back or sides). Thus, the best way to handle wind and waves is directly head-on. You'll get pounded, but you'll remain stable while you seek accessible landing spots. If you can't more forward, aim for a lee (out of the wind) shore, or land in the direction you are being blown.

If waves overtake you from astern and threaten to capsize you, follow the advice for reaching a beach.

REACHING A BEACH

If by choice or desperation you must come in through a surf line, determine whether the waves are so big that it's safer to simply ditch your boat and swim ashore. The waves will likely push the boat to shore anyway. If it's a sit-in kayak, consider lifting your legs out of the cockpit and over the side to make a quick exit if needed.

To paddle in, approach the beach backward. Position your bow facing the oncoming waves and raise your rudder (if you have one). As a wave approaches, paddle toward the wave so you take it on your bow, and then as it passes, back-paddle toward shore. Repeat till you're ashore.

If you wind up sideways to the waves, in a "surfing position," lean into the wave and brace with your paddle into the whitewater.

COPING WITH TIDAL CURRENTS

Tidal currents will be strongest in the middle of channels. If facing a strong current on a waterway, paddle as close to the shoreline or the inside of a bend as possible.

CROSSING A CHANNEL

Just like a pedestrian at a busy street, kayakers should take the straightest line across a busy channel. And like pedestrians, kayakers have the right of way. However, if you've ever crossed a busy street, you know that vehicles don't always abide by this rule. Time your crossing and choose your course to keep a wide berth from other vessels.

INTERNATIONALLY RECOGNIZED HAND SIGNALS

HELP/EMERGENCY Wave paddle from side to side.

ALL CLEAR Point paddle in direction that is "all clear." For straight ahead, hold paddle straight up.

STOP Hold paddle horizontally above your head.

ALL OKAY Pat top of your head.

WAKESURFING, TUBING, AND "TOWABLES"

Today, wakesurfing, wakeboarding, and riding inflatable tubes and other "towables" are more popular than waterskiing. Combine fun and safety by learning the right techniques.

PREPARING TO TOW AND SAFETY PRECAUTIONS

○ Know how a boat handles before towing; check the ladder and safety gear.

○ Know the currents and winds; don't tow in busy channels; and maintain a safe distance from all fixed objects: docks, channel markers, oyster beds, reefs, and shorelines. Imagine a clear, 300-foot circle as your "safe zone."

○ Everyone should wear bright life jackets and know hand signals (see page 53).

○ Designate a spotter: Most states require a spotter to instantly relay signals from a rider or to announce a wipeout, so drivers can focus on driving.

○ Your boat will tow a rider better if the tow rope is attached to a center-mounted, stern ski-tower pole or a bridle that hangs from both eye loops at the stern. Tow ropes fastened only on one side can dangerously affect boat handling.

○ Don't "weight" or ballast a non-wakesurf-specific boat to create a surfable stern wave. You can sink—easily.

○ Ensure the engine is not spewing exhaust into a rider's face. Carbon monoxide kills (page 54).

TOWING TECHNIQUES

- For tubes, use around 100 feet of rope; for waterskiers, 75 or so. Wake-surfers will want to be closer to utilize the wake—but maintain a safe distance from the propeller or a belching two-stroke motor.

- A slalom ski or wakeboard requires a full-throttle launch to get the skier up and riding. A surfboard, longboard, or tube can be launched and driven much more slowly. A surfboard can be planed at 10 mph, a wakeboard 15 or so. A slalom skier may need 25 mph or better.

- Slow down for turns. A boat turning at 20 mph means the rider at the end of the line is easily going twice that speed. Wipeouts that fast can result in critical injuries.

- Be aware of your wake's impact on other boaters, docks, and the shoreline. A heavy wakesurfing boat moving at 10 mph creates a more powerful wake than a planing waterski boat going three times as fast.

- Always watch the tow rope to keep it clear of the propeller.

There is nothing–*absolutely nothing–half so much worth doing as messing about in boats.*

—from *The Wind in the Willows*, Kenneth Grahame

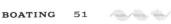

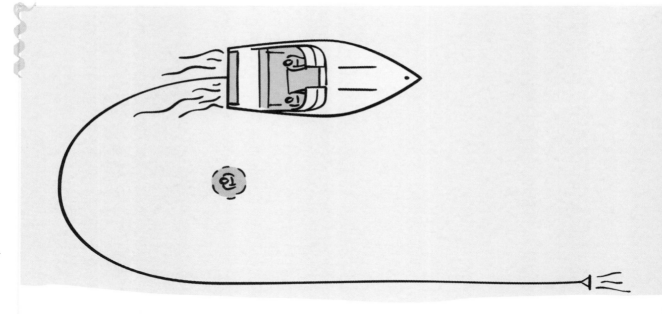

RIDER (AND SWIMMER) RECOVERY

- If a rider spills, the spotter should immediately yell "Wipeout!" or "Rider down!"

- The spotter should watch downed riders constantly. Other boaters may not notice them. Some states require boaters to raise an orange flag. Riders should raise their ski or board to alert other boaters of their vulnerable position.

- Drop speed to idle (very slow) and bring the boat around in a U-turn—so that the trailing line makes a U with the rider inside at the bottom. As the boat goes forward, water drag will bring the rope to the rider. Keep your boat between the rider and other boats; if possible, stay downwind/down current of the rider.

- Once the rider grabs the line, shift to neutral or cut the engine.

- When the rider wants back onboard, always kill the engine to prevent a propeller strike.

- Once the rider is aboard, ensure the ladder is up and that the rider, passengers, and gear are secure before moving.

TOWING RIDER HAND SIGNALS

FASTER

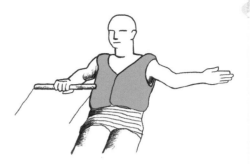

RIGHT (STARBOARD) TURN

LEFT (PORT) TURN

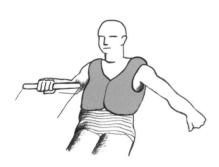

SLOWER

STOP

SKIER OK AFTER FALL

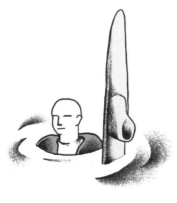

**PICK ME UP OR FALLEN
SKIER—WATCH OUT**

CUT MOTOR

SPEED OKAY

CARBON MONOXIDE KILLS

Carbon monoxide (CO) is a colorless, odorless, tasteless gas produced by combustion from engines, generators, cooktops, and heaters. CO buildup is a particular danger on boats: It can occur in a sealed cabin while cooking or from a poorly ventilated cabin heater. You can be exposed to heavy doses while idling, motoring slowly with a tailwind, or when being towed behind the boat and inhaling engine exhaust. Never "teak surf": for example, grabbing the stern and bodysurfing behind the boat.

PREVENTING CO BUILDUP

- CO can collect if you're moored against a seawall or other structure (even another big boat). Maintain fresh-air circulation around the boat. Open cabin windows.

- Do not sit and idle, especially in still air, which can envelop everyone in a cloud of CO.

- When motoring slowly, exhaust readily "backdrafts" into the stern (aka, the "station wagon effect"). Be wary if running downwind at the speed of the breeze.

- Keep your motor well-tuned or upgrade your engine: The worst are older, outboard, two-stroke engines (Evinrude E-Tec two-strokes are an exception). For lower CO, get a post-2011 inboard engine with a catalytic converter or a newer, noncatalytic, four-stroke outboard. But never let your guard down.

CO POISONING SYMPTOMS AND TREATMENT

Carbon monoxide binds to hemoglobin and prevents red blood cells from absorbing oxygen. Both quick high-concentration inhalations and prolonged low-concentration inhalations can kill. Note that CO poisoning symptoms can be mistaken for seasickness or drunkenness, and that exercising exacerbates the effects of exposure. Symptoms include eye irritation, headaches, nausea, weakness, and dizziness. If you suspect someone has CO poisoning, do the following:

- Immediately move the victim into completely fresh air and disable the source of CO.

- Have the victim lie down and watch for worsening condition.

- Summon medical help or call 911.

- If the victim loses consciousness, immediately perform CPR (page 200).

FOUR GREAT USES FOR **A DRY BAG**

Dry bags—or wet bags, as they're also known—are great for keeping your gear dry, but alternative uses include serving as makeshift pillows and saving your life. Here are a few ways they can help you in a pinch, on and off the water.

Makeshift PFD: Dry bags are neither meant to float you nor are they USCG-certified PFDs, but if you find yourself adrift with one on hand, you're (sort of) in luck. Simply pack it with as much air as you can and roll it three times before clipping. You may have to reinflate it after several hours, but it will keep you afloat and give a place to rest your weary head. Orange and red are good color choices for this reason.

Catch bag or cooler: If you're in cooler climes, or have cool water or ice available, a thick dry bag is a great way to keep certain critters alive and fresh, especially shellfish like clams, which are best when kept wet and cool. Don't leave the bag in the sun when bearing fresh catch, and don't put anything too craggy inside, like oysters, which might tear it. This also keeps beer cool, of course.

Free dive or spearfish float: Tether your inflated dry bag to your speargun or dive belt, and this makeshift float will alert boat traffic and your diving buddy to your position. Again, orange and red are best.

Buoy or marker: While not always legal, your dry bag can serve as a marker for a water hazard, or you can use it as a buoy for a shellfish pot. (Be sure to attach your name, phone number, and possibly address and/or vessel name and registration number.)

BOOKING A CHARTER BOAT

If you lack a boat, gear, insurance, and expertise, but not a yearning for the sea, book a charter. Which kind, you ask?

PRIVATE CHARTERS

Private charter captains are accustomed to fishing in rough seas, and experienced charter clients know this. So consider: Do you get seasick? Are you comfortable with being 20, even 50, miles offshore? If unexpected weather kicks up 10- to 12-foot ocean swells and 20-knot winds, the fishing trip won't necessarily be cancelled or deposits returned. Will you mind? Do you understand the experience you've booked and know, say, that fishing the iconic sand flats of the Bahamas means standing in direct sunlight all day with no cover?

PARTY FISHING BOATS

Often referred to as "booze cruises," open or "party" boats can have a rough atmosphere that isn't always suited for children. Find out whether you'll need to bring your own gear and how many other clients are expected aboard. You might share the boat with anywhere from ten to forty people.

ETIQUETTE AND TIPPING

Regardless of the type of charter, know that the captain is in charge and follow orders. Excessive boozing and/or tomfoolery is not tolerated because it puts everyone in danger and might land you in jail.

Want superlative service on your next outing? Tip well. Mates and crews work mostly for tips, and hard as it is to believe considering a charter's cost, captains can barely afford to cover their own bills. Generally, follow the same formula for tipping in US restaurants, and do not charter a boat unless you're prepared to tip at least 15 percent of the trip's cost. If you're thrilled, upwards of 20 percent is just peachy.

PERMISSION TO COME ABOARD:
LOADING, BOARDING, AND SEATING

The smaller the boat, the more important this often overlooked skill becomes. First, remember to load your boat evenly from the center so it rides flat, or at "trim," and enter the boat at the center, keeping the dock lines taut. Never step on the gunwale, especially on a smaller boat. When loading gear, put it on the dock and load it from the boat. It's even better if someone hands it to you.

When driving, if you load weight too far forward, the boat will plow through the water instead of jumping on an efficient plane. Exceeding your boat's listed capacity is also a no-no. The heavier your boat is loaded, the more likely it will unintentionally "ship" water, making it susceptible to swamping. When you're on the beach, board or load from the bow, then while hanging on the sand, turn the boat around to face bow out. (See How to Pull onto a Beach, page 33.)

AVOID THE SWAMP: KNOW YOUR BOAT'S CAPACITY

How many people and how much weight can you carry? Check the boat's capacity plate, usually found near the helm or at the transom. For a boat rated for eight persons or 1,225 pounds, you could carry more than eight people, but 1,225 pounds is the legal weight capacity, excluding an outboard motor. It's not a federal violation to exceed stated capacity, but it could be a violation in your state or locality; the Coast Guard might cite you for unsafe operation, and insurance may not cover an accident.

If your boat lacks a capacity plate, the USCG recommends this formula to determine the maximum number of passengers: boat length (in feet) multiplied by width, divided by fifteen.

OPERATE A BOAT IN AN EMERGENCY

These instructions are not meant to replace a proper boating course. But it doesn't hurt for all passengers to know the basics of operating a boat—for instance, if the skipper becomes incapacitated or falls overboard (page 64). If the captain appoints you as second-in-command, bookmark these pages. To radio for help in an emergency, see page 236.

UNDERSTANDING THE HELM

1. Compass (the white line indicates direction of travel)

2. Chart plotter/GPS

3. Steering wheel or tiller

4. Gearshift/throttle (three positions: forward, neutral, reverse)

5. Trim/tilt switch (raises/lowers engine out of/into water)

6. Ignition (may have an "emergency stop" quick-release lanyard that, when removed, stops the boat)

7. VHF radio

8. Fuel gauge

9. Tachometer/RPMs

10. Side view of lanyard attachment to console

11. Battery switch (a saucer-size dial usually near the stern)

12. Fuel primer or primer bulb (an egg-like bulge on fuel line that, when pumped, gets fuel into engine)

13. Engine temperature gauge

14. Trim/tilt indicator gauge

15. Voltmeter

16. Switches for bilge pump, lights, and power to console

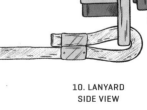

10. LANYARD SIDE VIEW

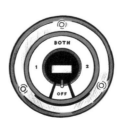

11. BATTERY SWITCH

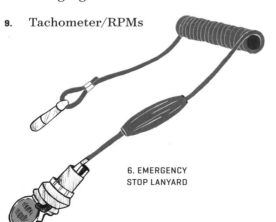

6. EMERGENCY STOP LANYARD

12. PRIMER BULB

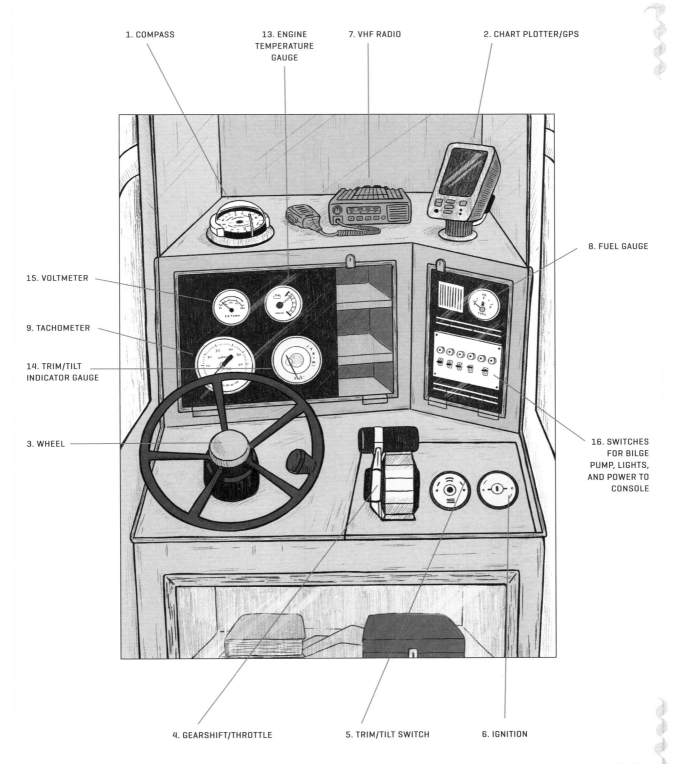

1. COMPASS

13. ENGINE TEMPERATURE GAUGE

7. VHF RADIO

2. CHART PLOTTER/GPS

8. FUEL GAUGE

15. VOLTMETER

9. TACHOMETER

14. TRIM/TILT INDICATOR GAUGE

3. WHEEL

16. SWITCHES FOR BILGE PUMP, LIGHTS, AND POWER TO CONSOLE

4. GEARSHIFT/THROTTLE

5. TRIM/TILT SWITCH

6. IGNITION

TAKING THE HELM

The main concern is stopping and starting the boat. Once you're driving, just don't go too fast for conditions. For driving tips, see page 62.

STOPPING THE BOAT

In an emergency, stopping the engine is the fastest way to stop the boat. Turn off the key; if there's a lanyard or cut-off switch in the ignition, yank it out. To stop the boat while keeping the engine running, pull the throttle back to center or neutral position.

STARTING AN INBOARD OR OUTBOARD MOTOR

1. Ensure the dashboard power switch, if present, is on and the dial battery switch, if present, is set to 1, 2, "on," or "both."

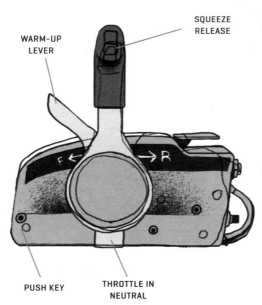

WARM-UP LEVER

SQUEEZE RELEASE

F ← → R

PUSH KEY

THROTTLE IN NEUTRAL

2. Blower: If present, engage blower for at least a minute before starting engine to purge explosive gas vapors.

3. Turn on navigation lights.

4. Click the gearshift/throttle into middle, neutral position.

5. Press the trim/tilt "down" to lower propeller into the water.

6. Pump the fuel bulb a few times, until it feels very firm.

7. Ensure lanyard/cutoff switch, if present, is in place in the ignition.

8. To start the engine with a warm-up switch or lever: While in neutral, turn the key and raise the warm-up switch. Once the engine revs, lower back down to idle before engaging the gearshift.

9. To start the engine without a warm-up lever: Shifter will instead have an outward-sliding warm-up control on the gearshift. Pull gearshift out sideways a quarter-inch or so to run up throttle in neutral for warm-up. Slide back inward to engage gearshift.

10. To drive the boat, gently engage the throttle or gearshift. You may need to depress a trigger button to engage forward and reverse. Slide forward to accelerate, and slide backward to reverse. Reversing too quickly can swamp the boat.

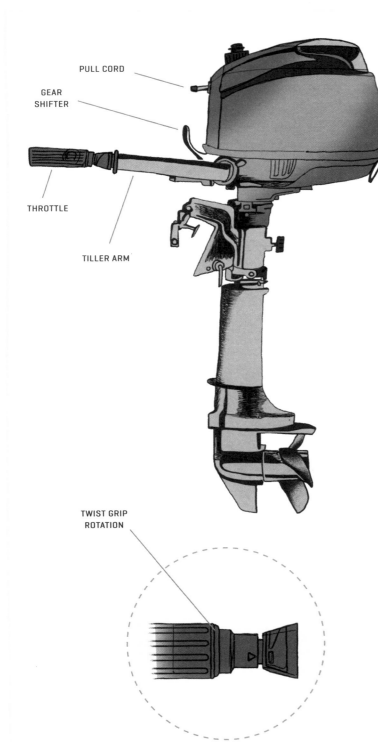

PULL CORD

GEAR
SHIFTER

THROTTLE

TILLER ARM

TWIST GRIP
ROTATION

STARTING A TILLER-STEERED MOTOR
A tiller-steered motor should have "start procedure" instructions on the engine.

1. Before starting, ensure the gear-shift is in the neutral position.

2. Pump the primer/gas bulb on the fuel line until firm.

3. Pull the ripcord hard. This may take several attempts. If the engine won't start, turn the throttle handle grip starboard (the boat's right) to "throttle up," and try again. After the engine starts, "throttle down" by turning the throttle to port (the boat's left).

4. If there is an emergency cutoff lanyard, put it into position and slip it onto your wrist.

TRIMMING, PLANING, AND STEERING: ESSENTIAL DRIVING SKILLS

Driving a boat can seem even simpler than driving a car, but boating well, and safely, requires three essential skills.

OUTBARDS & STERNDRIVES

TRIMMING "OUT" EXCESSIVELY

TRIMMING "IN" EXCESSIVELY

NEUTRAL TRIM FOR CALM WATERS

Trimming: Keeping your boat properly trimmed creates a safe and steady ride, minimizes fuel consumption with maximum speed, and keeps you from looking like a kook. "Trim" refers to the way the boat sits on the water while moving, and you adjust trim by tilting the motor. (Can't find that button? See "Operate a Boat in an Emergency," page 58.) To find the "sweet spot" for a neutral trim (with neither bow nor stern raised), test yourself both while motoring slowly and while planing.

Planing: At low speeds, a boat simply pushes water out of the way. At intermediate speeds (before planing), the stern sinks, the bow rises dramatically (limiting visibility), your boat hogs gas, and it creates a powerful, potentially dangerous wake. Thus, unless safety requires a low speed, the best way to travel is by planing. At high speeds (14 to 20 mph), a boat planes when it rises above its bow wave and levels off. The bow wave shrinks dramatically, and it's more fuel efficient and stable.

Steering and handling: A boat handles differently than a car because it's typically driven from the stern. Practice turning at low speed to learn where your vessel pivots.

Boats also handle unpredictably because waves, wakes, and currents make the water an unpredictable surface. The faster you go, the more difficult handling can be, and if you feel you're going too fast, you probably are. Turn too hard at speed in chop and your boat may roll over instead of turn. That's no good for anyone.

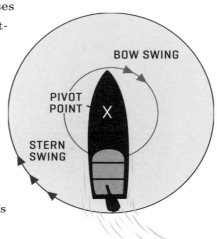

BOW SWING

PIVOT POINT

STERN SWING

GOING FOR A SWIM:
VOLUNTARILY AND INVOLUNTARILY

When boating, sometimes you want to swim, and sometimes you don't. Here's advice for swimming safely and avoiding overboard accidents (page 64).

SWIMMING OFF THE BOAT—VOLUNTARILY

Always make sure your anchor is well set and the engine is off before letting anyone jump off the boat. Then, be aware that tides and currents can change, and consider keeping someone onboard all the time to retrieve anyone who gets swept away.

- Swim only during the day.

- Stop well before you get tired.

- Don't dive off the boat—only enter feet first.

- Children and nonswimmers must wear PFDs.

- Trail a long, floating, or buoyed line that swimmers can grab if necessary.

SWIMMING OFF THE BOAT—INVOLUNTARILY

A prepared boat is key to accident prevention: Keep the deck free of hazards, maintain hand and guard rails, have a pull-down ladder, and keep lines and PFDs ready for rescue. When the water's rough, make sure every person has a whistle and perhaps even a safety harness or line. Then avoid these common human errors:

- Urinating into the ocean is a constant source of "man overboard" accidents. Use a cup or bucket, or the head below decks, especially if you're not strapped in.

- No one should be on deck alone, especially at night.

- Drugs, alcohol, and boating don't mix.

"CREW OVERBOARD!": A RESCUE PRIMER

The Coast Guard reports over fifteen hundred people fall overboard every year. To rescue a drowning swimmer, see page 195. Here's how to retrieve someone who involuntarily leaves the boat.

INITIATE RESCUE

1. Shout, "Crew overboard to [location: starboard, port, stern]!"

2. Sound six or more short horn blasts.

3. Have someone besides the captain point continuously at the victim and keep them in constant sight.

4. Get the victim flotation immediately: Throw in a floating boat cushion, life ring, rescue sling, inflatable throw bag, a ski rope with a PFD, even a surfboard. Cold water can quickly incapacitate the healthiest victim.

5. If you fear losing sight of the victim, toss in a buoy, smoke signal, or floating light, or mark their location with GPS. Even a line of garbage can lead you back.

6. Evaluate the victim's condition: Are they conscious, unconscious, or injured? Are they heavily dressed? Wet clothes can make it almost impossible for a solo rescuer to bring a victim aboard.

7. Talk to and calm a conscious victim. Give them advice for handling cold shock and conserving heat; see "Cold Shock and Hypothermia," page 226.

8. If an emergency "mayday" call is warranted, immediately alert the Coast Guard and nearby boaters (page 236).

WILLIAMSON TURN

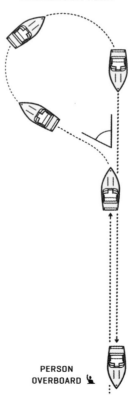

PERSON
OVERBOARD

POSITION THE BOAT

Ensure no lines have been pulled overboard that could wrap in the propeller, then turn the boat around. Maneuver next to the victim while staying on their downwind or down-current side, so you don't drift over them. If wind and waves are strong, get no closer than 10 feet, and approach dead slow—at speeds above 1 knot, it's impossible for a victim to hold a line.

The best way to position the boat depends on your boat and the situation:

- In a powerboat, shift throttle to idle, turn toward the victim on the side they went overboard, using a simple "destroyer" turn.

- In a sailboat, if the victim is in sight, initiate a "quickstop" turn: Turn into the wind and turn back to the person in the water. Don't drop sail immediately, even if you'll ultimately motor into position. After passing back by the victim, drop sail and turn toward them, approaching bow-first.

- If you can't see the victim, initiate a "Williamson" turn: Put the helm over, turning hard toward the side where the victim fell (if known), until you've changed heading 60 degrees. Then come around 240 degrees until you're on the exact reciprocal course to your original course. This will put you on the best line to the victim.

QUICKSTOP TURN

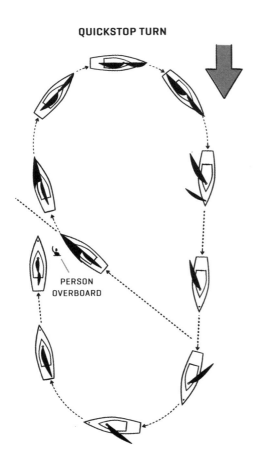

PERSON OVERBOARD

DESTROYER TURN

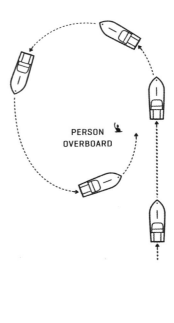

PERSON OVERBOARD

BOARDING A CONSCIOUS VICTIM

Avoid entering the water to help a conscious victim. That may only increase the number of people needing rescue. Based on your gear, your boat, and the conditions, decide the best way to bring the person aboard.

Most of all, especially in cold water, it's more important to lift the victim from the water horizontally, if possible, than to get them out quickly. Lifting vertically causes all the blood to rush to the lower body and away from the brain and heart, which can lead to unconsciousness or even death.

- Provide a way for the victim to climb or be lifted aboard. Deploy a line, rescue net, or aluminum rescue ladder. To create a makeshift ladder, string three lines at staggered heights from cleats on the side. A simple loop tied into a line can provide a vital foothold (keep a line prelooped and ready).

- Choose the safest place to board. On a bigger boat, that's often the side; avoid the transom (or stern) in heavy seas, since the boat can crush a victim. For a small boat that's low in the water, using the transom (or even the bow) might be necessary to prevent capsizing.

- Distribute weight to the opposite side of the boat to prevent capsizing as the victim boards.

- All rescuers should tie or strap themselves to the opposite side to avoid being pulled overboard during rescue.

- To pull the victim from the water with only one rescuer: Have the victim face outward, away from the boat. Grab their arms with a mountain climber grip. If rescuing at the side, use the boat's rocking motion to your advantage. As your side lowers, coordinate your actions so the victim kicks while the rescuer pulls with all their might.

- To pull a victim with two rescuers: One rescuer grabs under the shoulders or by the arms while the other grabs under the knees, so the victim is lifted horizontally.

- If the victim must be winched aboard (i.e., using a sailboat's winch), ideally use a rescue device like a LifeSling Overboard Rescue System (a buoyant horseshoe-shaped device that loops beneath the arms). Then, rig the rescue line to a windlass, block and tackle, boom vang, or mainsail halyard, and winch them up. Again, if possible, lift from two points— under the shoulders and under the knees—to keep the victim horizontal.

- In a sailboat, you might lower the jib sail into the water and lift the victim aboard inside it.

BOARDING AN UNCONSCIOUS VICTIM

If the victim is unconscious, don't attempt a solo rescue if there's any chance you may also end up in the water. Instead, wait for help to arrive.

If one person can swim while another person remains onboard, have the swimmer put the victim in a rescue device, or else run a mooring line through a cleat and get the line underneath the victim's arms. Tow the victim to the boat. Once they're alongside, loop another line under the victim's knees and heave them aboard horizontally.

If you have a sturdy net, improvise a "Jason's Cradle." Roll the victim into the boat horizontally.

POST-RESCUE CARE

Treat any overboard victim as if they are critically ill, and seek medical attention immediately. Lay the victim down with their head toward the stern and legs slightly elevated in order to keep the blood flow toward the head while the boat is under way. Administer oxygen if available. Treat for hypothermia (page 226).

Beware of post-rescue collapse: Never tell a victim to relax until they are fully stable under medical supervision. Instead, tell them to keep fighting. Sometimes people are so relieved at being rescued that they can pass out and even die. Even free of the water, they are still fighting for their life.

JASON'S CRADLE

ESSENTIAL NAUTICAL KNOTS AND TURNS

These are the twists and turns no sailor can live without.

BIGHT, **TURN**, and **ROUND TURN** are the foundation of our knots.

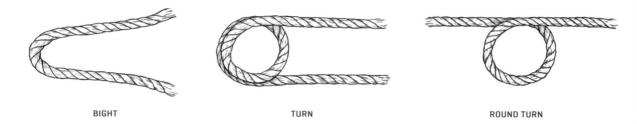

BIGHT   TURN   ROUND TURN

HALF HITCH: Rarely used alone, a half
hitch usually secures a primary knot.

SINGLE HALF HITCH   TWO HALF HITCHES

BOWLINE: An easy, secure loop to be
used under load.

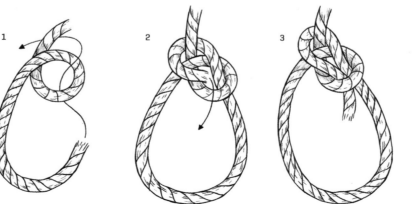

RUNNING BOWLINE: Sliding loop or noose, good for lassoing.

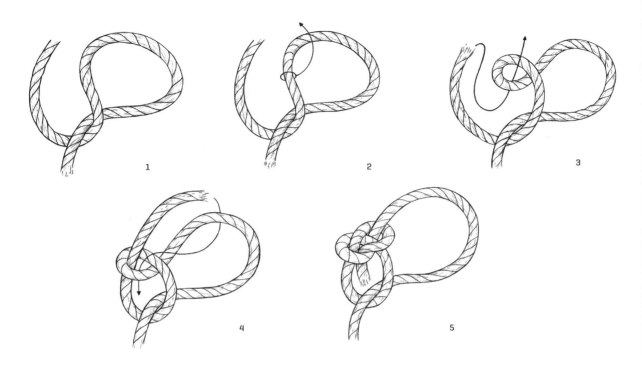

FIGURE EIGHT FOLLOW-THROUGH: Super solid knot for securing the line to a ring, harness, or carabiner for climbing (especially up a mast).

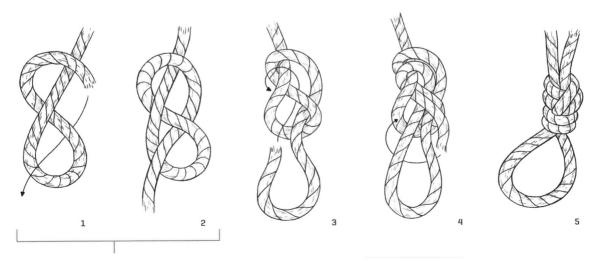

FIGURE EIGHT: Quick stopper knot.

ANCHOR BEND [A.K.A. FISHERMAN'S LOOP]:
Anchors the line to a chain/shackle; attaches
fishing line to tackle.

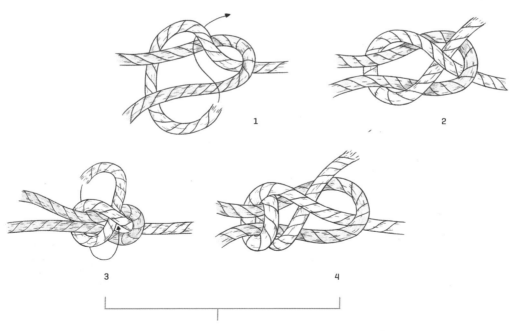

DOUBLE-SHEET BEND

SHEET BEND: Adjoins two lines, especially of different diameter. More secure than a square knot.

1   2   3

CLOVE HITCH: For tying boat fenders to railings; simple quick-release hitch to tie the line to a secured line or post. However, it slips when the object it's tied to slips or is not under constant pressure. Best secured with two half hitches.

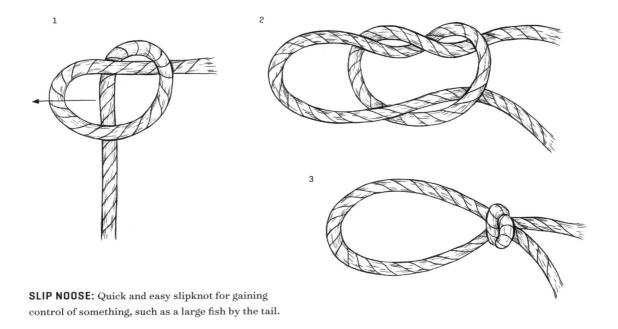

1   2

3

SLIP NOOSE: Quick and easy slipknot for gaining control of something, such as a large fish by the tail.

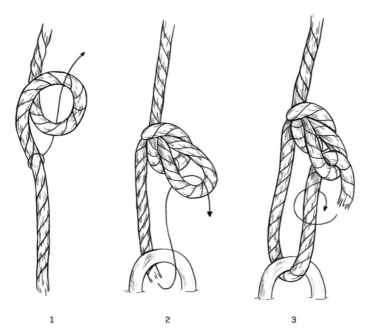

TRUCKER'S HITCH: Straps objects to roof racks or boat rails; secures loads and tarps.

Tie a slippery half-hitch in the middle of the rope. Make a turn around a bar, cleat, or the like. Pull very tight.

1   2   3

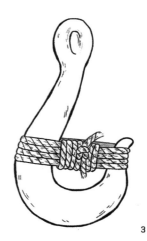

1   2   3

MOUSE A HOOK: Prevents a line or spring from slipping off a hook; prevents a hook from straightening under a load; replaces a missing pin on a shackle.

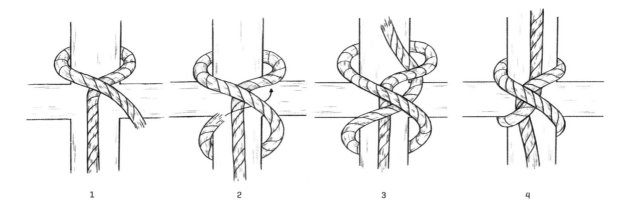

1 2 3 4

TRANSOM KNOT: Binds rigid materials, such as wood, at right angles.

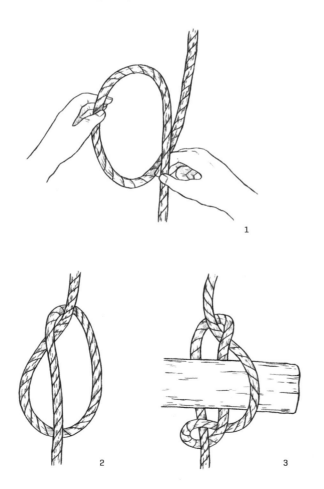

1

2 3

4

LADDER HITCH: Can be used to form a ladder by stringing hitches vertically and on either end of horizontal spars. Very helpful in an overboard rescue!

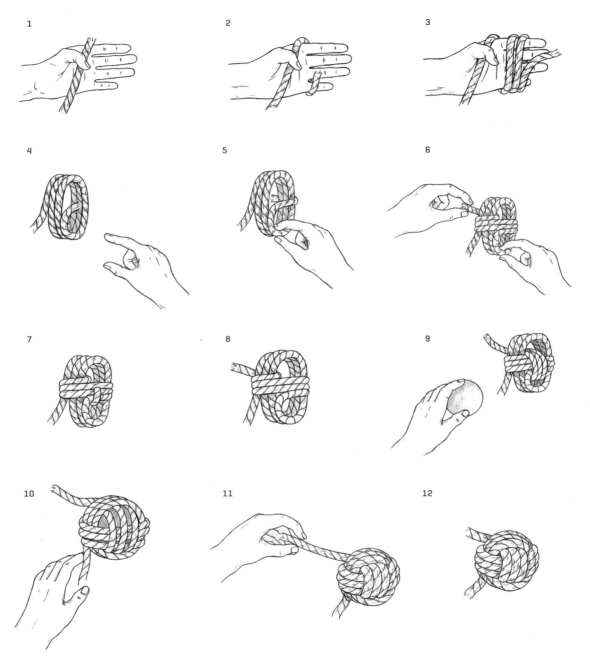

The **MONKEY FIST KNOT** is so-called because it resembles a clutched monkey's paw. Insert a weighted ball or a rubber ball inside the "fist" to make a heaved line go farther or to make it float.

Humans have taken animals on boats for, arguably, as long as humans have been going to sea. Today, many recreational boaters bring their dogs. Here are nine tips for a nautical canine.

1. Provide lots of food and water, and bring newspaper or paper towels for accidents.

2. Dogs can get seasick and throw up, just like humans. Or drink too much saltwater and become dehydrated. Also watch for signs of lethargy, disorientation, and lack of balance.

3. Provide shade, both to protect their feet from hot decks and to avoid heat exhaustion. Watch for very heavy panting and drooling.

4. All dogs can swim, but not all are good swimmers, particularly short-legged dogs. Others may tire quickly. Watch out for a floundering dog, and consider a pet life jacket, which makes retrieving a dog far easier.

5. Don't let your dog jump into a busy or current-filled waterway. Or consider not letting your dog swim. A sopping wet, waterlogged dog is heavy. Wear a life jacket when retrieving your dog—since you could end up in the water, too.

6. If you visit islands or preserves, ensure they aren't protected or pet restricted (which could result in hefty fines). Regardless, keep your dog from disturbing birds, other wildlife, foliage, or fellow humans.

7. On beaches and in shallows, think of paws. Sharp shells, oyster beds, coral reefs, and sea urchins can lacerate feet.

8. To help dogs board a boat from land, a surfboard or standup paddle-board can take the place of a ramp.

9. Keep all fishing gear away from dogs—and beware of back casts. Your dog may view a shrimp-baited hook as a snack or jump in to retrieve a well-cast lure.

WHERE AM I?: NAUTICAL CHARTS, COMPASSES, AND LANDMARKS

Learning to navigate the ocean is something like going down a rabbit hole. The more you know, the more you realize there is to know. For traditional Polynesian societies, it's sacred knowledge passed down through generations. For modern sailors, it's the work of a lifetime.

Thankfully or not, modern technology like GPS has made it possible to know your position without any calculations or nautical knowledge whatsoever. However, you should know how to decipher a nautical chart, read a compass, and get a visual fix on your position using landmarks. This not only might save lives in an emergency, it's the sort of knowledge that will make you a sailor.

NAVIGATING A NAUTICAL CHART

Locations on a nautical chart, and anywhere on the globe, are measured precisely in intersecting, imaginary latitude and longitude lines, wrapping Earth in a grid. Latitude is always named first, longitude second.

"Parallels of latitude": These horizontal (east-west) lines form circles around the globe and measure distances north and south, starting at the equator.

"Meridians of longitude": These vertical (north-south) lines go pole to pole and measure distances east and west, starting from an imaginary line called the prime meridian. This longitude line passes through the Royal Naval Observatory in Greenwich, England, and is the source for GMT, or Greenwich Mean Time.

Distances for both latitude and longitude are measured in degrees (°), minutes ('), and seconds ("). This is abbreviated as DMS and appears as DD°MM'SS". These numbers refer to exact distances, which get progressively more refined.

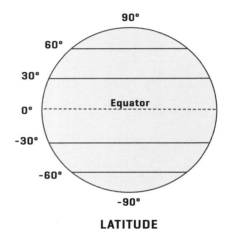

LATITUDE

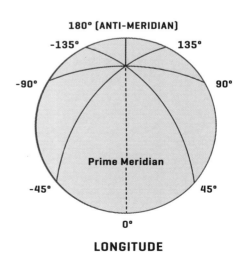

LONGITUDE

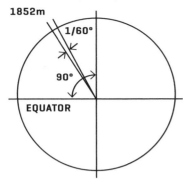

NORTH POLE

1852m

1/60°

90°

EQUATOR

LAT/LONG: A MATTER OF DEGREES

Degrees of latitude and longitude are calculated relative to their imaginary "starting points." Latitude starts at the equator, which is zero degrees (0°) latitude. North of the equator, degrees of latitude are positive numbers, and south of the equator, they are negative numbers. Thus, the North Pole is latitude +90° north, and the South Pole is -90° south (add up all four 90° quadrants and you get 360°, or a circle).

In case you were wondering, the distance from the equator to the North Pole is 5,400 nautical miles, which makes the circumference of the entire Earth 21,600 nautical miles, or 21,600 minutes.

Longitude lines are measured from the prime meridian at Greenwich, which is zero degrees (0°). West of the prime meridian, degrees are negative numbers, and east of the prime meridian, they are positive numbers (up to the point they reach the anti-meridian, on the exact opposite side of the globe, which is 180°).

The intersection of latitude and longitude can be given for any location on the planet. As an example, here is the location in degrees, minutes, seconds (DMS) for the Statue of Liberty in New York City:

Latitude: N 40°41′21″
Longitude: W 74°2′40″

Just to confuse things, GPS renders DMS into decimals, and while it's a useful skill to know how to convert decimals into DMS, and vice versa, it's enough to know that both mean the same thing. For instance, the decimal or digital location of the Statue of Liberty is: latitude 40.68916, longitude -74.0444.

TRUE NORTH: USING A COMPASS

A compass is a simple device that makes use of a magnetized needle or disk to indicate the direction "north." The needle consistently points north because of the pull of the earth's magnetic field.

Every compass has a "compass card" that marks each direction as part of a 360° circle: North is 000°, east is 090°, south is 180°, and west is 270°.

Seems simple, but there are two dangers with a magnetic compass. One is called deviation. Since the needle is magnetic, any nearby iron-containing metal can attract or influence it, so that the needle won't point north but to that metal object. To avoid deviation, read the compass far from any such metal.

The other issue is variation. In fact, the planet's "magnetic north" is slightly different than the planet's "true north," which is the North Pole. Depending on where you are, this variation can be nonexistent or off by several degrees—and thus, hundreds of miles.

Thankfully, all nautical charts have a compass rose with arrows that indicate magnetic north (on the inside) and true north (on the outside, indicated by a star). Variation can be accounted for by simply counting the degrees of difference between magnetic and true north. To get a true heading, read your compass, then add degrees for west variation, and subtract for east variation.

LANDMARKS: GET YOUR FIX

Establishing your location using landmarks—which the Coast Guard might need in an emergency—is known as your fix. While boating, keep a running mental log of your position in relation to a few specific coastal landmarks—lighthouses, headlands, harbors, river mouths. Don't try to remember everything. Just name for yourself a few notable ones.

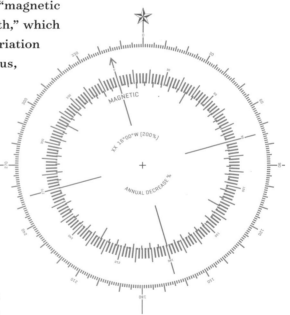

A NAUTICAL CHART FEATURES A COMPASS ROSE LIKE THIS ONE.

Depending on the location on Earth, it will indicate both "true north" and "magnetic north," which is either east or west of true north. The outer 360° ring with the star up top represents true north. The inner 360° ring represents magnetic north.

Lines of position fix: To determine a fix, it's easiest to establish lines of position (LOP). Line up two objects or landmarks on a nautical chart and draw a line on the chart from those to your vessel. This at least determines that you're on a line between those points. Now establish another LOP and draw that line on your chart. The point where those two LOPs intersect is your position or fix. For more accuracy, use three LOPs.

A bearing fix: Select two or more identifiable physical landmarks or aids to navigation (AToNs) on your chart, such as a buoy. If you only use two, make sure the angle between you and the landmarks is as close to 90° as possible. Head your vessel toward or aim a handheld compass at the marks. The direction of the landmark or AToN from you is its bearing. Once you have the bearings of these marks, check the deviation on the chart.

Boating in a straight line: Establish a transit. Line up two objects—any two objects, a telephone pole, a dock, a church steeple, a prominent tree. Keep those objects lined up and head toward them. If they come out of line, adjust your course accordingly to bring them back into line.

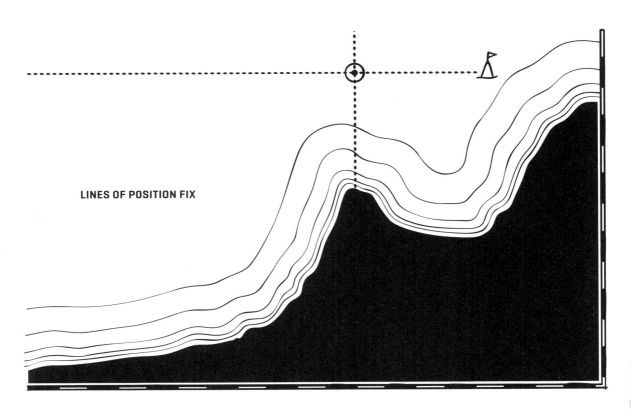

LINES OF POSITION FIX

TO **BECOME A SAILOR,**
GO TO THE SEA

AS TOLD BY LIN PARDEY
With her late husband, Larry (who sadly passed away in 2020), Lin Pardey
sailed over 200,000 nautical miles and coauthored over ten books about their
adventures. Lin is, quite simply, the most experienced female sailor on Earth.

I'm originally from Detroit. My husband, Larry, was a professional
skipper when I first met him. We built our first boat together and
launched it in 1968 and set off for six months. We came home
eleven years later. It was just so cool.

Sailing away—I get asked about this constantly. We've spent
our lives trying to guide people so their dream isn't destroyed.
It's the choices you make right in the beginning. The first thing I
tell people is that comfort and safety do not exactly equal adventure and freedom. Cruising isn't easy. If it was, everyone would be
doing it. The only way to become a sailor—and these are Larry's
words—is to go to the sea. People take so many courses—so many
classes, seminars, and books. People spend too much time learning and not enough time actually on the boat doing.

So my first advice is to get out sailing with other people. Get
out on as many different boats as possible. But choose the people
you sail with carefully. Are they fun to sail with? Do they know
what they're doing? Before you buy a cruising boat and sail away,
your first sailboat should be small, 14 or 15 feet long, so that you
really learn how to sail.

We sailed over 200,000 nautical miles and have had the good
fortune of never damaging a boat in our voyaging. We never
had a gear failure at sea except for one spinnaker halyard. The
thing that makes sailing so unique is that the basic machine you
use—your sailboat—is actually very simple. It depends on the
sails working, the rudder working, the mast standing up, and the
hull not leaking—and that's it. Our boat *Taleisin* was 29 feet and
6 inches. She was very beamy, designed for extremely light wind
sailing, and she was beautiful.

She also had no engine. Sailing engine-free we call it. Being
down here now in New Zealand, we're very aware of these Polynesian voyages. Sailing engine-free connects us with that nautical

history—the vastness of the oceans. Every time you add one more complication to that equation, instead of making your life easier in the long run, it might cause more problems than it's worth. Electric winches. Oh, great, they take some of the work out of sailing. Well, the minute the electricity doesn't work, you don't have that power to help you anymore. Then you spend hours and hours getting it fixed.

Living in close quarters together—that's not as much of an issue as people think. If both people decide to go sailing, it isn't the close quarters that gets to them. It's learning to take care of the boat. Remember, you're taking care of all the facilities of a city—by yourselves. That includes creating your own water, electricity, a propulsion unit, and a sewer plant. You don't do that in real life on land. So what gets people down is gear breakage—that ruins more cruises than anything.

The average person can go cruising on a $15,000 30-footer that they buy from a storage yard. You don't have to be rich. That 50-footer that many folks want is a hell of a lot of boat for two people. So many things can go wrong. You don't need a big boat. Get out there for a while in a smaller boat and learn to take care of it—and yourself.

I spent my formative years living on a 33-foot boat and sailing around the world with my family. As a 12 year old, I did the "dogwatch" alone, 2am to 6am, with infinity above me and six miles of ocean below. The incomprehensible vastness insists that child acknowledge an inner world, this inner world is not ephemeral, it is highly coloured and clearly defined, populated by any ever changing cast. My so called "muse" is not separate from me, it is "me" and it's all I have. I have done some terrible things to her but nevertheless she has not deserted me. She goes quiet sometimes to escape noise but is always there.

—Katie Jane Garside, lead singer of Daisy Chainsaw, Queenadreena, and Ruby Throat.

THE BEAUFORT WIND SCALE

All sailors know that too much sail in too much wind can produce fatal results.

Fortunately, in 1806, Sir Francis Beaufort, a captain in the British Admiralty, helped figure this out. He modified a wind chart originally developed to measure the speed of windmills. Beaufort, a brilliant sailor, described twelve wind and sea states that determined how much sail a British Man O' War could safely unfurl and how fast the ship would then travel. Rather than describing the wind in knots, he chose a "force" scale, which goes from 0 (calm) to 12 (a hurricane), or in Beaufort's immortal words, "That which no canvas could withstand."

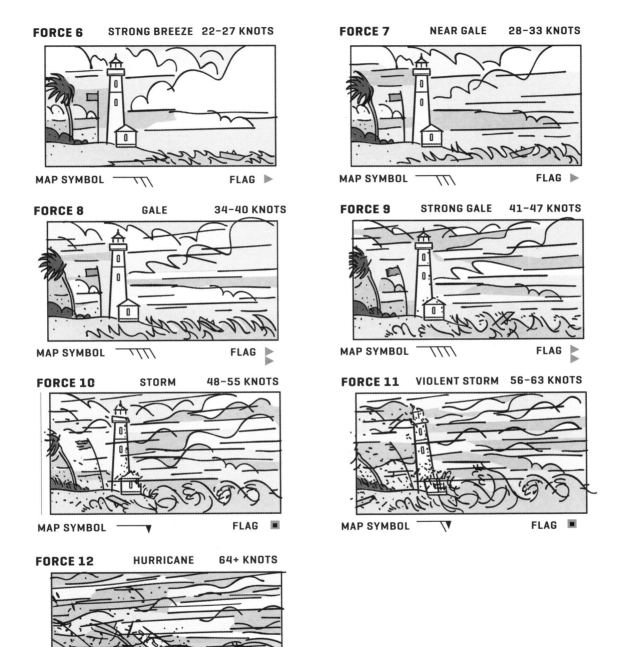

FORCE 6   STRONG BREEZE 22–27 KNOTS
MAP SYMBOL   FLAG

FORCE 7   NEAR GALE   28–33 KNOTS
MAP SYMBOL   FLAG

FORCE 8   GALE   34–40 KNOTS
MAP SYMBOL   FLAG

FORCE 9   STRONG GALE   41–47 KNOTS
MAP SYMBOL   FLAG

FORCE 10   STORM   48–55 KNOTS
MAP SYMBOL   FLAG

FORCE 11   VIOLENT STORM 56–63 KNOTS
MAP SYMBOL   FLAG

FORCE 12   HURRICANE   64+ KNOTS
MAP SYMBOL   FLAG

DROWNING IN INK:
PROPER **NAUTICAL TATTOOS**

Show me a man with a tattoo and I'll show you a man with an interesting past.

—Jack London

Compromised as they may seem, sailor's tattoos once held significance, and occasionally they still do. In collaboration with Christina Sun at Bowsprite, here's a compendium of sailor tattoos and their respective meanings.

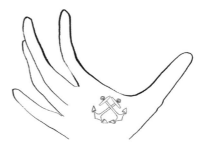

HOLD written on one set of knuckles and **FAST** written on the other is meant to give a sailer good grip in the rigging.

A **NAUTICAL STAR** or **COMPASS ROSE** was traditionally given so that a sailor could always find his or her way home.

CROSSED ANCHORS on the webbing between the thumb and index fingers are for a bos'n's (or boatswain's) mate.

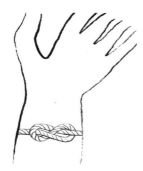

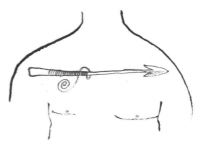

A **ROPE** tattooed around the wrist suggests a sailor is or was a dockhand.

A tattoo of an **ANCHOR** tells that a sailor has been a part of the Merchant Marines or crossed the Atlantic.

A **HARPOON** marks a member of the fishing fleet.

A **SPARROW** or a
SWALLOW tattoo goes
to a sailor for every
5,000 nautical miles
they travel—a swallow
because it can always
find its way home.

A **SHELLBACK**
TURTLE or **KING**
NEPTUNE is earned
when a sailor makes it
across the equator.

Royal Navy sailors during WWII
who took part in Mediterranean
cruises were tattooed with a **PALM**
TREE, as were US sailors who spent
time serving in Hawaii.

A **DAGGER THROUGH**
A ROSE proves a sailor
is loyal and shows a
willingness to fight any-
thing, even something as
sweet as a rose.

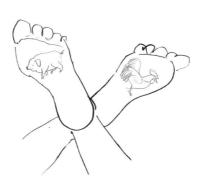

During WWII, **PIG AND**
ROOSTER tattoos (sometimes
one on each foot) were worn to
prevent a sailor from drowning. Pigs and roosters were
boarded in crates that floated,
and subsequently, are storied
to have been the only survivors
of some wrecks.

A **FULL-RIGGED SHIP** displays
that a sailor has been around
Cape Horn.

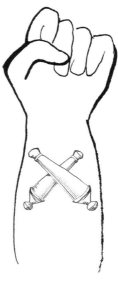

GUNS or **CROSSED CANNONS**
signify naval military service.

SURFING

THE RISE OF MODERN SURFING

AS TOLD BY STEVE PEZMAN

Steve Pezman is the founder and publisher of *The Surfer's Journal*. He was also a long-running publisher of *Surfer* magazine. Through the decades, "Pez" forged relationships with surfing's seminal photographers, writers, visionaries, and iconoclasts.

Early California history books tell stories of Hawaiian natives crewing on sailing boats to California. Richard Henry Dana wrote of incredibly skilled Hawaiian crewmen in his book *Two Years Before the Mast*. Hawaiians came to California for ranching when San Diego was just a pueblo, and it's hard to imagine that they didn't come ashore, look at the perfect waves, and surf. What we know for sure is that, in 1885, three Hawaiian princes who were in the United States shaped boards out of redwood and surfed the mouth of the San Lorenzo River in Santa Cruz.

At the turn of the twentieth century, surfing almost died out in Hawaii. The people who led the revival learned from Hawaiians but weren't full-blooded Hawaiians themselves. Alexander Hume Ford was a journalist from Charleston, South Carolina, who promoted surfing for commercial reasons. He and a Hawaii-born Irishman named George Freeth took Jack London surfing in 1907, which London wrote about in *Cruise of the Snark*. Freeth was in love with surfing, and he did the first mainland public demonstrations in 1907 at Redondo Beach.

Then came Duke Kahanamoku, surfing's Johnny Appleseed. He was Hawaiian and a 1912 Olympic gold medal swimmer, which gained him huge credibility and attention. Wherever he went, he introduced surfing, even constructing surfboards to use and leaving them. Those boards became the seeds. Take Corona Del Mar, California. Duke created a clan of surfers there that eventually included Lorrin Harrison and others who would become seminal California figures. Duke traveled to the East Coast, New Zealand, Australia, Europe. He spread the stoke far and wide.

In 1957, the bestselling book *Gidget* came out, which was based on a young Jewish girl from The Valley named Kathy Kohner and her time spent learning to surf at Malibu. Two years later, the movie *Gidget* arrived, a romantic fairytale that made surfriding very appealing to the masses. Its effect was profound. Up to then, parents tried to imbue their kids with values they'd learned during the Great Depression, and the main focus was obtaining security—the next meal, a home, the basic accoutrements of life. After *Gidget*, surfers threw that off. They said no—the ride, the experience, the cosmic connection, the exhilaration, the pleasure was the real reward of life.

At the same time, something just as important happened: foam. Hobie Alter (developer of the Hobie Cat) and Gordon "Grubby" Clark, who was just an outright genius, developed cheap, lightweight, easy-to-shape foam surfboard cores. Until then, surfboards were shaped from balsawood, but after *Gidget*, the number of surfers went from thousands to millions, and there wasn't enough balsa, so foam surfboards filled demand.

Decades later, Sean Collins founded the game-changing Surfline, which brought surfing into the twenty-first century. Sean wasn't a trained meteorologist, but he taught himself to be an incredible surf forecaster. Surfline started as a telephone forecasting service, then a fax service, and then a website featuring incredibly detailed forecasts and beach cameras. Rather than commodifying material like surfboards or clothing, Sean commodified information. He allowed people to cherry-pick good times to surf instead of having to spend all day at the beach waiting for the good moments. That allowed people to live away from the beach, pursue a career, have a family, and still get to surf when it was good. He completely changed the sport's dynamic. It was as if Native Americans were suddenly able to find a herd of deer by calling in their location instead of finding them by looking through the forest.

In a way, that was sad. All these things changed surfing culture from being a little secret thrill that relatively few knew about to a mass industry. The more popularized surfing became, the less specialized one needed to be. What it meant to be a surfer changed.

Yet surfing has maintained its allure, even after it got crowded. The modern world can't ruin surfing because the ride still exists—the push of the wave and the connection to the cosmic energy of the universe. Sun, weather, and wind create the swells that we're riding. There's a cosmic aspect to it. Even if you don't think of it that way, some part of your psyche is making that ancient connection when you're sitting out there looking at the horizon, waiting for a set.

How fast do you go on a giant wave? I installed a propeller on one of my towboards at Jaws, and it showed we went 40-something miles an hour, just on the wave. But the sensation, that's very different. Imagine you're on a racetrack, and the racetrack—the wave itself—is also moving at 22 miles an hour. If you're going downhill at another 40 miles an hour, the sensation of speed is increased immensely. On a really big wave it's close to what a downhill skier experiences. It's the maximum speed you can deal with as far as a human's ability to react.

A wave—especially a wave like Peahi—always feels faster because, the thing is, it's alive. When you're on skis or a mountain bike, the mountain doesn't move. With surfing, it's as if you were in an earthquake and the whole hill was sliding. Or like snowboarding on top of an avalanche. That's the sensation of the ocean and a wave.

—Laird Hamilton

DO YOU REALLY WANT TO START SURFING?

A CHAT WITH WILLIAM FINNEGAN

Of all the things you can do in life, few, if any, match the physical and spiritual rush provided by surfing. This can be wonderful and life-changing, but that attraction is also fraught with peril. Arguably, no human has done a better job of describing this perilous addiction than William Finnegan, the Pulitzer Prize–winning journalist and author of *Barbarian Days*. The following is a condensation of a conversation Finnegan had with Chris Dixon, who is himself intimately familiar with how a surfing obsession can impact one's life.

I include in *Barbarian Days* a conversation I had with a guy named André, a big-wave surfer from Oregon. We met in Madeira, and he was really young, so I was surprised to hear that he was divorced. He started telling me his stark little story. Surfing broke up his marriage. He said, "These women gotta know what they're getting into. It's like if you or I hooked up with a fanatical shopper. You'd have to accept that your entire life would be traveling around to malls. Or, really, more like waiting for malls to open." He was actually hilarious, but he wasn't trying to be funny. He was just thinking it through from the other side. While we were talking, we were driving around looking for waves, and it wasn't good, the tide was too high, so we ended up sleeping in the car by a surf spot waiting for the tide to drop— just a couple of shoppers waiting for the mall to open.

I never really experienced that kind of stark conflict with girlfriends over surfing: *What do you mean you're going surfing?!* For one thing, my life was rarely that settled or domestic when I was young. More often, with a girlfriend, we'd be traveling. So I might be dragging her to Maui or Sri Lanka or wherever. These girlfriends had more smarts and education than I had, but they just weren't sure what they wanted to do in the world yet, which left them open to my agenda, which almost always involved looking for waves. I usually had a portable project like working on a novel—so I was okay with living in a hut in the jungle near the coast in Sri Lanka. But the whole enterprise was driven by my surf mania.

Looking back, I can see now how thoughtless, how stubborn, I was. My plans about where to go were pretty much nonnegotiable. If a girlfriend, even a serious girlfriend, had said, *Why don't we go live in Nepal because I'm interested in something there?*—that would have been out of the question. No, it's not on the coast. Actually, I did live inland sometimes. I lived in London and later spent three winters in Montana. But those stints were pretty much on my terms, too. I think I was just a general prick. I was so bullheaded, and surfing usually played heavily into whatever that was. I'd do almost anything to make sure I got waves, even when I was deeply in love.

Writing *Barbarian Days* forced me to look at the life I didn't choose. There was a pregnancy when I was eighteen. We didn't go through with it, but talking it over with my childhood sweetheart, even now, forty years later, was quite emotional. What might have been, what we might have had, if we had become parents then. I was so callow; I really didn't think about it at the time. Now I can, and I can't just say, *Oh, that would've been a disaster*. It would have been a different life. It might have been a more demanding, richer life. I would have had to grow up faster. In surf terms, it would've been more cramped, obviously. I couldn't have left the United States after grad school and bummed around the world, chasing waves. But that wouldn't necessarily have been the worst thing for my soul. It's the path not taken.

Later, when I got serious about making a living as a writer and decided to live in New York, I really had to fight the tidal pull of surfing. I was living at Ocean Beach, San Francisco, getting tons of waves. When I first moved, I thought, *This is it, there are no waves around here, I'm screwed. Maybe I'll take the odd surf trip when work allows, become a vacation surfer. Arggh.* Luckily, I was wrong about New York. There are waves. But I was fairly freaked out.

I was also really lucky with the woman I married. We met in 1980 in Cape Town. She had zero interest in surfing. Refused to even watch me surf. Has never taken a pic of me surfing, to this day. But the flip side to all this extravagant indifference has been a ton of tolerance. She has never objected to my surfing, never moaned about it. If I want to go, I should go. She's good at amusing herself. Even when I've had close calls in bigger waves, she hasn't asked me to dial it back. She says she trusts my judgment—not sure about that call. I know a lot of surfers who've had problems with their partners about the amount of time they spend chasing waves—endless negotiations, especially once they have kids.

I actually have more conflict with my daughter. We'll be in Martinique, or someplace, on vacation, and I'll see some waves. I'll see some boards and think, *Ah, I can borrow a board, get some waves, alright*! And she can read my mind and just puts her foot down. She's fourteen. She's like her mother—not interested in surfing—but without the tolerance. She says, "You're not leaving me sitting on the beach." What can I do? I can't scream and pout. I'm an adult. She's the most important person in my life. We go snorkeling.

THE WAY OF THE
WARRIOR SURFER

BY ANDREW MANZI

Andrew Manzi is the founder of the Warrior Surf Foundation and a 2018 CNN Hero of the Year.

When I was sixteen, I was taking my driver's license test, and that happened to be on September 11, 2001. I was in Iraq not even eight months after I graduated high school. We went to Fallujah. It was known to be a bad area, but we had no idea how bad. There was no frontline—it was everywhere, just a hotbed of madness.

We did everything. We were the only light-armored reconnaissance unit in country at the time. We took a lot of casualties and went through a ton of shit together. We had, like, fifty-three Purple Hearts. Eight were KIA.

Everything had been so intense for so long, then all of a sudden I was out. I came home. I was lost. I didn't know what traumatic brain injury or post-traumatic stress was. I had no understanding of what had happened to me.

One thing, though. I had this ratty old surfboard that I got in Wilmington, North Carolina, in 2006 for fifty bucks. A 9-foot Pride longboard. The first place I ever truly surfed was a place called Point Panic, Rhode Island—thirty minutes from my house. I paddled out in a scuba suit. It was fricking cold and I got my ass kicked. But I felt good out there. Maybe it was the 40-degree water pushing into my face that made me forget about anything else in life. A weight was lifted, and it just turned into something else. Surfing gave me some mental stability. To know I could count on something to wash the worries away. I refused medications. I didn't want any of that stuff. I had surfing. And it kind of took over just enough. In the middle of winter, its 20 degrees out, 20-knot gusts. I'd get done surfing. I'm sitting in the back of class shivering. But I loved it.

In 2013, something told me to come down to Folly Beach, South Carolina. I started working at a bar and making good money. Then one day Josh Wilson, who owned Charleston Surf Lessons, said, "Yo, I need some help pushing people into waves." Once I saw the joy that people were getting out of it, I was hooked.

The next year, I started meeting a lot of vets on the beach and offering them a surf lesson. There was one dude in particular, a Green Beret just back from Afghanistan. I said, "You're probably feeling a little weird right now. I'm surfing tomorrow. I'll teach you what I know." We went out and he just lit up like a Christmas tree.

The whole combat deal. You wait and wait and wait for something bad to happen. And something bad's gonna happen. That's what you trained for. You kind of want to get into it because that's what you're there to do. Surfing, you wait and wait and wait, and you paddle for this wave. You drop in, and something amazing happens. It's one of the few environments I've found where I can take a deep breath and let everything go away. The ocean takes it all.

Really, the Warrior Surf Foundation doesn't do anything. It's all the ocean's work. Sometimes I obsess on paddling over a wave about to break. There's an offshore wind, and you get that rainbow spray. The ocean will bitch slap the best in the world. But it also provides therapy. We're all hurting in some way. Or maybe we're not. Maybe we just want to be out there with people like us. Ultimately, though, I think it's being out there and just not knowing. You don't know what's coming. That's what we thrived on, once upon a time.

FIVE BIG WAVES TO SEE (AND MAYBE SURF) BEFORE YOU DIE

Banzai Pipeline, Ehukai Beach, Oahu, Hawaii: In winter, cylindrical barrels of comical, mutant proportions break over a frightfully shallow reef, thundering so close to the beach you can see the fear in a surfer's eyes. Post up in a beach chair as the best surfers in the world compete for your amusement amid a paradisiacal gladiator field of blond sand, cerulean ocean, and swaying palms.

The Wedge, Newport Beach, California: In summer, southerly swells run up against the 1,900-foot-long Newport Harbor jetty, creating a mutant peak mere feet from howling onlookers. Surfers, bodyboarders, skimboarders, and bodysurfers are launched into the sky, swallowed by gaping tubes, and obliterated by whitewater. Visit before 10 a.m. and after 5 p.m. when waters are open to board riders.

Teahupoo, Tahiti: During the Southern Hemisphere's winter, at the base of a stunning valley, waves steam in from 4,000-foot depths and explode atop a 5-foot deep reef. Thanks to that reef's perfect orientation to the swells, you can sit atop a surfboard or a boat in the relative safety of deep, crystalline water, while a few yards away, surfers are swallowed by the most beautiful barrel on the planet.

Jaws, aka Peahi, Maui, Hawaii: In winter, at Peahi, a pinnacle of reef is aligned alongside a deepwater canyon that focuses tremendous North Pacific swell energy. In terms of perfection, Jaws is considered the marquee big wave on the planet. Take a seat on the cliffs overlooking this wonder with binoculars. The surfers look like ants set against azure skyscrapers.

Nazaré, Portugal: In winter, swells focus into monsters before a five-hundred-year-old fort along the rocky Portuguese headland. Nazaré has only been widely known since 2011, when Garrett McNamara stunned the surfing community with a world record 78-foot-high wave. Nazaré's titanic peak happens thanks to a 125-mile-long offshore canyon. From a safe hilltop vantage, you can sip wine a stone's throw from a true wonder of the world.

NAZARÉ, PORTUGAL

Surfing is equal parts sport and culture, life and lifestyle, feat and fantasy. Here is a highly subjective list of iconic films that capture surfing in all its guts, glory, and cosmic weirdness.

A FEW FAVORITE DOCUMENTARIES

Endless Summer (1966): Simple in concept, grand in execution, Bruce Brown's tale of two surfers chasing warm weather and waves around the planet is one of the few films to translate surfing's magic to the masses.

Pacific Vibrations (1970): Produced by Surfer founder John Severson, *Pacific Vibrations* placed surfing squarely at the center of the profoundly disruptive zeitgeist of the psychedelic era.

Step into Liquid (2003): An ambitious, gorgeous film, Bruce Brown's son Dana wisely showcased women surfers Layne Beachley and Rochelle Ballard alongside stupefying footage of Laird Hamilton at Jaws and Mike Parsons at Cortes Bank.

Riding Giants (2004): Stacy Peralta's masterful history of big-wave surfing unfolds as a fascinating, gut-wrenching tale of outsized egos and titanic waves.

Surfwise (2007): Dorian "Doc" Paskowitz and his opera singer wife, Juliette, rejected modern society and raised seven kids in a small camper on beaches across North and Central America, revealing how a surfing obsession is both a blessing and a curse.

A FEW FAVORITE FEATURE FILMS

Gidget (1959): How did Gidget and her Malibu boyfriends launch the sixties' surfing explosion? Because what they were really espousing was a radically new way to live.

Ride the Wild Surf (1964): By far the best of the sixties "beach movies." Despite its share of cheese, this film features terrific surf footage by icons Greg Noll, Mickey Dora, Butch Van Artsdalen, to name a few.

Big Wednesday (1978): Some say John Milius's portrayal of three friends in the 1960s is overly sentimental. But it's among the most successful surf films ever, and for surfing's baby boomers, it was real life.

Apocalypse Now (1979): "Charlie don't surf!" Watch Milius and Francis Ford Coppola's masterpiece after *Big Wednesday*, if only for its infamous combat surfing scene. The films are two sides of the same coin.

North Shore (1987): A hilarious, ludicrous, but engaging tale of an Arizona wavepool surfer who challenges Lance Burkhart—played by a young Laird Hamilton—at Banzai Pipeline. Introduced millions to Hawaiian culture, dialect, and Laird.

WETSUIT 101

Only in the warmest water can surfers forgo a wetsuit, but even in Hawaii, you'll want some neoprene sometime. Note that wetsuits differ for surfing and diving, so buy specific suits for each activity.

HOW WETSUITS ARE MADE

Wetsuits are built around remarkably thin, tough, closed-cell rubber foam panels called neoprene, which is made from either petroleum, limestone, or straight-up tree-sap rubber. Neoprene allows for very light water seepage, hence the name "wetsuit," and the millions of bubbles in the foam create incredible insulation: The thin layer of water against your skin warms with your body's heat. For softness and strength, wetsuits are lined with flexible nylon, Lycra, or polypropylene.

Wetsuits come in all colors, shapes, and sizes. What you need depends on where you surf. There are armless vests and pull-on "jackets." "Springsuits" have short arms and short legs, while "short johns" have no arms and short legs. "Fullsuits" have long arms and legs, and some include a hood. Wetsuits are typically measured in millimeters by the foam thickness of main panels. The thinnest neoprene is 0.5 mm; the thickest reach 8 mm. Thus, a "6/5/4 fullsuit" has a 6-mm torso, 5-mm legs, and 4-mm arms. A "3/2 fullsuit" has a 3-mm torso with 2-mm arms and legs. A "2/2 suit" uses 2-mm neoprene all around.

Manufacturers balance softness, flexibility, and durability. Stiffer foamed suits are denser and last longer but aren't as comfortable. Sewn seams on cheap, entry-level suits are "flat stitched" without seam-sealing glue; they're tough, but leak like a teabag. Blindstitched suits (where the needle doesn't completely penetrate the rubber) with glued seams are much warmer. Warmer still are suits whose seams are bonded and taped inside and out with liquid glue. "Smoothskin" suits are warmest of all: The outside torso panels are coated in smooth, waterproof rubber—great for windy conditions.

WATER TEMPERATURE GUIDE

Wetsuits let you avoid hypothermia (page 232). How much neoprene you need depends on water temperature and weather. Also, the longer you're out, the colder you'll become, especially your hands and feet. Below 55°F, a dunking can bring on an excruciating "ice cream headache." Here's your guide:

WATER TEMPERATURE		PROTECTION
80+°F/ 26.7°C	Tropical	Lycra rashguard for sun
70–79°F/ 21.1–26.1°C	Warm	A 1–2 mm wetsuit vest or shirt for sun and wind chill
65–70°F/ 18.3–21.1°C	Cool	Springsuit or long-sleeve surf jacket
59–64°F/ 15–17.8°C	Quite Cool	3/2 fullsuit
48–58°F/ 8.9–14.4°C	Cold	4/3 fullsuit, 3–5 mm booties, maybe 2-mm gloves and hood
40–48°F/ 4.4–8.9°C	Frigid	5/4/3 fullsuit (or 6/5/4), 3–5 mm gloves, 5–7 mm booties, 5-mm hood
39°F/3.9°C AND BELOW	Mortally Cold	6/5/4 or thicker fullsuit, "lobster-style" 5-mm gloves, 5–7 mm booties, 5–7 mm hood

WEARING A WETSUIT

The best wetsuit is one you don't know is on, as if it disappears. Wetsuits should fit tightly everywhere, without being baggy or uncomfortable. Be picky, especially around the groin and beneath the armpits, which are prone to rashes from chafing. Gloves and booties should fit like a snug sock, with no extra room at the end of fingers and toes.

Know front from back—nothing IDs a kook faster than a backward wetsuit. When surfing, fasten your surfboard leash below (not around) your suit's ankle (or water might pool at your calf), and don't attach a calf leash over a fullsuit or you'll wear a hole in the neoprene. When wearing booties and gloves, roll the wetsuit over the top; if you tuck the wetsuit into booties and gloves, they fill with water. Finally, put on gloves last or zipping will be nearly impossible.

SURFING RASH

Surfers can contract a wicked, itchy rash due to chafing in their wetsuit or rubbing exposed skin against a waxy, sandy deck. This is why rash guards were invented.

In particular, wetsuits bother the "spaces in between"—that is, armpits, groin, and neck. Wear a tight-fitting Lycra rash guard underneath your wetsuit, but if this is too tight, improvise. On your neck and armpits, apply generous amounts of petroleum jelly or similar, non-water-soluble concoctions like cocoa butter. Even rubbing rashy areas with slimy, oily kelp provides relief. Afterward, thoroughly clean your wetsuit.

For rashes at the groin or legs caused by contact with your surfboard's rails, ointments will make you slippery, so opt for long Lycra shorts; a pair of soft, long surf trunks; or full-length "yoga-style" surf pants.

Meanwhile, "wetsuit acne" can arise because your skin can't sweat or breathe beneath a tight suit. To prevent these pimples, keep your suit and skin particularly clean before and after surfing and remove your wetsuit right after surfing. Use acne medicine, and know that broken skin beneath a rubbing wetsuit can induce infection.

WETSUIT CARE

Modern wetsuits are tough, but if not properly cared for, they can fall apart and even make you sick. Protect your investment.

- Don't change your wetsuit on rough pavement, rocks, sand, or an abrasive boat deck. Stand on a towel or mat so you don't damage the rubber and Lycra.

- Take care pulling the suit over your feet. Putting it on, slide it over your heel gently. Taking it off, peel it down, turning it inside out as you go; don't wrench a big chunk over your heel and overstretch it. The ankle seal will last longer.

- After use, always thoroughly rinse your suit with freshwater, and wash it regularly with a mild soap (like all-natural Pau Pilau Biological Wetsuit Cleaner) to keep it clean and supple. Dried salt makes a suit stiff and tough to get on. Meanwhile, wet neoprene is a wonderful breeding ground for bacteria, which can infect cuts or irritated skin. Never use a dry cleaner or bleach (harsh chemicals), a washing machine (too rough), or a clothes dryer (melted goo).

- Dry your suit inside out first, and then right-side out.

- Ultraviolet light damages neoprene, so don't leave a suit hanging in the sun.

- Never hang wetsuits over metal that can rust, like a thin, wire hanger. Thin hangers can also distort the shape. Use a thicker plastic hanger and don't fold. Store fully dry and unzipped.

- Try not to pee in your wetsuit. Mildly acidic, urine can cause the equivalent of diaper rash. Urine can also degrade the seals, glue, and rubber in the crotch areas. Plus, it stinks.

"THE MOST CHALLENGING SIMPLE THING": BODYSURFING

Bodysurfing is the most challenging simple thing you will ever

do in your life. There are four things you need to know.

1. Know how to swim.

2. Make sure your trunks will stay on.

3. Kick like hell.

4. Come out of the water smiling.

And if you don't do the last one, you're doing it all wrong.

—Mark Cunningham

To practice surfing at its simplest, become the board.

Your initial forays into bodysurfing should be at a sand-bottomed beach with gently rolling waves. Like bodyboarding, first hitch a ride into rolling whitewater and work up to unbroken waves.

The technique is simplicity itself: Watch for an incoming wave. When it's 10 or so feet away, kick off the bottom toward shore, flatten your body, head down, and swim hard to match the wave's speed. If you catch it, you'll feel yourself pushed forward. As you're propelled, exhale slowly through your nose to keep from inhaling water and extend your arms forward to help planing and to protect your head and neck in case you're slammed to the bottom.

You can't see with your head down, but this helps keep your body flat. With practice, try popping your head up while maintaining a flat body, and try launching yourself sideways to follow the wave as it peels left or right. Kick out of the wave with a sideways somersault.

As you gain experience, strap on a pair of swim fins—not diving fins, which create enormous drag—and try bodysurfing in slightly deeper water. Fins give an explosive takeoff speed. Try with your arms at your sides, and spread out like wings—but always keep palms flat to increase the planing area.

Really want to become the board? Bodysurf with a small handplane. These handheld mini-surfboards strap onto one hand and drastically increase bodysurfing speed. Rules for catching waves are roughly the same, but swim fins are a must, since you can't paddle. One hand, preferably two, must hold the handplane. When angling down a wave's face, go in the direction of the hand that holds the plane: To go right, use your right hand; use your left to go left.

However, be very careful extending a handplane. It's very easy for your arm to be swept back over your head, dislocating your shoulder. Hold the plane loosely and jettison at the first hint of trouble.

BOOGIE, MAN: **BODYBOARDING**

In 1971, a fiendishly inventive Southern California surfer named Tom Morey wanted to get up close and personal with "unsurfable waves"—those that crashed over dangerously shallow sandbars and coral reefs in Hawaii. Morey handcrafted a flexible, hydrodynamic, 4-foot-long slab of soft polyethylene and called it a "Boogie Board." As it happened, this prototype bodyboard provided easy rides in gentle waves, too—becoming the perfect gateway drug to standup surfing.

A foot or two of swell, a bodyboard, a leash, and maybe a set of swim fins are all you need. For your first forays, forego the fins, pick a sandy beach with small waves, and simply catch the whitewater of an already-broken wave. Grab the board's rails near the top, and as the wave arrives, launch shoreward atop the board. As you gain experience, lean from side to side to turn the board, and catch unbroken waves, riding the break's momentum.

To tackle bigger, more powerful waves in deeper water, purchase a set of bodysurf-specific swim fins. These provide more propulsion and enable you to "duckdive" through oncoming waves (rather than swimming over them or getting rolled). As balance improves, also paddle using your arms.

Remember: *Steep waves can be dangerous.* If you're about to flip, quickly roll off the board and into a ball to prevent your spine from being bent backward and "scorpioning" from being driven headfirst into the seafloor. Another danger is when the board's nose drives into the sand and your abdomen folds across the tail. Whenever you lose control, let the board go.

HOW TO DUCKDIVE A BODYBOARD

1. Kick or paddle hard toward a wave to gain momentum.

2. With the wave a body length away, grasp the board's upper rails, take a deep breath, and sink the nose of the board with a "push-up" motion.

3. With one knee, push down on the rear of the board, and kick hard with the other leg, diving beneath the breaking wave. The wave will push you farther, and once it passes, raise the nose of your board and "cork" to the surface.

SHOREBREAK, RIP CURRENTS, AND ROGUE WAVES

So-called "sneaker" or "rogue waves" are unusually large waves that arrive without warning, sweeping unsuspecting swimmers out to sea. Shorebreaks, meanwhile, are tall, powerful waves that crash in dangerously shallow water. Shorebreaks are created when a seafloor rises steeply near the shoreline, and the strongest tend toward high tide, when wave energy passes unimpeded over outer sandbars or reefs and slams ashore.

Both can be accompanied by irresistible rip currents that pull swimmers into deep water or along shorelines. Rogue/sneaker waves and shorebreaks are among the most dangerous and unrecognized hazards at any beach, so whether you're swimming, bodyboarding, or surfing: Keep your eyes on the ocean, and expect the unexpected. It's also wise to check surf forecasts via websites like Surfline, Stormsurf, Surf-forecast, and Magic Seaweed.

SWIMMING IN SHOREBREAK

First, avoid a wave's crashing lip at all costs. Waves vary in size and power, but don't underestimate any. If caught "under the axe" in deeper water, face the wave, submerge yourself butt first, feet downward, and curl up into a ball, covering your head. Try to simultaneously relax and brace for impact. If the wave slams you to the bottom, push off the bottom with your feet to quickly regain the surface.

Remember, waves come in sets. Once the last wave in a set passes, run or swim for shore.

If you're in shallow water close to shore and wave impact is unavoidable, submerge, sit down, ball up, cover your head, and roll with the punches. When you can stand, run like hell for the beach. Diving under an actively breaking wave, in any direction, risks a head slam into the sand.

On the other hand, if you're between breaking waves and the beach, float at the surface, face the incoming whitewater, and let the broken wave push you shoreward. Exhale through your nose as the wave passes over, and swim toward shore as the turbulence subsides, keeping up with the back of the wave. The water beneath waves often pulls one back out to sea, so try to remain in the surging whitewater near the surface. The moment you feel ground beneath your feet, run, high-stepping to avoid the pull of the returning wave.

SHOREBREAK WITH A SURFBOARD OR BODYBOARD

If you're on a surfboard outside the breaking waves and need to reach the beach, consider taking the leash off so you won't be entangled with your board. Bodyboards are soft, so remain attached to it for flotation. Wait for a lull, then try to paddle in with the lull or at the back of the last wave of a set. When you reach waist-deep water, roll off the board, and run onto the beach with the incoming surge. If you're slammed while on a surfboard, let the board go, and follow the advice for swimming.

If you're being swept into a pier or jetty, do your damndest to avoid it—even if it means getting slammed by a wave. If you'll definitely impact, remove your leash to avoid entanglement and use only your feet or board to fend off the obstacle. Get through the pier as fast as you can. A jetty will often have a powerful laminar current right alongside that can carry you back out to sea where you can safely regroup.

CAUGHT IN A RIPCURRENT

Water is pushed ashore by waves as whitewater. It then creates or follows a deeper water trench that funnels it back out to sea as a rip current. If you're pushed out, relax, flip on your back faceup and float or swim and ride the current out while swimming parallel to shore. Keep protecting yourself and angling for the beach when it's safe. Don't worry about reaching a specific spot; anywhere safe will do. Realize too, rips cannot possibly exist everywhere. Eventually the current will release its grip and you can swim in. If you're amid waves, dive beneath them and swim, riding the current until outside of breakers, then rest and regroup and swim in, or float and wave for help.

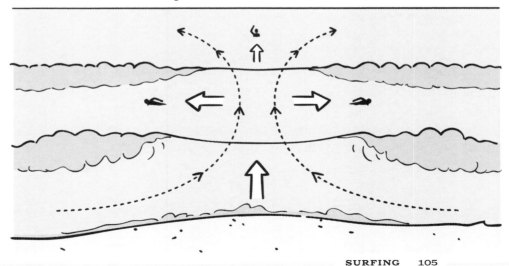

THE ULTIMATE SURF VAN

If—eventually, inevitably—you become addicted to surfing, you have three options: (1) move to a house near the beach; (2) buy a sailboat to reach remote coastlines; or (3) buy or build out a surf van so you can roam the coast in a portable beach house. Given sailing's commitment to ocean living and the cost of coastal real estate, the most popular choice among surf addicts is #3. Happily, the #vanlife options of today dwarf those of 1951, when VW first sold its Westfalia camper.

CHOOSING YOUR CRAB SHELL

For some folks, a pickup truck with a camper shell or an SUV work fine. But a van embodies the "hermit crab" ethos of the surfing life: As you self-sufficiently bear your coastal home on your back, you can work virtually; comfortably change out of soggy gear; store all your stuff; eat, sleep, and pee in peace; and jump from your living space to driving instantly, taking off at the first hint of trouble.

Whatever you choose, stay within your van's design parameters and load ratings. Overloading creates dangerous handling and awful fuel economy, while outsized tires and lift can overstress drivetrain and suspension. If funds are limited, forego lift kits, solar panels, heavy-duty bumpers, furnaces, refrigerators, and electronic wizardry. These are useful when you're broken down in a parking lot, but focus first on mechanical necessities.

Expensive upgrades include fuel-efficient diesel engines and four-wheel drive, which can keep you out of trouble in soft sand. For beach driving advice, see "Go Pound Sand," page 133; we recommend traction aids rather than dangerous bumper winches.

Finally, if you want to stand up inside, you need a high-roofed model, a tent-based "pop-top," or a fixed fiberglass high top. Going to garage it? Measure before you buy!

VINTAGE VS. MODERN

It's true that VWs are considered the gold standard among surfinistas, and older VW vans are charming, unsophisticated, and functional. But before buying that dreamy vintage rig, make sure your mechanical skills can handle the expected breakdowns. Built from 1980 to 1991, VW's Type 2 Vanagons are comfortably spacious, very maneuverable, and safe, but they're underpowered, lack decent climate control, and need constant TLC and hard-to-find replacement parts. They're best when upfitted with a modern motor. Still, they have a thriving online community. Though not as sexy, Ford Econolines are reliable and common as dirt across North America, making parts and service easy to come by.

After the mid-1990s, vans became much tougher to fix, but airbags, antilock brakes, and traction control make them far safer. Excellent choices in modern rigs include Ford Transits, Mercedes Sprinter and smaller Metris (Vito in Europe), and Dodge RAM Promasters (Ducato in Europe). Though not currently sold in the United States, VW still offers excellent rigs in Europe.

POWER AND ELECTRONICS

Unless auxiliary A.C. is necessary, forego a generator, and avoid onboard propane tanks, which are hazardous in a crash. Also consider the following:

- A simple plug-in voltage meter to monitor your alternator and batteries.

- An auxiliary "deep cycle" battery, separate from the main battery, to run lights, fridge, and other gear.

- A marine-grade charger that plugs into shore power to maintain the auxiliary battery.

- A marine-grade power inverter that converts 12-volt car power to 120-volt household power.

- An onboard data reader to troubleshoot computer-controlled engines from the mid-1990s to present.

- A modern, compressor-driven, 12-volt fridge, which is quiet and efficient but fairly expensive. Avoid cheap, power-gobbling, "thermoelectric" and household units, which are neither efficient nor reliable.

- A 100-watt solar panel to power both the auxiliary and house batteries (using appropriate voltage converters). Removable panels can follow the sun.

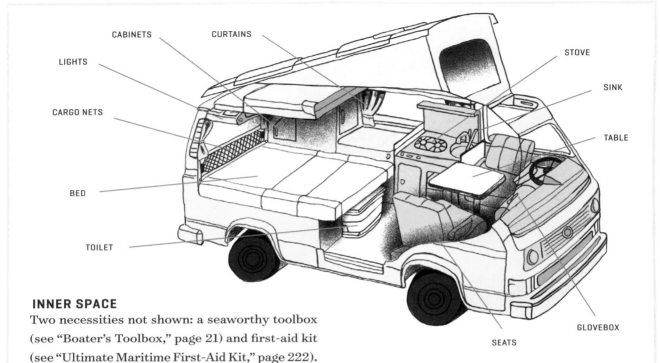

CABINETS CURTAINS LIGHTS STOVE SINK CARGO NETS TABLE BED TOILET GLOVEBOX SEATS

INNER SPACE

Two necessities not shown: a seaworthy toolbox (see "Boater's Toolbox," page 21) and first-aid kit (see "Ultimate Maritime First-Aid Kit," page 222).

◎ **Glovebox:** Holds camera, journal, headlamp, cards, extra fuses.

◎ **Cabinets:** Old VWs and custom campers have excellent cabinetry, or make your own.

◎ **Bed:** If not pre-equipped, build your own.

◎ **Water supply:** A tank-supplied sink with a sailboat-style, foot-operated or electric pump is nice, but simpler is a 2-gallon plastic tank wand sprayer or solar shower. Roof-mounted shower tanks affect handling.

◎ **Cooking:** A permanent interior stove is nice, but a portable butane or propane stove is cheap, convenient, reliable, and works indoors and out. When operating inside, crack a window to avoid carbon monoxide buildup.

◎ **Rotating front seats:** Key to turning any van into a room; vastly increases space, comfort, and "campability."

◎ **Portable toilet:** A lifesaver on the road. Use solely for "number 1"; for "number 2," a large coffee can lined with plastic bags lets you "catch and release" (pooping inside is, uh, smelly). A folding camp shovel lets you dig a latrine.

◎ **A table:** For eating and laptopping.

◎ **Overhead interior lights:** Stick-on LEDs are cheap and long-lasting.

◎ **Cargo nets:** Hold lots of gear.

◎ **Window curtains and screens:** Curtains for privacy (also hang behind front seats), and screens keep out bugs.

OUTER SPACE

- **Rear hatch:** Liftable hatches—typical of VWs—shield you from weather when loading/unloading. Swing-out twin doors can be opened even when loaded with gear.

- **Tires:** Use normal all-terrain tires. "Mud-terrain" tires are too noisy.

- **Roll-out awning:** The best include a zip-in room for added space. ARB is the gold standard.

- **Window tint:** Heat-blocking tint keeps the van much cooler.

- **Roof rack:** Forego spendy, drag-inducing sky boxes for basic bars. Secure gear with simple thumb-button or ratchet straps.

- **Front bumper:** Bolt-on fishing rod holders can be as simple as a PVC pipe.

- **Rear bumper:** Receiver-style trailer hitch to attach all manner of racks and gear in wind slipstream—saving fuel.

- **Heavy-duty hand pump or 12-volt compressor:** Necessary to reinflate tires after airing down for beach driving.

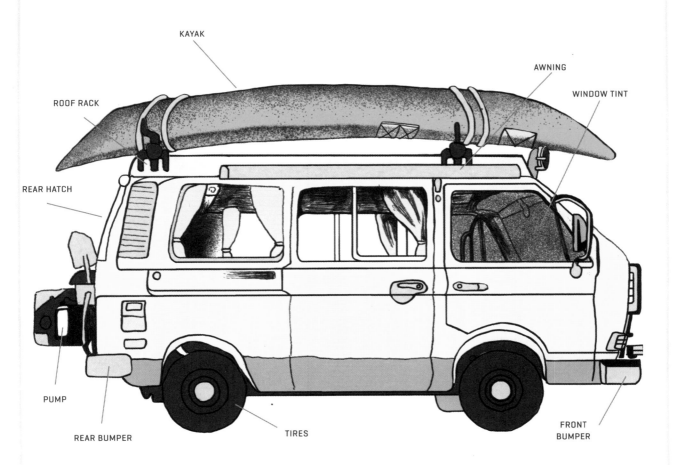

KAYAK

AWNING

WINDOW TINT

ROOF RACK

REAR HATCH

PUMP

REAR BUMPER

TIRES

FRONT BUMPER

AUNTIE RELL:
THE QUEEN OF MAKAHA

AS TOLD BY KATHY TERADA

Kathy Terada is a nurse practitioner from the West Side of Oahu and a former world-champion tandem surfer (with Brian Keaulana). Kathy considers surf legend Rell Sunn as her mentor, surf partner, and best friend. Learn more about the Rell Sunn Educational Fund at www.rellsunn.com.

The aloha spirit is real simple. You give and you give and you give and give from here [the heart], until you have nothing else to give.

—Rell Sunn

I actually met Rell Sunn doing hula because my kuma (hula master) told me about these wonderful hula sisters in Waianae. So I started dancing for Rell's hālau. It's funny, Rell's sister, Kula, was already a famous female surfer in Hawaii—and I always wanted to be like her. But in 1982, Rell is the one who became the top-ranked professional longboarder in the world. We danced hula together, surfed together, and she was a lifeguard. Eventually, the beach kind of took over for us and hula took a back seat.

Rell's grandmother gave her the middle name Kapolioka'ehukai, which means "Heart of the Sea." She broke a lot of barriers. She was the first female ocean lifeguard in Hawaii, a diver, a canoe paddler, a bodyboarder, a shortboarder, and a professional longboarder who helped form the Women's Professional Surfing Association. She was just as respected as any of the men. She did what she loved and made a career out of it. At the same time, she was also a single mom raising her daughter, Jan. The lifeguards at that time were all from the community—Rell, Buffalo, and Brian Keaulana—and they were all surfers, divers, fishermen. They didn't have Jet Skis or ATVs. They had to be in incredible shape and know the ocean, the currents. They had to rely on their knowledge and strength to rescue people. And they rescued a lot of people.

Today, the beaches are more crowded, and lifeguards spend more time in the towers. Lifeguards back then—especially Rell— were so personal and social. Rell would walk up and down the

beach and talk to everybody. She'd set up her chair with her dogs and talk story. She was one of the best storytellers.

Whenever you interacted with her, she made you feel like you were special to her. And you were. That's why everyone would say, "I was a really good friend with Rell." She was "Auntie Rell" to everybody. Especially the kids.

When my kids came along, Rell would make little surf contests just for them. She judged their rides and gave each a special prize, like—you had the best barrel, even if they didn't get barreled, you had the longest ride, the biggest shorebreak wave. She did so much preventative work with the kids—taught them and played with them so they'd grow up knowledgeable about the ocean. It wasn't classes she was teaching—it was a way of life.

The other thing about Rell: Her house was always open. She would feed whoever. Teach whoever. If someone was in trouble, she'd take them in. She shared whatever she had—and she didn't have a lot. I don't know any other female who could dive and spearfish the way she did. She did it to feed her family. Because of who she was, people would always sponsor her for different things. That's because she didn't ask for help for herself. It was always to help somebody else—another family, a group of kids, or to run her Menehune Surf Contest, which her daughter still runs today. Whenever she helped someone, it always came back to her.

Rell learned she had breast cancer in the early eighties and fought it for fourteen years. Even before she had cancer, my friends and I thought she was a real-life hero. Then when she was diagnosed, she got a job with my clinic as a navigator—a person who helps women in the community not be afraid to get cancer screenings. Then if they were diagnosed, you know, she helped them navigate their treatment and get the support they needed.

The film *Heart of the Sea* is about Rell. It was filmed during the last year of her life, when she was having a hard time. She told me, these two came to do a documentary and they want to know what my life is like. So I'm gonna make 'em bodyboard, canoe, dive, head out on the reef. All those things. So they could see what a day in her life was actually like. I always thought that was pretty cool.

Rell always said that Makaha was God's country. There's no other place like Makaha. Well, that's partly because of people like Buffalo, Brian, and Rell. She, to me, is Makaha. I'm sad that some people will hear of her but won't know her. It was such an honor to have been part of her life, you know?

ON YOUR FEET, YE SCURVY DOG:
LEARNING TO SURF

Score a big, fat beginner board and familiarize yourself with these foundational techniques. We strongly recommend taking a lesson; nothing beats in-person instruction.

THE BASICS: PADDLING AND SITTING

Before surfing, first learn to paddle and balance atop the board. In calm water—a flat ocean, lake, or swimming pool—lie prone on the board to get a feel for its balance point. It should lie nearly flat on the water, with the nose slightly up.

Next, straddle the board in the middle like you're riding a horse, nose just up, tail just down. While sitting, practice spinning around by lifting the nose, grabbing the rail edges, leaning back, and kicking your feet in opposite, circular strokes.

Paddle with a simple crawl stroke: Keep head and chest up, and feet together or crossed. Dangling feet off the side creates drag. Bend your arms at the elbow as you paddle and keep them close to the board during extension. Reach fairly deep into the water; pull until your arm is extended behind you (as the other extends out front). Don't dig your shoulders into the water.

THE POP-UP: MAKING YOUR STAND

When surfing, you stand with one foot in front, one behind, along the board's centerline. Left foot forward is called "regular foot"; right foot forward is "goofy foot" (since it's like being left-handed). Either way doesn't matter, but most people prefer one over the other.

Practice out of the water to build muscle memory. Place your surfboard on a bed with fins hanging off, on a carpeted floor with fins removed, or in soft sand with holes for the fins. Lie on the board with toes just at the tail. Simulate a couple of paddling strokes, look straight ahead, and bring your hands to the board's rails (edges) as if preparing for a push-up ("cobra pose" position).

1. Place your toes on the board to help you pop up.

2. Spring to your feet in a single motion, swinging your front foot forward between your arms and trailing your back foot. Assume a low, knees-bent, sideways stance. Do not pop on your knees first.

3. Make sure your feet straddle the board's centerline, with your arches on the line.

4. Maintain contact with your hands and stay low until you feel balanced.

5. Slowly rise to a standing position, feet just beyond shoulder-width apart. Extend arms

outward to help balance. Keep knees bent to maintain a low center of gravity; this also enables a quick return to "four point" position for balance recovery. Practice pop-ups on a tippy board to improve balance.

SOUP CATCHIN': RIDING YOUR FIRST WAVES
For your first waves, pick an uncrowded, sandy beach with small, gentle waves, and bring a friend for backup. Like any surfer, size up the ocean from shore. Where are the waves breaking? How long are the lulls? Are there any hazards?

Pick your spot and walk the board out until waist deep, always keeping the board's nose pointed into oncoming waves. When breaking waves hit a board broadside, they knock you down, hard.

Your first goal is to "catch soup," aka white-water. It's far easier to learn to surf on already-broken waves, which give plenty of push and little trouble. While standing in the water, point your board toward shore. As the whitewater reaches you, launch yourself onto your board and ride it prone toward shore. Do this several times to get a feel for the board; first go straight and then lean side to side to turn. When you're ready, pop up and ride a few standing.

To end your ride, sit on the board and drag your legs, or jump off to one side feetfirst and grab the board as you hit the water. Don't let the board fly away, and don't ride it onto the sand.

PADDLING OUT: BEYOND BREAKING WAVES

To paddle outside breaking waves, you must get past incoming waves. If waves are fairly small, one method is to paddle forward with some speed, then do a push-up on the board as each wave arrives. This eases you through low whitewater and carries you over the top of cresting waves.

For larger waves, you must "turn turtle." Paddle hard as the wave approaches, then roll the board over upside down, gripping the rails near the nose, pointing straight toward the wave. "Hide" underneath the board as the wave rolls over. This is also a good way to protect yourself from an onrushing surfer. For better grip, wrap your legs around the board.

If waves are so big you feel compelled to bail your board and dive for the bottom, the waves are too big to ride. Loose, flying boards are a serious danger to others, so never bail your board if anyone is behind you. If someone is behind and a wave is bearing down, turn turtle, hold the board in a death grip, prepare for impact, and take your lickins.

SITTIN' ON TOP OF THE WORLD: CATCHING BREAKING WAVES

Once you're comfortable surfing soup and paddling out, it's time to catch an unbroken wave. Again, learn on smaller, gentler waves. When you eye a likely looking swell, paddle straight toward shore with a steady, strong stroke. As the wave lifts you, and the board starts to move on its own, take one more big stroke, and before the wave's face steepens too much, arch your back and pop up.

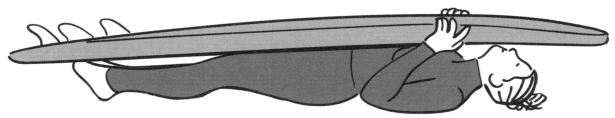

Turning turtle beneath a wave

A common mistake is popping up before you're moving at the speed of the wave. If you do, the wave will either roll on by or you'll nosedive (pearl) as it overtakes you too fast. To prevent pearling, after popping up, quickly shift your weight back a bit.

At first, surf straight to shore. Once you're completely comfortable with that, try a few gentle turns by shifting your weight toward the tail and smoothly leaning where you want to go. After much experience, you'll be ready to surf "down the line"—following the unbroken face of the wave. At that point, we promise, you'll be utterly addicted.

THE END OF THE RIDE: HANDLING WIPEOUTS

By choice or not, a ride often ends before you reach the beach. See "Shorebreak, Rip Currents, and Rogue Waves" (page 104) for handling large waves, and if you're getting thrashed repeatedly, or scared, surf another time or in another place. Most of all, before a wipeout, take a deep breath and relax.

- As you fall or jump, try to land either beside or "upstream" from your board, so it doesn't hit you.

- Never dive off your board, whether into a wave or for the bottom. Shallows or rocks may be closer than you think and can break your neck.

- Safe ways to land in soft soup (whitewater) are to belly flop forward or to "starfish" (arms and legs out) flat on your back.

- In very shallow, sand-bottomed water, jump off feetfirst with knees bent to absorb the shock.

- While in the washing machine, cover your head with your arms in case the board "rubberbands" back and hits you (thanks to your leash). Mostly just "go with the flow" until the turbulence subsides enough to surface.

- When you surface, have a 360-degree look around. Any surfers coming at you? If so, dive deep. Any rocks in your path? Reel in your board and paddle away from them.

- If you find yourself dragged over a shallow reef, lay very flat, with feet pointed toward shore. If you can, climb atop your board, but keep your hands on the deck so you don't smash your fingertips.

SURFING'S TWELVE COMMANDMENTS

Few things are more frustrating to advanced surfers than a flailing, inexperienced, even dangerous beginner in their midst. Thus, to become a skillful surfer requires more than mastering the mechanics of waveriding. It also means mastering the social dynamics and somewhat variable laws of the sacred surf lineup.

1. THOU SHALT BE PARTICULARLY RESPECTFUL IN HAWAII—BEER HELPS

Hawaiians rightfully consider surfing their gift to the world. Show your appreciation. In Hawaii, before paddling out, respectfully introduce yourself to the locals and Hawaiians on the beach and in the lineup. The locals are the fittest and most tan and have the prime viewing spot, the best peak, and the heartiest laughs.

Unlike many other surf locations, Hawaiians generally want to know who you are, where you're from, and if you like their island. They consider it the pinnacle of respect if you ask them, first, *if* it's okay to paddle out, and second, *where* it's best to paddle out. To make fast friends, chat while offering a cold six- or twelve-pack of beer (Primo, Bud, or Kona Longboard Lager). This is especially helpful at Makaha (locals will be sitting on the wall or at the picnic table under the trees), Launiupoko Beach Park (picnic tables under the trees), or Ala Moana (along the rock wall or around a local's truck). You'll likely be greeted every time thereafter and given access to a vinegar jug to douse jellyfish stings.

Then, after paddling out, don't assume you can now sit on the main peak amid the regulars. Sit to the side and catch scraps. Eventually, a local will call you into a nice wave. Don't blow it.

If you get yelled at, eye-to-eye contact is considered aggressive behavior in Hawaiian culture. Divert your gaze and apologize for your transgression. Later, offer beer.

2. THOU SHALT CHECK THY EQUIPMENT

Wax your board well to avoid slide-off injuries, ensure fins are secure to avoid slide-out injuries, and make sure the leash is solid to avoid drowning, knockout, or laceration injuries.

3. THOU SHALT ASK THE LIFEGUARD

If you don't know a beach, ask a lifeguard about the lineup and why, for example, that perfect-looking wave is empty. They'd rather help you onshore than rescue you offshore.

4. THOU SHALT SURVEY THE LINEUP

Survey the lineup before paddling out. Where and how are the waves breaking, where are the rip currents, who are the best surfers, and are they tightly packed together? Are beginners out? Is there an uncrowded, out-of-the-way spot where you can surf? Honestly assess if waves are too challenging. No harm in picking another day.

Once in the water and outside the break, survey the lineup again. Surfers in front of you are in line for waves. Watch who takes off, and where, and identify any alpha dogs. Treat them with extra respect.

5. THOU SHALT PADDLE OUT AWAY FROM OTHER SURFERS

When paddling out, go around the break and stay away from surfers. Riders already on a wave always have right of way, so don't paddle into their path. Watch their angle of approach and adjust yourself so they can surf past you safely.

If you must choose between being hammered by whitewater or getting in the way of a surfer, grab your board in a death grip and take your lickings in the whitewater. If a runover is unavoidable, either bail your board and dive or turn turtle with your board to protect yourself. Getting run over can damage people and surfboards. At any break, this can get you sent in—or punched. Apologize, apologize, apologize.

6. THOU SHALT NOT DROP IN

For beginners, the most important rule is that the surfer closest to the breaking whitewater moving down the line, aka the curl, has the right of way. This means: *Always glance over both shoulders when paddling for a wave.* If you're paddling next to someone who's nearest to the curl, let them go; quit paddling, grab your rails, and sit upright, weighing down the board's tail to stop.

Sometimes, the person who's up and riding first can claim rights to the wave, but this law is abstract and nuanced. You're never wrong to follow the "closest to the curl" rule. If someone is about to drop in on *you*, hoot or whistle to alert them to your presence. This may or may not help, depending on the vibe in the lineup.

If you accidentally interfere with a surfer's ride (known as a "burn" or "snake"), do your best to get out of their way. If that's impossible and you stuff them back in the whitewater . . . apologize, apologize, apologize.

Finally, some waves break two ways; the peak peels right *and* left. If so, you can offer to "split the peak" with the adjacent surfer, but ensure you go in opposite directions.

7. THOU SHALT WAIT FOR AND TAKE THY TURN

All lineups function loosely on the turn system, so wait your turn. However, few things piss surfers off more than wasted waves. Once your turn comes, you have one chance to not look like a kook. Paddle with determination and surf the wave well. If you don't think you can catch it, or it's too imposing, back off in plenty of time for another surfer to catch it. That said, position sometimes trumps turn. If someone's in a clearly better position for an incoming wave, that person will likely—and is usually expected to—go ahead of someone who's waited longer.

8. THOU SHALT AVOID "TUNNEL VISION"

When still learning, you're often so focused on improving skills and catching each wave that you forget everyone else. "Tunnel vision" leads to all kinds of mistakes: dropping in, running over paddling surfers, bailing your board into others. Be situationally aware of the whole lineup.

9. THOU SHALT GIVE WAVES AWAY

Sometimes, even if it's really your turn, you build goodwill by giving a good wave to someone who looks hungry. If someone paddles to test you, back off and let them go, but ensure you both know you were being generous.

10. THOU SHALT SHARE WAVES FAIRLY—ESPECIALLY ON A LONGBOARD

A longboard makes it easier to catch waves farther out than a shortboard. If surfing amid shortboarders, let them have a fair share of waves.

11. THOU SHALT CONTROL THY BOARD

A loose surfboard is a danger to you and any surfer shoreward of your position. In general, but especially when paddling out (page 116), don't "bail" your board if it might hit anyone. Hang on for all you're worth.

12. THOU SHALT NOT WEAR OUT THY WELCOME

Traditionally, surfers go to the same spot over and over. They become "regulars." You can slowly endear yourself to this regular crew if you're cool, friendly, don't hog waves, and generally understand and respect the surfing commandments. If you haven't reached that stage, don't spend all day in the same lineup. Get a few waves and move to another peak. There are always (usually) many other waves.

TEACH A KID (OR FRIEND) TO SURF

Surfing, at its best, fosters community and "shares the stoke." Teaching others can be a life-changing gift—if done properly and if you already know how to surf.

As the teacher, realize that one bad experience, especially for children, can trigger a crippling fear of the ocean. When pro big-wave surfer Peter Mel was six years old, his dad took him out at Santa Cruz. After one wipeout, an entanglement with slimy kelp, and an icy dunking, Mel didn't try surfing again until he was thirteen.

Before teaching someone, ask two questions, and answer them honestly. How much experience and comfort does the person have in the ocean? And do you have enough surfing and basic rescue experience to provide a smooth, safe introduction? Kids especially trust you to take care of them. When in doubt, pay for professional lessons first until the person masters the basics. Then continue learning together.

GO SLOW AND KNOW YOUR STUDENT

Defuse any nervousness with encouragement and fun, but don't force someone into surfing if they're terrified. With young kids, first swim in a variety of conditions, and put them on a soft, foam, 9-foot surfboard with rubber fins in calm water. Simply let them play: Snorkel off it, jump from it, stand atop it, work on balance. For a more stable platform, lay one board over another crosswise.

A good approach is to tackle first waves atop a bodyboard. This gets novices used to the ocean's surges, swells, and power one step at time. However you do it, make sure they know how to handle rip currents and waves—and if appropriate, cold water in a wetsuit—before adding the complication of a surfboard. Practice getting rolled in nearshore whitewater and small waves to develop self-confidence for inevitable wipeouts. Watch a lineup and discuss what surfers are doing.

Then again, some kids are fearless and will get themselves in trouble fast until they learn a healthy respect for the ocean. Never take your eyes off any child or student. Provide 100 percent supervision until you're positive the person doesn't need it anymore. Make your student prove they're ready to fly solo.

FIRST WAVES

When your student is ready to surf, follow the instructions in "On Your Feet, Ye Scurvy Dog" (page 113). Practice pop-ups on land, then start in gentle whitewater. Proceed slowly, and at every stage, let someone develop confidence in the new skill before tackling the next one. It's all about honing technique while having fun.

For very small kids, the best way to ride a first wave is to put them in a life jacket, plop them on the board's nose, paddle into tiny surf, and belly-ride waves together. Demonstrate how to control the board and turn. Next have kids pop up to their knees, and then their feet, as you both ride the wave.

If kids are too little to paddle or swim to safety, always make them wear a life jacket while you push the board into waves. Older kids and adults should always use the surfboard's ankle leash, even in gentle whitewater.

TAKIN' A LICKIN': THE FIRST WIPEOUT

No matter how careful you are, eventually your student will endure a scary and/or painful wipeout. This is the moment of truth. Will they pop up, ready to go again? Or will they call it quits?

Your challenge is to soothe fears and restore confidence. Get creative. Instead of quitting immediately, suggest a fun experiment: You both can ride one wave together, and afterward, see if the person still feels the pain of the wipeout. A good wave can erase pain and fear. Focus on the great things the student did before, or even during, the wipeout. Console your student with the knowledge that what they experienced is a natural part of this amazing sport.

KNOW THY SURFBOARD

In the 1950s, two legendary California surfboard shapers—Hobie Alter and Gordon "Grubby" Clark—began experimenting with an explosive soup of formaldehyde, sulfuric acid, nitric acid, benzene, and other chemicals. They hoped this mad scientist's cocktail would result in a material that would supplant balsawood, then the heavy core of most surfboards. As luck would have it, their dangerous trial-and-error eventually yielded a polyurethane foam that, when dried, was light, tough, inert, and easy to shape. To make it waterproof and strong enough to be a surfboard, they poured this foam into a 10-foot mold around a strength-enhancing wooden stringer, planed and sanded the dried "blank" into shape, and then laminated it beneath nasty, resin-saturated fiberglass cloth. The result? The modern surfboard. Foams, resins, and stringers have evolved into greener and lighter polymers, but even today's hard-shelled, high-performance models share the same basic design as Hobie and Grubby's original Frankenstein.

LEXICON OF A SURFBOARD

1. **Blank:** The foam core—polyurethane or Styrofoam—at the heart of most surfboards.

2. **Cloth:** Made of woven fiberglass or carbon fiber, cloth is laid between the blank and the resin for strength.

3. **Resin:** Liquid epoxy or polyester. Mixed with a hardener, it cures to form the hard "outer shell."

4. **Rails:** Sharp transition from bottom equals snappier turns. Soft transition equals more forgiving performance.

5. **Tail:** Shape affects handling.

6. **Nose:** A surfboard's tip.

7. **Skeg or fins:** Shape and number affect handling.

8. **Stringer:** A strip of wood bisecting blank from tail to nose; adds strength.

9. **Rocker:** The amount of curve from nose to tail. Flatter is more stable; more curve improves turning.

10. **Hull:** Refers to the shape of the board in cross-section. There are many variations, including flat (most stable), belly (rounded concave), concave, and V-hull (similar to V-hull boat).

11. **Delamination:** Separation of fiberglass from foam.

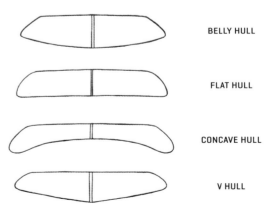

BELLY HULL

FLAT HULL

CONCAVE HULL

V HULL

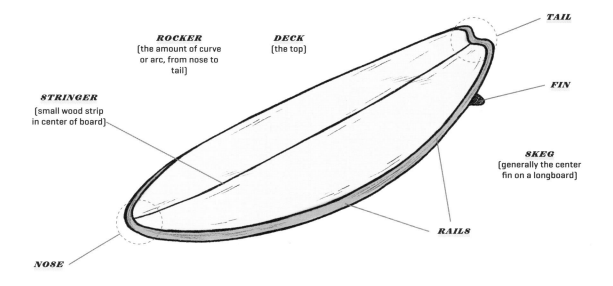

ROCKER
[the amount of curve or arc, from nose to tail]

DECK
[the top]

TAIL

FIN

STRINGER
[small wood strip in center of board]

SKEG
[generally the center fin on a longboard]

RAILS

NOSE

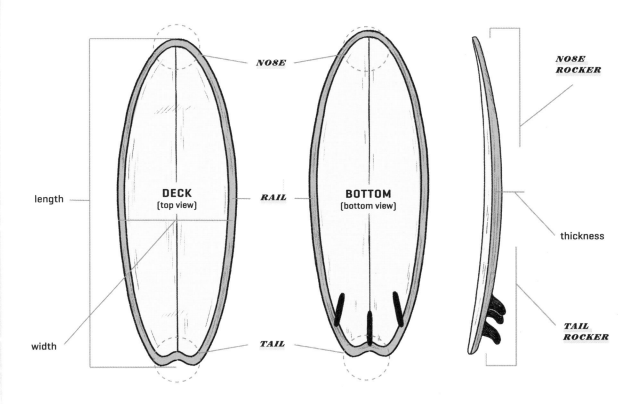

NOSE

NOSE ROCKER

length

DECK
[top view]

RAIL

BOTTOM
[bottom view]

thickness

width

TAIL

TAIL

TAIL ROCKER

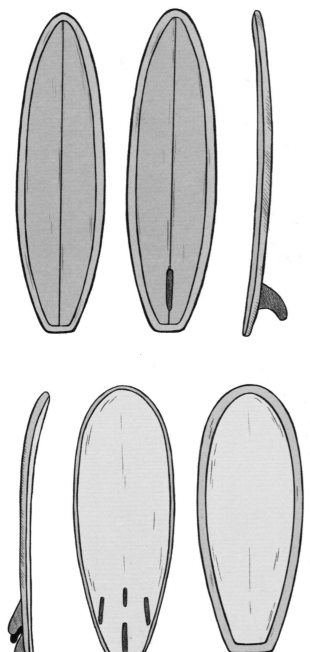

TYPES OF SURFBOARDS

Longboard: Between 8 and 12 feet long, longboards are surfing's workhorses. They're rounded at the nose and at least 20 inches wide and 2 inches thick. Longboards typically have a single center fin (aka skeg) and sometimes a smaller pair of side "bite" fins for stability and added thrust. Longboards are best for beginners because they're stable and their paddling speed enables surfers to catch waves easily. Performance longboards are narrower and feature a curvier rocker. Old-school "log"-type longboards are fat, flat, and designed for long cruises and "hang tens" off the nose.

Funboard/funshape or hybrid: From 7 to 8 feet, with somewhat rounded noses and multiple fin setups, funboards or hybrids are more maneuverable than longboards and more stable and forgiving than shortboards. They're perfect for intermediate surfers not yet ready for a shortboard. The more "longboard"-like model is known as a Mini-Malibu.

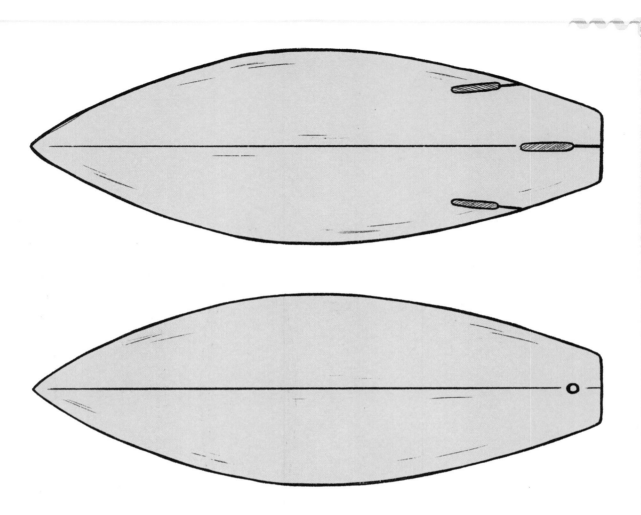

Shortboard: From 4 to 7 feet long, depending on size of rider and intended use, shortboards have two to five fins, sharp noses, thin rails, and a curvy rocker. A shortboard is the Jet Ski of surfing: unstable, difficult to catch waves with, and hard to balance. The tradeoff is an ability to "pump" down a wave face for tremendous speed and to perform gouging cutbacks, vertical "off the lips," soaring aerials, and other maneuvers on steep, big, fast waves.

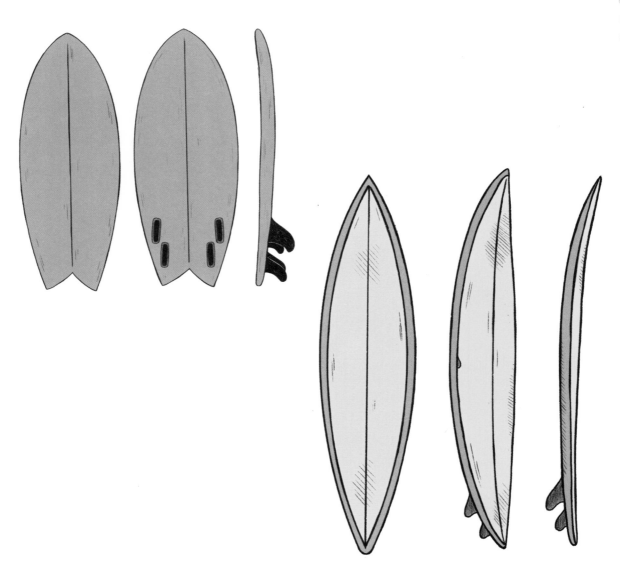

Fish and eggs: Wider in the nose and midsection than a standard shortboard, with a thicker profile and flatter rocker, fish (with a split tail) and eggs (very ovoid and fat) are great for generating speed and pulling off shortboard maneuvers in smaller, mushier waves.

Big-wave gun: From 9 to 12 feet, guns are narrow, thick, and pointy. An arrow-angled tail and multiple fin setup are terribly important for holding a solid line and not spinning out while dropping in on a 30-footer at 50 mph. When you need a gun, you'll know.

DON'T SURF STORMWATER

Immediately after it rains, the surfer's ocean playground can become a temporary toxic-waste dump, particularly when towns and farmland live upstream. Many health departments officially advise the public to stay out of the surf for seventy-two hours after a rain. In reality, the "safe" period can vary considerably. So understand the risks and use your judgment.

What's the problem? In addition to stuff you can see—plastic garbage, cigarette butts, hypodermic needles—rainwater runoff from lawns, driveways, roads, and parking lots (and carried through storm drains) picks up a slurry of invisible toxins: animal waste, fertilizer, pesticides, poisonous metals from brake dust, oil, transmission fluid, and raw sewage.

The amount and type of potential water contamination depends on the amount of rain, the local watershed development, and the proximity of the pollution source to a particular beach. Even if you're surfing a pristine tropical area, consider what's upstream of the river mouth. Farms, for example, can result in animal waste in the water.

The dangers are all too real. Here are some potential illnesses; most require antibiotics.

- **Gastroenteritis:** "Montezuma's Revenge" is the most common stormwater-borne illness; it results in fever, cramps, vomiting, diarrhea, and dehydration.

- **Methicillin-resistant *Staphylococcus aureus* (MRSA):** Considered a "superbug," this can cause painful red sores, headaches, potentially fatal fevers, muscle spasms, and delirium.

- **Meningitis and encephalitis:** Spawned by viruses and animal-spewed bacteria, these cause swelling around the spinal cord (encephalitis) or the brain (meningitis). Symptoms include stiffness in the neck, severe headache and fever, clumsy gait, confusion, light sensitivity, seizures, and drowsiness; can lead to coma and death.

- **Vibrio vulnificus:** The dreaded, legendary "flesh-eating bacteria" is a growing problem in Florida. Most victims, however, suffer only from vomiting, diarrhea, and abdominal pain.

- **Leptospirosis:** A bacteria expelled from the urine of infected livestock, dogs, and wild animals, leptospirosis can cause nausea, diarrhea, vomiting, fever, chills, muscle aches, jaundiced skin, red eyes, and rashes. Can also cause liver failure, respiratory distress, and even death.

BUYING YOUR **FIRST SURFBOARD**

Beginners buying their first surfboard want a "foamie." These soft boards are mass-produced, durable, and perfect for learning.

Beginners tempted to jump immediately to a "real" board should realize that the first thing a hard surfboard teaches is how easily it can damage its rider. Pointy noses can cut lips, hard rails can bash skulls, and sharp fins can slash ankles. Plus, by paddling out on a foamie with textbook awkward form, you instantly broadcast your beginner status—which might cut you some slack in the lineup.

BEGINNER'S ONLY: THE FOAMIE

Choose something wide, thick, and rounded, with soft, rubber fins, a leash with a metal swivel to prevent tangling, and a good bit of upturn in the nose (aka "rocker") to prevent nose-diving on steeper waves. Soft boards can be "abrasive" to your skin, so wear a nylon rash guard, longer trunks, a wetsuit, or swim yoga pants.

Do *not* buy a cheap, fabric-covered Styrofoam surfboard or bodyboard at a touristy beach shop. These are dangerous junk that will disintegrate.

A decent soft surfboard runs at least $90. For more performance, consider a higher-end, more-expensive ($200 and up) "slick-skin" foamie. These are covered in shrink-wrapped vinyl and waxed like a regular board. They're lighter and stiffer with precisely shaped rails, and their fins are "foiled," or curved like an airplane wing for speed and control. These can serve well past the bare beginner phase.

CHOOSE YOUR [FOAM] WEAPON

	OPTION	PERFECT FOR	WHY
1	Shortboard, multifin, 5 to 6 feet long	Kids up to age 7, 50 to 60 pounds	If your little ripper's proficient with a skateboard, or athletic, consider a smaller foamie or slick-skin board in the 5- to 6-foot range. "Fish"-shaped twin-finned surf-boards are wider and most stable, while narrower tri-fins are more maneuverable. Both resemble what Kelly Slater or Carissa Moore might ride, and they allow for real surfing as kids improve—and kids improve *rapidly*.
2	Longboard, 8 feet long, at least 21.5 inches wide, 3 inches thick	Ages 8 to 13 and smaller adults, up to 110 pounds	For smaller riders, the 8-foot foamie longboard is wide and stable enough to catch almost any wave. Caveat: If your board comes with a leash that lacks a detangling swivel, upgrade to a better leash from a surf shop.
3	Longboard, 9 to 9.5 feet long, at least 24 inches wide, 3 inches thick	Ages 13 and up, up to 190 pounds	Like boats, surfboards increase in stability with increasing size. Most beginning teens and adults will do best with this wide and stable 9-footer.
4	Longboard, 10 feet long, at least 25 inches wide, 3 to 4 inches thick	Adults, 200-plus pounds	Big adults need more stability and a bigger board. If you're buying this big, consider a 10-foot soft standup paddleboard instead. Arm paddling and straddling is more difficult (paddle on your knees), but now you can surf *and* SUP (page 134).

SURF'S UP: HARD SURFBOARDS

When your foamie is holding you back, start hunting for your first hard surfboard. There are two basic types: Polyester fiberglass resin poured over polyurethane foam, and epoxy resin poured over Styrofoam. The latter is generally lighter and stronger, but a bit more difficult to repair and work with.

Go to a local surf shop guru for advice about the type of board that's best for your skill level and the breaks you want to surf.

For a new board, consider going straight to a local shaper, which sometimes avoids the retail markup. Shaping is a tough, low-margin business; expect to pay between $500 and $1,000 for a custom board, which is a great deal. Plenty of shapers are happy to help newbies, so if your first choice acts condescending, move on.

To buy a used board, look for deals on Craigslist or for a good used board at a well-outfitted surf shop. Whatever you do, don't go to a shop and waste their time if you plan to go elsewhere for a used board. Examine used boards closely for potential damage and the quality of repairs:

1. **Delamination:** This is when the fiberglass or epoxy deck, rail, or bottom detaches from the underlying foam and forms a "bubble." Press your fingers over the board's surface; anywhere it springs back is delaminated. Unless well-repaired, "delam" will spread, compromising the board's integrity.

2. **Dings:** Examine all ding and hole repairs. If the foam around a former ding is very dark, considerable water has seeped in—and may still be there. This can weigh the board down and compromise the foam.

3. **Creases and cracks:** Is the board free of hairline cracks or creases? These indicate great stress from breaking waves. As with dings, any dark foam under a crack indicates water intrusion.

CARE AND FEEDING OF SURFBOARDS

Direct sunlight and heat are the bane of all surfboards, which will delaminate when left exposed to either. Turn foam boards bottom or fins up when in the sun, and store hard boards in a reflective bag out of direct sunlight. Avoid storing boards in hot cars, and consider a very light-colored or white surfboard for its heat-reflective properties.

Water intrusion ruins boards. Fix damage promptly. On regular foam boards, dings can usually be repaired with marine silicone glue. For hard boards, use the appropriate resin—don't stuff a hole with wax or plop on a sticker and expect the patch to last.

Successful beach driving requires the right conditions, a vehicle with adequate clearance, and usually deflated tires.

1. Consider the sand. Fine sand—like Daytona Beach—packs densely and is very drivable. Coarse, pebbled, or loose sand is slippery and shifting, requiring higher clearance and deflated tires.

2. Consider the tide. Low is best, since the sand below the high-tide line will be damp and denser. Driving in saltwater will ruin your car.

3. As necessary, deflate tires down to 10 to 15 pressure square inch (psi). Bulging tires create a beach-ball effect, resulting in more tread contact, so vehicles "float" without digging in.

4. Follow the tracks of other vehicles. This already-packed sand acts almost like rails.

5. Drive slowly, turn gently, and maintain momentum. Avoid stopping before your destination. Look ahead and figure out your route as you keep moving.

6. If you slide, steer with the skid—like in snow. If traction slips, accelerate slightly to improve traction without spinning your wheels.

7. If you encounter tidal pools, pass on the inshore side; sand between tidal pools and the ocean can be mushy.

8. Never say, "Hey, watch this."

GETTING UNSTUCK
Don't drive on sand without a shovel and a cell phone (to call for help if this doesn't work).

1. Dig gently sloping ramps ahead of and behind the vehicle. Dig far enough so the vehicle is resting evenly only on the tires.

2. For traction, put upside-down floor mats in front of and behind the drive tires. Far better are MaxxTrax, which are built for this.

3. Keep wheels straight. Gently drive forward, then when traction erodes, stop, roll back, and when momentum reverses, gently accelerate again until traction erodes.

4. Repeat this back-and-forth rocking process, building momentum and creating ruts that allow you to roll out.

Winch warning: A winch is useful but dangerous. Attach it to something absolutely immoveable, and keep others far away. A snapping cable can kill.

WHAT'S S.U.P.?: **STANDUP PADDLEBOARDS**

Humans have been standing atop watercraft and catching waves using long paddles for at least a thousand years, when ancient Peruvians surfed atop reed canoes. In Hawaii in the 1930s, the Waikiki Beach Boys used long paddles aboard massive koa-and-redwood surfboards: These helped them take pictures of surfing tourists, spot distant wave sets, and easily catch Waikiki's long rolling swells.

Yet standup paddleboards (SUPs) didn't really catch on until the early aughts, when Laird Hamilton and others paddled out at Malibu, Waikiki, and Makaha. Now the sport is mainstream, and SUPers are not only using paddleboards to surf but to replace kayaks and cruise down coasts, cross lakes, and even roll down rivers like the Colorado.

WALKING ON WATER

Teach yourself the basic mechanics in a pool, harbor, or lake, somewhere utterly calm.

1. Stand in the middle of your board facing forward, feet shoulder-width apart, and paddle on either side. Walk up and down the board. Practice turns by digging the paddle in behind you, with its raked sweep pointed away.

2. Practice changing your stance from side-by-side to front-to-back: Use side-by-side for paddling, front-to-back for negotiating and riding waves. If your feet are side-by-side as you drop in, you'll be knocked backward or faceplant.

3. Spend lots of time swimming with your paddle, since you will. Get used to levering it, so it isn't a hindrance. Make the gear an extension of your body.

To catch an incoming wave, paddle toward it, then turn toward shore and accelerate to match the wave's speed.

PADDLING OUT AND JOINING THE LINEUP

For your first waves, as always, choose an uncrowded beach with glassy conditions and small, easy rollers. Always wear an ankle leash so your board doesn't mow someone down (and know the leash's length to maintain a safe distance).

First practice paddling into oncoming waves from your knees, and then practice standing up. Paddle directly toward the waves, and as a wave bears down, shift one foot (or knee) slightly backward to lift the board's nose. As you rise over the wave, shift your weight forward, almost like jumping hurdles. Pick up your nose at the right moment, dig in the paddle, and pull yourself over that first hurdle.

Once you're comfortable paddling out, head for the lineup. Just paddle around and get used to how the board behaves when swells roll under you from different angles, especially side to side. Balancing is far more difficult.

CATCH A WAVE

SUPs paddle faster than surfboards, so you can sit farther out. Pick a likely swell early, and begin paddling 20 to 30 yards before the wave arrives. However, make sure no one else is paddling for the wave. If so, defer to them—that is, until you're no longer a rookie.

If the wave is breaking to the right, paddle hard on your right side to gain momentum. When the wave is almost on you, switch to paddling on your left to angle into the wave. As you transition to being carried by the wave, quickly shift your feet front-to-back, with more weight on your back foot.

If you don't wipe out, you'll accelerate rapidly. To make turns, gently lean or drag your paddle hard behind you. If the wave slows, dig the paddle in for a burst of speed. After a few rides, try crouching and planing the paddle behind you—while varying the pressure. The paddle greatly extends your reach, allowing you to get high and tight to the wave face and, eventually, into the tube of a wave.

HANDLING A WIPEOUT

Many surfers get hit and injured by errant SUPs. Do all you can not to fall and bail your board—that is, let whitewater drag the SUP to the end of the leash.

Instead, learn to kick your board back out over waves as you fall. As the wave approaches, launch yourself backward from the board's tail and kick the nose up and out to sea as it shoots forward. In most cases, this will send the board over the wave, putting it next to you when you surface.

Remount as soon as possible. If successive waves don't give you time, turn the board to the beach, watching out for people on the inside, and hold the board's tail for control without letting go. Or, hold the leash at the fabric railsaver at the board's tail with one hand and the paddle in the other, and pull the board through the whitewater.

If this is too difficult, find an easier spot or SUP on a smaller wave day.

SURFING **COMMANDMENTS, PART II:** S.U.P. RULES

SUPers must abide by all the Surfing Commandments (page 118), along with a few SUP-specific rules. Thanks to former world champion surfer-turned-SUPer Ian Cairns for the wisdom.

1. THOU SHALT SUP AMID THE FEWEST SURFERS

Paddle out to the spots or breaks with the fewest surfers, and never SUP amid surfers if you can't control your board.

2. THOU SHALT NOT LORD OVER THY NEIGHBOR

Many traditional surfers regard SUPs as unwelcome foreign objects, even boats. To minimize annoyance, don't stand and hover over everyone. Sit or kneel in the lineup, chill out, and wait your turn. Be sociable and consider sitting farther over on the shoulder. SUPs paddle faster than all but the best longboards, so you should still be able to catch waves from the shoulder.

3. THOU SHALT NOT BAIL THY S.U.P.

If you fall on a wave, do everything to grab and control your board (see "Handling a Wipeout," page 136). Hitting another surfer in the lineup is grounds for instant dismissal and fuels the surfer argument that SUPs don't belong.

4. THOU SHALT CALL SETS

Standing SUPers can see the set waves coming before traditional surfers can, so whistle or tell the surf crew that a set is coming and maybe even which wave looks better.

5. THOU SHALT NOT BE A WAVE HOG

SUPers can catch waves unreachable by others because SUPs are so buoyant and fast. Be aware of your wave count. Too many and you'll be considered a wave hog. Get a few good ones and find another peak, or catch waves on the shoulder for a while.

6. THOU SHALT USE A SHORTER LEASH

Use the shortest leash possible, around 6 or 7 feet long. This keeps the board close, speeding your ability to retrieve the board quickly after a wipeout. This also leads to fewer leash tangles and step-ons and shows that you're not a kook. A coiled SUP leash is best.

SURF WAX

Whichever brand of surf wax you prefer, purchase the right wax for the water temperature. Warm- and tropical-water waxes are harder and melt only at high temperatures. Cool- and cold-water wax is softer, melting at lower temperatures. Using tropical wax in cold water can make your deck pretty slick.

You need basecoat wax, topcoat wax, wax-removing citrus solvent, and a wax comb. First, remove any old, cruddy wax. Use a hair dryer or if it's sunny, leave your board out, waxed-side up, till the wax warms and softens. Then scrape using the wax comb (or a credit card), and wipe clean with solvent.

Wax only the part of the deck where your feet and body will be. Longboarders, who walk their boards, usually wax their whole boards, while shortboarders wax roughly the back two-thirds.

1. Start with a basic pattern—circles, stripes, cross-hatch—of coarse basecoat wax. This gives your topcoat wax something to stick to.

2. Apply topcoat wax, creating raised bumps, about the height of a dime, all over the waxy surface.

3. Wax to the board's rails, or edges, but don't cover them.

That's it. Now keep your waxed board out of the sun or a hot car. Melted wax is nearly impossible to remove from upholstery, but not from clothes.

GETTING SURF WAX OUT OF CLOTHES

Don't toss your favorite T-shirt or lucky boardshorts when they get a surf-wax infusion. Zog, founder of Mr. Zog's Sex Wax, recommends you try these approaches:

○ For small stains, place a paper towel between the fabric and a warm iron. As the wax melts, it sticks to the paper. Cotton can handle higher heat, but use a fairly cool iron with meltable synthetics.

○ If a big blob accidentally gets washed and dried in your pocket, slowly heat in a pot of water until the wax melts and floats to the top. Scoop it out.

○ Finally, try a citrus-based wax remover (though these can leave an oily residue) or acetone (which may ruin some fabrics). When all else fails, try your dry cleaner.

But to-morrow, ah, to-morrow, I shall be out in that wonderful water, and I shall come in standing up, even as Ford and Freeth. And if I fail tomorrow, I shall do it the next day, or the next. Upon one thing I am resolved: the Snark *shall not sail from Honolulu until I, too, wing my heels with the swiftness of the sea, and become a sun-burned, skin-peeling Mercury.*

—from *The Cruise of the Snark*, Jack London

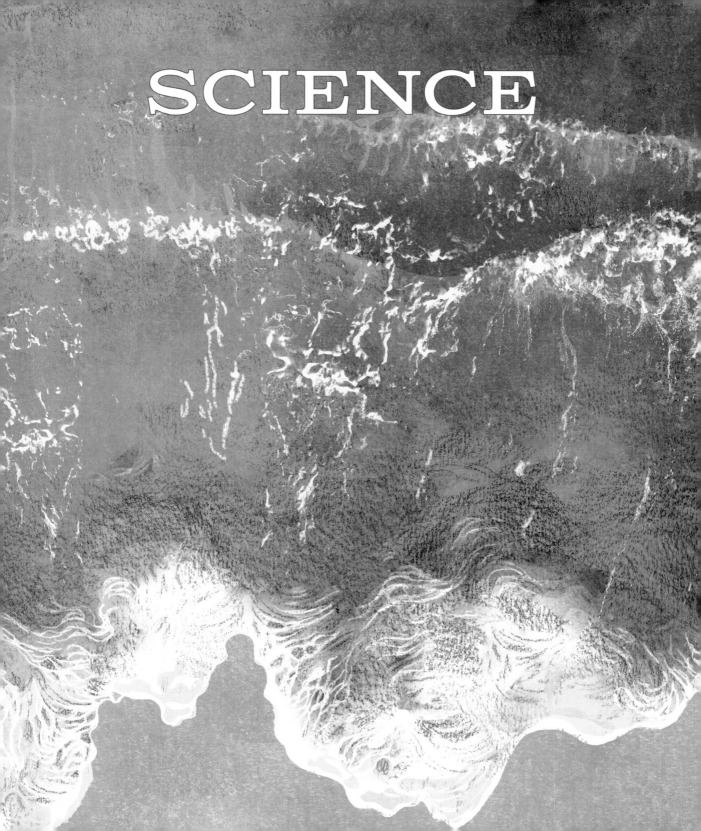

SCIENCE

WHY OCEAN EXPLORATION MATTERS

AS TOLD BY DR. ROBERT BALLARD

On September 1, 1985, Dr. Robert Ballard and a team of navy and Woods Hole researchers discovered the wreckage of the R.M.S. *Titanic*. In ensuing years, Dr. Ballard discovered the wreckage of the *Bismarck*, the *Yorktown*, and a perfectly preserved shipwreck from 350 BC. Yet Dr. Ballard considers his 1977 discovery of hydrothermal vents, and his 1979 discovery of "black smokers," as his most important discoveries. Thriving in a realm devoid of sunlight, these places have fundamentally changed our understanding of life on Earth. Follow Dr. Ballard's work at Nautilus Live (www.nautiluslive.org).

Titanic. I can't escape that ship, you know? I remember when my mother called me after I'd been on every talk show. She said, "It's too bad you found that ship." I said, "Mom, are you okay?" She said, "I'm fine, but hydrothermal vents are far more important. Now your epitaph is written. The man who found *Titanic* died today, not the man who found hydrothermal vents—and the origin of life on the planet."

Why explore the ocean? I've done over 150 expeditions. But still, we know so little. There are three million shipwrecks—three million chapters of human history—but I doubt we've found a few thousand. There's more history in the deep sea than in all the world's museums combined. The ocean produces half the oxygen we breathe. Who knows what medicines have yet to be created from marine species. Yet how much of the deep sea have we seen with our own eyes? You could argue, maybe 5 percent. We're totally in the dark.

The basic fact is that 95 percent of the human race lives on 5 percent of the Earth's surface, and 72 percent of the Earth's surface is the ocean. Do you realize that half of our country is underwater—and we haven't even mapped it in any detail? We have better maps of Mars than we do of half the United States.

I have a ship, the *E/V Nautilus*, which is owned and operated by the Ocean Exploration Trust. They're off Canada right now exploring seamounts. What makes our ship different is that it's run by the inmates. We're always frustrated by how government and private business often don't get it right, so *Nautilus* is run by oceanographers and explorers. That's very rare.

We're always bitching and moaning because people spend so much more on exploring outer space than inner space—God's up there, and we go where the devil is. But we're really entering a very exciting time because of these autonomous vehicle systems. Aboard the *Nautilus* we have two remotely operated vehicles, *Hercules* and *Argus*. We can live stream video from our ROVs. Unlike manned deep-sea submarines, *Argos* and *Hercules* can stay down exploring all the time. It's going to be a total game changer for humans.

Why take the fragile human body to the bottom of the ocean? On the screen I'm still looking out of a window and operating the same robotic manipulator—remotely. In the command center, I'm looking at fifty monitors and integrating it all. We do this live now, too—interactive broadcasts in museums across the United States. Using telepresence for exploration is so cool. While I'm talking to you, I'm at home watching *Nautilus* at sea. If they find something cool, anyone following us online can be alerted too.

It's literally spirit moving. We're setting up camp in the Pacific. It's a third of the Earth. We plan on being there for quite some time. One day, we could have thousands of autonomous underwater vehicles roaming the ocean. Wind 'em up, send the suckers out, and they come back in a few hours and tell us what's out there. When we add in autonomous vehicle systems where ships are totally unmanned, we're gonna finally figure out what the heck's underwater.

Because the ocean is the answer. We're toast without it.

OUR FOSSIL WILL BE PLASTIC

AS TOLD BY MARCUS ERIKSEN
Marcus Eriksen is a former US Marine and the founder and director of the Five Gyres Institute
(www.5gyres.org).

My awakening goes back to 1991 when I was in the first Gulf War. I remember during the ground war, sitting in a foxhole and talking to a friend: "If we survive this, we should build a raft, like Tom Sawyer and Huckleberry Finn, and raft the Mississippi." Remember the oil wells Saddam Hussein lit up on his way out of Kuwait City? I was very close to them. The wind would blow over and turn day to night. The ground was black for miles in all directions. The beach was trashed. Lots of loss of human life. It was devastating.

I finally made good on that rafting promise in 2003. At Lake Itasca, Minnesota, where the Mississippi begins, I started a ten-month trip to my hometown of New Orleans. Along the way I saw tons and tons of trash and junk floating down the river. Before that trip, I had been to Midway Island for a research project. There I saw albatross with plastics exploding out of their stomachs. So a few things got me interested in plastics: Going down the Mississippi. Seeing the source of all this plastic: our wars for resources. And those albatross.

When I got to New Orleans, it turned out that Captain Charles Moore—the guy who discovered the Great Pacific Garbage Patch—lived 30 miles from me. Afterward, I worked with him for about six years—doing research and education programs on plastics. That's when I met my wife, Anna Cummins. I was on Carlie's boat, the ORV *Algalita*, in the middle of the Pacific Ocean when I asked Anna to marry me. I also said, "I wanna build another raft." That became the junk raft, which was made of six pontoons filled with 15,000 old plastic bottles. Our cabin was the fuselage of an old Cessna 310 airplane.

On June 1, 2008, I sailed that raft from LA to Hawaii with my good friend Joel Paschal, with Anna as our ground support staff—a three-month odyssey at sea. Then Anna and I sailed back, and we've since done twenty expeditions around the world together.

I once collected a fish in the mid-Pacific, and out of its stomach poured seventeen particles of plastic. We've discovered over 1,200 organisms that have either eaten or been entangled by plastic. We're creating a very vulnerable and beleaguered ocean with a lot of organisms eating our trash—filtering out the small stuff. That plastic enters the food chain. With some fish we eat, we're eating plastic, too.

If we can one day stop the flow of trash into the sea, those plastics will ultimately break up and be filtered through organisms, and those will sink to the seafloor and become sediment. The geological layer of microplastics will be evidence of this moment in time. From 1950 to 2050—our fossil will be plastic.

MOST COMMON TYPES OF OCEAN PLASTIC

OBJECT	PERCENT POLLUTION (By Unit Count)
Food Wrapper/Containers	31.14
Bottle Container/Caps	15.5
Bags	11.18
Straw/Stirrers	8.13
Beverage Bottles	7.27
Take-Out Containers	6.27
Lids	4.9
Cigarette Butts	3.66
Cups (Hard Plastic)	3.13
Utensils	2.79
Cups and Plates (Foam)	2.02
Other Jugs/Containers	1.13
Personal Care Products	1.05
Balloons	1
Cigarette Lighters	0.84

A DIP OF THE NET:
PLANKTON AND PLASTIC

In 2007, *National Geographic* photographer David Liittschwager unveiled a remarkable, beautiful photo of tiny plankton he had collected by dipping a small mesh net off the south coast of Hawaii's Big Island. Though the viral photo was incorrectly reported as the contents of a single drop of ocean water, the photo nonetheless revealed an astonishing array of life. In 2018, a trawl in almost the exact location again revealed a tremendous diversity of phytoplankton, but with a troubling difference: This time, the trawl was almost as full of plastics as with tiny creatures.

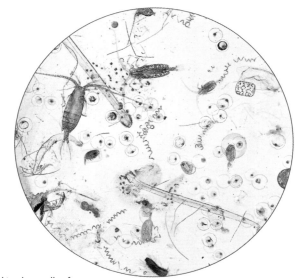

Phytoplankton in one dip of a hand net photographed off Kona, September 20, 2006.

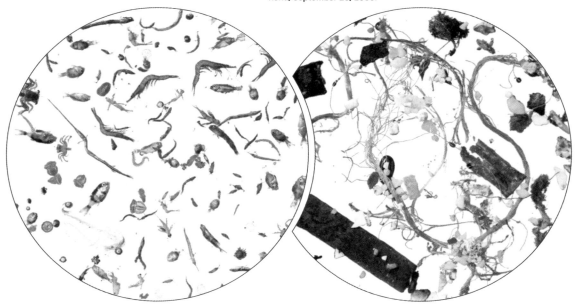

The contents of a trawl photographed in almost the same location in 2018 with phytoplankton (left) separated from plastics (right).

KNOW YOUR **SEA MONSTERS**:
THE LARGEST CREATURES IN THE SEA

The biggest creature that has ever lived on Earth still swims the oceans: the 108-foot-long blue whale. But the honor of "longest animal" belongs to the frightful, deadly lion's mane jellyfish, a venomous, tentacle-laden horror that stretches out to 120 feet. What other giant monsters might you meet in the deep blue sea? We're so glad you asked. . . .

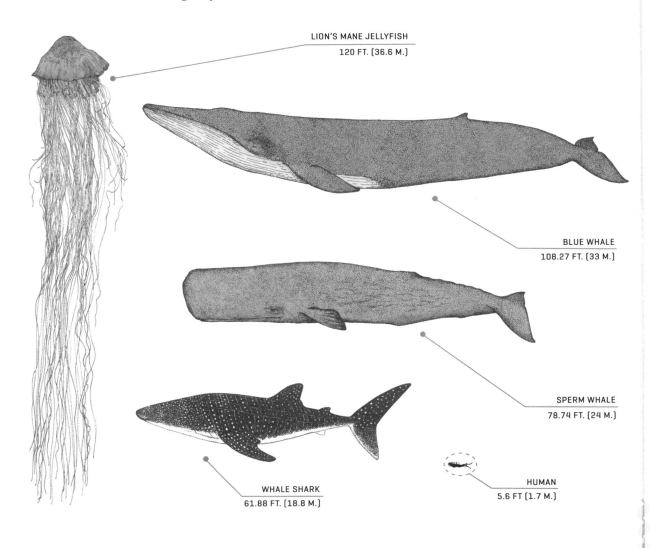

LION'S MANE JELLYFISH
120 FT. (36.6 M.)

BLUE WHALE
108.27 FT. (33 M.)

SPERM WHALE
78.74 FT. (24 M.)

WHALE SHARK
61.88 FT. (18.8 M.)

HUMAN
5.6 FT (1.7 M.)

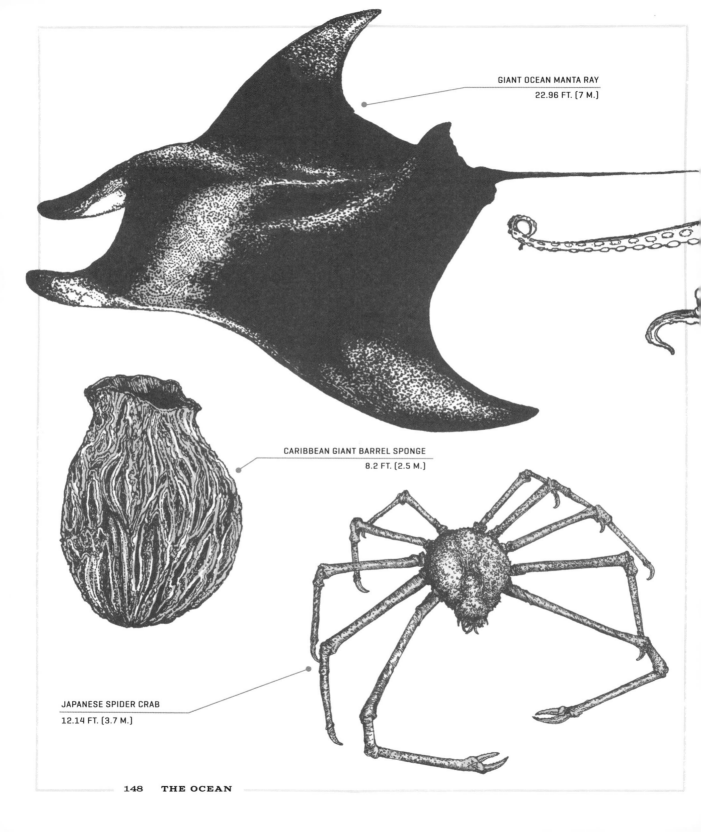

GIANT OCEAN MANTA RAY
22.96 FT. [7 M.]

CARIBBEAN GIANT BARREL SPONGE
8.2 FT. [2.5 M.]

JAPANESE SPIDER CRAB
12.14 FT. [3.7 M.]

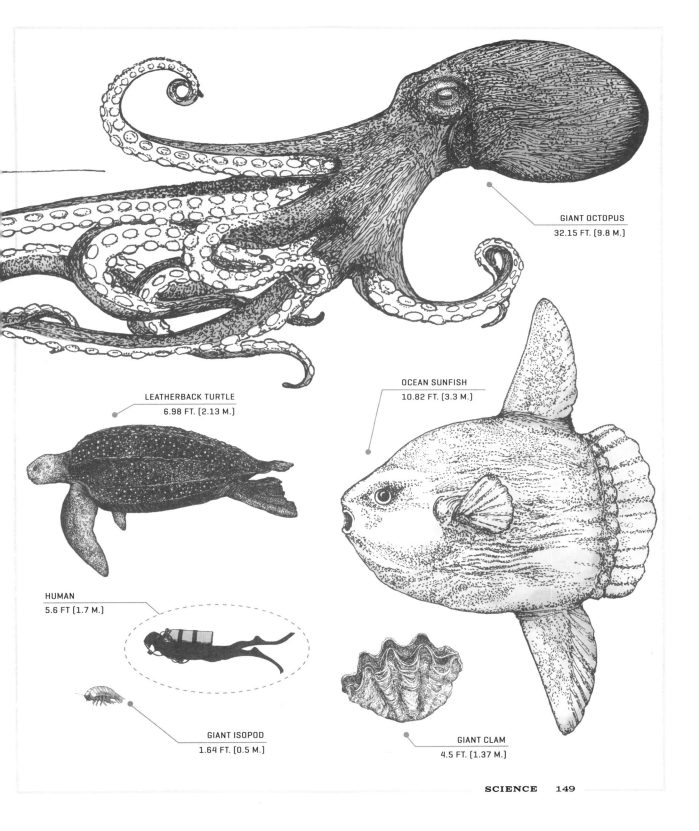

GIANT OCTOPUS
32.15 FT. [9.8 M.]

OCEAN SUNFISH
10.82 FT. [3.3 M.]

LEATHERBACK TURTLE
6.98 FT. [2.13 M.]

HUMAN
5.6 FT [1.7 M.]

GIANT ISOPOD
1.64 FT. [0.5 M.]

GIANT CLAM
4.5 FT. [1.37 M.]

TIDEPOOLS 101

AS TOLD BY DR. STEPHEN R. PALUMBI

There are four overlapping zones in a rocky intertidal area. The splash and spray zone, the high tide zone, the low tide zone, and the submerged zone.

At the top, the splash zone, almost all the creatures are terrestrial. They get hit by waves at really high tides and maybe water splashes over them every once in awhile if the moon is at the right phase, but at the very top of the intertidal, marine organisms are out of the water longer than they're in the water. That puts strong physiological stresses on them—drying out, heating up, getting encrusted with salt. There aren't many lifeforms that can live up there and handle the physical environmental stresses.

At the bottom of the zone, things are exactly the opposite. Only every once in awhile at very low tide is this section exposed, and its creatures experience more biological interactions and stress than almost anywhere else in the sea. There are competitors and predators and parasites—all kinds of threats to species from the other species around them. It's among the most crowded and competitive marine habitats on Earth.

Famously at the top of the intertidal, in the splash zone, in addition to all the birds, is a small snail called a periwinkle—*Littorina littorea*. They're found all over the world and they're very good at drying out, heating up and not being damaged. In fact, if you plop them in a cup of water, they'll crawl out. That's because tidepool waters are full of crabs, anemones, and starfish: dangerous places for a succulent, thin-shelled snail.

The high tide zone is home to the limpet, another small and bountiful intertidal mollusk. They've been around for hundreds of millions of years. They're little snails that live in a conical shell that looks like a Chinese hat. They wander around at high tide eating little algaes on the rocks and at low tide they go right back to the same spot they started out the night before. And they're there so often that they wear off a spot in the rock that's exactly the shape of their shell. It's called a home scar and it's the spot they go to make sure they won't dry out at low tide. They do this without any workable brains or workable eyes. Somehow they have an internal compass, or map that they can always follow home.

At the lower levels and bottom are critters on the hunt—urchins and little fish like gobies, sculpins, and mudskippers. They lurk in the little cracks and crevices in tidepools and can live out of the water longer than you'd think a fish would. Barnacles can also blanket this territory. They're little shrimp-like animals that lie on their backs cemented to a rock. The individual barnacle builds a shell around itself in the shape of a volcano and sticks out its cilia, little hair-like legs that fan out and filter food from the water. People long assumed barnacles to be mollusks, but they're arthropods. Some of them get really big—the size of golf balls, and some species are considered delicacies. They taste like crabs.

Humans have been wandering the intertidal looking for food for a long time. Is it the most important habitat to the survival of humans? I don't think that's the question. Tidepool

SPLASH AND SPRAY ZONE

HIGH TIDE ZONE

LOW TIDE ZONE

SUBMERGED ZONE

creatures are endurant because they've evolved in environmental extremes and are a good example of critters who could survive climate change, pollution, or living next to a nuclear plant. Hundreds of species on Earth live nowhere else but the intertidal zone. Peering into a tidepool, you're like an aerial drone drifting above a neighborhood, just looking in on things. The creatures within them live very intricate lives in very small spaces. They're charming, they're beautiful, they're diverse and that's what makes them infinitely fascinating.

PORTRAIT OF A WAVE

Say you're bobbing atop a surfboard in the lineup along Hawaii's North Shore. A perfectly formed wave appears outside and you start paddling to catch it. How was that wave created? Where did it come from?

In essence, waves are generated by storms. In the Pacific, as the first breezes of an approaching cold front roll out to sea between Siberia and Japan, minute, vertical barometric changes cause tiny deformations atop the ocean—variously called ripples, capillary waves, or "cat's paws." As the breeze stiffens, capillary waves provide a rough surface for building winds to grab on to. Surface water molecules vibrate in a circular motion, forming tiny wind waves whose peaks form rows of miniature sails and whose valleys, or troughs, carry a rotating eddy of air that furthers them along.

By the time the gale pushes these waves 25 miles offshore, they're rolling orbital columns, something like a jumble of logs rolling downhill—perhaps 10 feet high, very steep, with 7-second "periods." A period measures the time it takes for a full wave, from trough to peak to trough, to pass an anchored buoy. Also, most wave energy lies below the surface—at this point, the orbital column might descend 40 feet. After 250 miles, the waves become rounded "swells," averaging 27 feet high, with a 13-second period, and an energy column now 400 feet deep.

Say barometric pressures plunge, and the storm grows to a monster, spanning half the Pacific, with 60-mph winds spiraling in the familiar cyclonic shape. Swells can grow into 50-foot-high, 17-second-period juggernauts—several miles across, 1,000 feet thick, their energy extending 1,200 feet down. These waves will now be traveling faster than the 60-mph winds that spawned them.

Eventually our storm will sweep off toward Alaska, or the West Coast, but the swells will continue to race outward like ripples from a rock thrown on a pond. A strange process organizes these "groundswells" over the next thousand miles. They drop in height, but not depth. The strongest, longest period waves pass through the shorter, weaker ones as they're sorted by period into swell trains, or sets, of five to fifteen waves.

The fastest swell trains roll eastward at around 35 mph. Bizarrely, the individual waves in the train travel twice as fast as the train itself. They conserve energy by drafting off one another, continually rolling from front to back, something like tank treads. Unimpeded by shallows, they can whipsaw halfway around the globe.

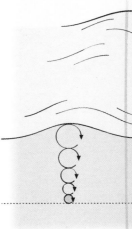

MOTION OF WATER MOLECULES

After a couple of days, this swell nears Hawaii, forming a defined front around 2,000 miles wide. The fastest, 25-second forerunner waves undulate along its leading edge in mile-plus-wide ribbons, with peak 15-to-17-second energy following several hours later. As the peak energy of the swell passes, the period drops and the waves slowly subside in strength.

Forerunners are rarely seen along continental shorelines. They're so deep that they scrape across the rising seafloor and are refracted, or deflected away, from land. Since the Hawaiian islands are mountaintops rising from deep seas, plenty of wave energy reaches the beach as waves are grabbed by the seafloor and bent toward the shore. Reaching shallower water, deep swell energy compresses. Waves slow and rise dramatically, becoming steep and unstable. The deeper part of the wave slows, while the shallower part keeps moving fast. When a wave reaches water roughly 1.3 times its height, it pitches forward and breaks.

Surfers seek waves that first run across a shallower spot, which slows part of the wave, while the rest of the wave continues to run faster in deeper water as it bends shoreward, breaking and peeling "down the line" as it goes. Slowly rising seafloors produce easier-to-ride, crumbly waves. Where the rise is abrupt, waves will be steep and hollow, forming a "barrel."

And so it arrives, the perfect wave. Then, just over a day after it's ridden on Hawaii's North Coast, surfers in San Francisco will ply the very same swells. The next morning, surfers from Malibu to Baja will hoot in excitement and start paddling.

OCEANS IN MOTION:
THE WORLD'S CURRENTS

Every July, why is the ocean so cold in San Diego, California, that surfers wear wetsuits, when at almost exactly the same latitude, the waters off Charleston, South Carolina, are like bathwater? The answer is currents. The California Current flows north to south carrying cold water from northern latitudes. Off Charleston, the Gulf Stream flows from south to north, bearing warm Caribbean waters and fueling hurricanes.

What creates currents? The complex interplay between atmosphere, sun, sea, tide, land, and the earth's rotation, but mostly, surface currents come from prevailing oceanic winds. These generally blow from one direction and, along with currents, serve as a sort of global climate control. Oceanic surface currents rotate broadly at speeds of tens or hundreds of centimeters per second around five enormous and relatively  calm patches of the ocean called gyres. On the western side of the gyres, north-flowing currents like the Gulf Stream are warm, strong, and narrow. On their eastern sides, colder south-flowing currents like the California are weaker but wider. Because their centers are relatively calm, gyres become great collecting points for oceanic plastic pollution.

Meanwhile, in the deep ocean, sinking cold water at the poles creates a massive deepwater current that circulates the ocean's waters very slowly around the globe. They're so plodding that one complete circuit of this "Global Conveyor Belt" could take a thousand years.

OF GODS AND MONSTERS: THE LEGACY OF **THE WHALESHIP *ESSEX***

In the annals of human suffering, the wretched, grinding misery endured by the crew of the Nantucket whaleship *Essex* ranks high. On November 20, 1820, Essex was attacked and sunk in the open Pacific by a massive sperm whale, an event that inspired Herman Melville's *Moby Dick*. Then, for three months, surviving crew endured such torture and starvation that they resorted to cannibalism. Remarkably, eight of the original twenty sailors—all pious Quakers—lived to tell the tale.

Plunge the harpoon deeper, however, and one wonders if the tragedy of Captain James Pollard and his crew was instead vengeance—and a warning—wrought by the gods. The *Essex* was emblematic of a society and an age that freely plundered

nature and destroyed cultures, whose deities had perhaps had enough. Here is a list of divine suspects:

MOTHER EARTH, GODDESS OF THE WAMPANOAG
The Wampanoag Indians called Nantucket home, and tilled its arable soil, for thousands of years. Up through the 1700s, they also skillfully crewed Nantucket whaleboats. But in 1764, an outbreak of "Indian sickness" killed 222 of the island's remaining 358 Wampanoags, and by the late 1700s, Nantucket was "a barren sandbank, fertilized with whale oil only," according to French American writer J. Hector St. John de Crèvecœur.

NEPTUNE, GOD OF THE SEA
The *Essex* went sperm whale hunting in the Pacific Ocean because, by then, Nantucket whalers had effectively cleared the Atlantic Ocean of them. A few days into her fateful voyage, *Essex* was nearly capsized by a squall line—and three of her six whaleboats were destroyed. Rather than sensibly return to Nantucket for repairs, Captain Pollard subjected his crew to a terrifying voyage around Cape Horn.

MAMA COCHA, INCAN GODDESS OF THE OCEAN
Mama Cocha, aka Mama Qucha, had surely protected Ecuador's Galapagos Islands from humanity's depridations for eons. Then whalers arrived, starting in the early 1800s, and denuded the islands of their beautiful, ancient giant tortoises, harvesting them for food. The *Essex* crew took 180 tortoises from Hood Island, and as a joke, helmsman Thomas Chappel set fire to Floreana Island. The ensuing inferno raged for days, charred the island for years, and rendered Floreana's tortoises extinct.

TA'AROA, GOD OF CREATION IN THE SOCIETY ISLANDS
Between 1804 and 1876, 225,000 sperm whales—perhaps 75 percent of the world's population—died at the hands of Pacific whalers. Thus, is it any wonder Ta'Aroa sent a whale to avenge this slaughter?

For the first time in recorded history, apparently enraged after the *Essex* killed three family members, an 85-foot-long, 60-ton sperm whale repeatedly rammed the 238-ton whaling vessel. "His aspect was most horrible, and such as indicated resentment and fury," cabin boy Thomas Nickerson later wrote.

The entire crew abandoned ship, boarding the *Essex's* three remaining whaleboats. Had they sailed with the wind, they might have reached the Society Islands in thirty days. Instead, the ship's first mate, Owen Chase, based on unfounded fears of cannibals on those islands, convinced Captain Pollard to sail in the opposite direction and against the wind for South America.

So Ta'Aroa sent ferocious gales and a marauding killer whale, whose attack introduced saltwater into the crew's bread ration. Eating it only made the crew thirstier. "[T]he violence of raving thirst has no parallel in the catalogue of human calamities," wrote Chase.

By mid-December, the desperate, famished crew had been blown only closer to the Society Islands. So they landed on a limestone outcropping called Henderson Island. After two weeks, they'd eaten nearly every bird, crab, and turtle and all the edible plants. So most of the crew resumed their voyage to South America, while three stayed to wait for rescue.

Once at sea, gales and waves again slowed their torturous eastward slog, and starvation quickly returned. Eventually, straws were drawn, and the unlucky loser was killed and eaten, a process the remaining crew repeated five more times. Curiously, five of the six men consumed were black, and the one white crewman eaten was Pollard's young cousin, whom he'd promised to look out for.

Then, three months after the whale's attack, two of the boats—bearing five wild-eyed, bone-sucking, emaciated men—were finally plucked from the sea off South America. The three men on Henderson Island were rescued as well.

OLOKUN AND HIS WIFE, ELUSU, WEST AFRICAN SEA GODS

In 1821, Pollard returned home, and he was generally forgiven by the Nantucket community, with the notable exception of his cousin's mother. In extreme cases like the *Essex*, cannibalism was simply "a custom of the sea." Indeed, five months later, Pollard was given command of the whaleship *The Two Brothers*. But perhaps Pollard's gastronomic transgressions were not entirely forgiven. In 1823, *The Two Brothers* was destroyed by a gale on the French Frigate Shoals, thus ending Pollard's career as a captain. Near the end of his life, Pollard was apparently interviewed by a Boston reporter, who mentioned he was distantly related to *Essex* crewman Samuel Reed. "You remember him, of course," said the reporter. "Remember him?" asked Pollard. "Hell son, I et him!"

MOTHER OCEAN

After the *Essex* disaster, sperm whales began fighting back. In 1835 and 1837, two whaleships were sunk by whales. In 1850, the *Pocahontas* was very nearly sunk, and in 1851, the year *Moby-Dick* was published, a vengeful whale destroyed the *Ann Alexander*. "Ye Gods," Melville wrote to a friend, "I wonder if my evil art has raised this monster."

Till then an adventurous sailor, whaleman, and novelist, Melville's own luck turned after *Moby Dick's* publication. The novel was neither a critical nor commercial success, and he never wrote another, though he did keep writing. Melville even met Pollard himself, then Nantucket's night watchman. "To the islanders he was a nobody," Melville wrote. "To me, the most impressive man, tho' wholly unassuming, even humble—that I ever encountered."

WHAT IS KELP AND WHY IT MATTERS

AS TOLD BY DAN REED

Dr. Dan Reed is the deputy director of the Marine Science Institute at the University of Santa Barbara. Much of his life's work has been devoted to the study of restoring and protecting the great kelp forests of the California coast.

Kelps take many forms. Some are short; some lay flat on the bottom. Most famous are the giant kelps like *Macrocystis*—the bull kelp off California. They form the massive floating canopies and undersea forests, growing to 20, even 30, meters high. A big kelp plant is like a bundle of ropes. Each rope is called a *stipe*, and attached to each stipe are blades, which look like leaves, that are attached with little gas-filled floats. That whole kelp unit is called a frond.

Kelp originated in the Northern Hemisphere and it spread south over millions of years—across the temperate seas of the world. Definitionally, kelp is a brown algae—a large, brown seaweed. I call them plants but they're really not. They're protists. Kelps don't have to invest in all those structural parts plants need on land. The water supports them. Kelps just need to hold onto the bottom, develop gas bladders, and float to the surface.

Kelp is a "foundation species" because it has a profound effect on the entire ecosystem. Kelp influences physical conditions and greatly enhances biodiversity and abundance. Because it grows up through the water column, kelp alters currents and even seawater chemistry. It changes the light and affects what grows beneath it, just like trees in a forest. Little fish will retreat to the blades of kelp and make their way deeper as they get bigger, as bigger species—fish and marine mammals like sea lions—use the forest as a foraging habitat for small prey. Some species eat kelp—various moon snails and turban snails, small shrimps and isopods. Then there are the detritivores. They wait for the blades and stuff to fall to them. Abalone are a perfect example. They've done radioisotope work tracing the carbon from kelp in Monterey Bay and have shown that 60 to 70 percent of the carbon in

BLADES

FLOAT

STIPE

HOLDFAST

FROND

urchins 1,500 meters down comes from kelp at the surface.

Sea urchins really like to feed on living kelp—no other creatures have their ability to mow down kelp. And sea otters love to eat urchins. Otters used to extend from the Curial Islands in Russia all the way down into Baja, Mexico, but they were extirpated by fur trappers in the 1700s and 1800s. Where you found the most luxurious kelp forests, that's where urchins were kept in check. Where there were no otters, you get these big areas called "urchin barrens" where no kelp will grow. This was the case for decades in California's Monterey Bay. But since the otters have returned, so has the kelp.

If you take away the kelp, you take away all the species that depend on it.

Something else comes into play. Kelp gets torn out by waves all the time, but it's such a dynamic species, it grows back. In some areas, kelp beds are persistent over time, but there's no such thing as an old-growth kelp forest. Our estimates suggest that the biomass in a kelp forest turns over ten times per year. It's really fast growing. A frond can grow up to a foot and a half a day.

When kelp is ripped out by waves, it either moves offshore and sinks into the deep sea or piles up on the beach in "wracks." The beach itself doesn't have primary producers in its food web, so that kelp is incredibly important. The little sand fleas and grazers and creatures that are drawn to the kelp that everyone finds a pain in the butt when they're on the beach—that's what the shorebirds and all the sand crabs feed on. Kelp fuels the beach food web, too.

Think about the beaches that get groomed by the beach cities—where they remove all the stinky kelp. Well, you groom the beach and you take out the main source of food. What have you done? You've created a desert.

FIND WORK ABOARD
A SCIENTIFIC EXPEDITION

AS TOLD BY DR. ROBERT HUETER

Dr. Robert Hueter has studied and written about sharks for more than forty years. He is the associate vice president for research, senior scientist, and director of the Shark Research Center at Mote Marine Laboratory in Sarasota, Florida. He is also chief science advisor for Ocearch, a marine research and education foundation.

I fell in love with the ocean from the beginning and grew up in the golden age of Jacques Cousteau and the rise of true oceanography. I realize now how lucky I was. I got into studying sharks in college in the mid-1970s. My summer work was tagging sharks with a group in New England. I tagged thousands and thousands of sharks and probably learned more about sharks in that boat than at any lab.

What always drove me and to this day still drives me is learning. I try to learn something new every day. Some of my fondest days go back to being a graduate student and hardly making any money, but every day was exciting.

If you want to join a vessel as a research scientist, there's lots of challenges these days. The students who come on board have that fire in the belly—that burning curiosity that's never really satiated. It's a desire for enlightenment—thinking it's so cool to unwrap these mysteries and reveal scientific truths. Those are the ones who'll succeed. Later, they go to graduate school, develop their own special interests, and come back on the research vessel—now as beginning experts.

People on the boat have to be serious about the science, but we're not joyless automatons—especially not the Ocearch crowd. We take our science seriously, but we don't take ourselves too seriously.

Something that is different in the digital age: Science is much more collaborative and team driven. When I was young, we trained as grad students to be solitary. Now it's complicated in the sense that, to maximize information, multiple expertises are involved. The days of looking into a microscope and describing what's swimming around in a slide are over. You have to be collaborative and socially adept, willing to help others and willing to ask for help.

Another thing: Ships are very expensive, and the number of institutes with their own research vessels has shrunk. Still, there are great opportunities for small boat coastal-type work, and that's where most of the work is getting done. The high seas, big animal stuff—there's simply less opportunities for that today. Diving skill comes into play in the coastal zone work; not so much on the big offshore ships. For us, valuable experience comes in the form of fish tags, undersea gliders, and offshore buoys, and expertise in remote sensing from satellites. One reason Ocearch is so popular is because we do *all* of this. Humans are involved; not just technology. People get to participate online, watching us get the animals and all the hands-on stuff we do. It's exciting for us, too. It's a blast.

Of course, the other thing that scientific ships need are trained, experienced crew all the way from captain to cook. You need mates, engineers, people who work on specialized scientific equipment—winches, trawls, the big A-frames and U-frames. The cook is probably the most important person on the ship—especially if they do a great job. I talk to the crew. I'm really interested in their work and how they got there. They all have different paths. A lot were in the Coast Guard or worked aboard a commercial vessel. What makes our crews different is that we want them to have an interest in the science side. They're contributing to knowledge as part of the team—in addition to keeping everyone safe.

It's more than a job.

And a good south wind sprung up behind;
The Albatross did follow,
And every day, for food or play,
Came to the mariner's hollo!

—from *The Rime of the Ancient Mariner*,
Samuel Taylor Coleridge

ALBATROSS

WHITE STORK

EMPEROR
PENGUIN

CORMORANT

1. ALBATROSSES

(Order *Procellariiformes*: includes petrels and shear-waters)

Some species spend their entire lives at sea (aside from nesting). With up to 11-foot wingspans, albatrosses can travel 10,000 miles without landing.

2. PENGUINS

(Order *Sphenisciformes*)

Flightless, but incredible swimmers. Emperor Penguins, the largest species, can grow to 4 feet tall and dive 500 feet.

3. STORKS

(Order *Ciconiiformes*)

With no sound-making vocal organ, storks communicate by bill-clattering. Instead of sweating, they defecate on their legs for evaporation cooling. Despite European lore, storks do not deliver human babies.

4. CORMORANTS

(Order *Suliformes*: includes anhingas, boobies, frigatebirds)

Skillful flyers, but often clumsy on land. Cormorants and anhingas hang their wings open to dry after diving.

GREBE

LOON

PELICAN

WHOOPING
CRANE

EGRET

HERON

5. GREBES

(Order *Podicipediformes*)

Small, duck-like birds with lobed toes and long necks. Very strong divers. Have elaborate courtship rituals and often carry hatchlings on their backs.

6. PELICANS

(Order *Pelecaniformes*: includes herons, egrets, ibis)

Members of this diverse order have long beaks and excellent hunting ability. Pelicans dive from great heights and catch fish in a massive throat pouch. Herons, egrets, and ibis stalk fish, crabs, and lizards in wetland areas.

7. LOONS

(Order *Gaviiformes*)

Long necks, large bills. Graceful in flight, but awkward on land, these skilled divers spend much of their lives at sea.

8. CRANES

(Order *Gruiformes*: includes limpkin, rails, crakes)

The stately whooping crane can exceed 5 feet tall, and secretive clapper rails can drink seawater. The limpkin's beak is specifically adapted to feed on only one species of Florida snail.

MALLARDS

OSPREY

SEAGULLS

BALD EAGLE

9. DUCKS

(Order *Anseriformes*: includes mallards, mergansers)

In addition to freshwater species, some waterfowl are purely saltwater species. Mallards frequent coastal saltmarshes.

10. GULLS

(Order *Charadriiformes*: includes auks, skimmers, puffins, plovers, sandpipers)

Hugely diverse order. Many species are highly social and fly long migrations. Some eat only specific prey. Laughing seagulls will eat your pizza.

11. BIRDS OF PREY

(Order *Falconiformes*: includes, bald eagles, osprey, kites)

Marine birds of prey like osprey and bald eagles are wickedly capable airborne hunters. Spying fish beneath the water's surface, they rely on keen eyesight, blinding speed, and sharp talons to pluck fish.

WHY SHARKS MATTER

AS TOLD BY DR. DAVID SHIFFMAN
Dr. David Shiffman is a shark biologist, science communicator, Shark Week debunker, and publisher of the blog, *Why Sharks Matter* [www.southernfriedscience.com/author/whysharksmatter].

As predators, sharks play an ecologically important role in structuring the food web, from consuming prey and keeping prey populations in check to other indirect effects. One is a process called *far ecology*. Even if a predator does not normally eat a prey species, it may still influence the species' behavior. A herbivore, for example, may choose not to forage an area because of predators. Sharks have that effect on sea turtles, some dolphins, and dugongs.

Actually, a recent modeling paper hypothesized that loss of sharks could be bad from a climate change perspective because sea grass is such an important carbon sink. When sharks are gone and dugongs forage in a new seagrass bed, it releases all this stored carbon into the atmosphere.

Where I'm from in western Pennsylvania, we used to have wolves. But we killed the wolves because wolves are scary. Who wants wolves in your backyard? Because of that, now there are too many deer. Deer don't have enough habitat, and they're malnourished and sick and wander into cities, where they cause billions in property damage. People say hunters keep the deer in check, but a wolf goes for the weak, old, and dying deer. A hunter goes for the biggest, strongest deer—and that has very different ecological effects.

A similar thing happens when you take away sharks. It's called predation relief, and it's very problematic. In the Caribbean, the loss of sharks is leading to a trophic cascade. Too few sharks equals more shark prey; in this case, grouper. More grouper equals less grouper prey; in this case, parrotfish. Without parrotfish to graze algae off the coral, algae takes over, and the coral dies. Coral is in trouble for a lot of reasons, but in some cases, the overfishing of sharks may be one of them.

Sharks are also economically important. For some coastal communities, a living shark on the reef attracts scuba divers to stay in hotels and eat at restaurants, and so on. That's more valuable economically than killing a shark and selling it. That's not true in all places, and overall, fishing is worth more than scuba in the global economy, but sometimes a shark is worth much more alive than dead.

In my work, I have, let's say, interesting days. I've seen thousands of sharks on five continents, and I still feel the same way as when I saw my first shark at age two at the Pittsburgh Zoo. It's just awe. These are incredibly powerful, graceful creatures, and some are quite large. In the right circumstances, they could very much be the end of me. Philosophically, I like the idea of wilderness. I like the idea that there's something that humans are not in control of—that my life is not perfectly safe.

Really, the most dangerous part of my job is not diving with sharks. It's driving to Miami to get to the research vessel. We're more dangerous to sharks than they are to us by multiple orders of magnitude. In a typical year, 650,000 Americans die of heart disease, 550,000 die of cancer, 50,000 die in car accidents, 3,300 drown, 80 people are killed by lightning. A shark kills less than one American per year, but the best estimate I've gotten is that 100 million sharks are killed annually by humans.

We shouldn't be scared *of* sharks. We should be scared *for* sharks.

What we've learned about white sharks with Ocearch is that everything we thought we knew is wrong in so many ways. It's fascinating putting this out in the public domain, which is a study in human psychology. When I give presentations and show 16-foot, 3,000-pound white sharks swimming along Florida coast sandbars near the surf zone, a shudder goes through the crowd. But I say, wait, what we're revealing is what these animals have always done. We just don't see white sharks bothering people. They have the opportunity, but they don't.

—Robert Hueter, OCEARCH

THE **AMAZING RAYS**
(AND SKATES)

BY ARNOLD POSTELL
Arnold Postell is the dive safety officer, senior biologist, and shark feeder and fanatic at the South Carolina Aquarium.

I swim amid rays all the time at the South Carolina Aquarium. They're amazing animals that fall under the same class of creatures—*Elasmobranchii*—as sharks. All share the common trait of soft, cartilaginous skeletons and multiple gill slits. Instead of teeth, most rays and skates have a strange, raspy plate of closely spaced teeth that look like a row of dentures. Rays give birth to live young, while skates lay bizarre, four-pointed eggs known as "mermaid purses."

One species of ray, the Atlantic torpedo, can generate over 200 volts of electricity to shock prey, but most rays protect themselves with a formidable stinger with a serrated barb on their tail. Rays whip the barb into attacking sharks or the ankles of unsuspecting bathers. The secretions around the barb are poisonous, and the pain is excruciating. Rays would rather not sting you, because, in most cases, the barb breaks off, leaving them defenseless for several months until they grow a new one. Skates don't possess tail barbs, but they do have sharp projections on their backs and tails.

Most rays feed on small fish and crabs. In summer, round stingrays cruise the California coast surf zones while southern stingrays lurk along the Atlantic coast. By burying themselves in the sand, the creatures find camouflage and protect themselves from breaking waves. (For sting advice, see "Spinal Tap," page 207.)

All rays and skates are extremely agile, relying on speed and maneuverability to escape sharks and other predators. They're not always successful; you often see rays with big chunks taken out of their wings by hungry sharks.

Rays and skates range in size from the foot-wide winter skate, the smallest, to the spectacular 26-foot-wide, 4,000-pound manta ray. Mantas have the largest brains of any fish. They're inquisitive, gentle filter feeders, who funnel tiny plankton into their mouths with strange-looking "cephalic horns." Mantas can swim better than 15 miles an hour, occasionally launching their massive bodies completely clear of the water. Their power is phenomenal.

RESTORING A REEF AND A WAY OF LIFE

BY INILEK WILMOT

Inilek Wilmot is a professional surfer, musician, oceanographer, and director of the Oracabessa Fish Sanctuary, Oracabessa, Jamaica.

There's a camaraderie here among the fishermen, but they're competitive, too—because they're all going out trying to catch the same fish. Yet when one is in trouble? Well, they could be enemies, but they have to depend on each other. The fishermen here in Oracabessa have an association, and they knew the fishery was in trouble.

One fisherman said, "A reef without fish is like an abandoned house. You take one look at it and you know there's no one taking care of it. Things are run down, overgrown, abandoned, dead." That's what the reef was like before.

One of the good things with the setup of the sanctuary is that everyone took a long time to make it happen. Really, it's simple: This effort established a 90-acre no-fishing area. If fish are protected in that one area, they will multiply and spread outside of the sanctuary, and you can catch *those* fish. But making it happen wasn't simple at all.

Our approach is trust and power— you have to build trust and equitably distribute power. You do that by taking people's concerns seriously—and compromise, compromise, compromise. The fishermen are involved. They're the game wardens. They plant the coral. They sign the checks.

In fact, everything about coral reef ecosystems represents balance between the physical environment and the biological community. The "pioneering" reef-building corals need an appropriate substrate to grow on and the right amount of light and temperature. The tiny coral animals that actually build the structure of the reef have a symbiotic relationship with microscopic algae. The algae produce food through photosynthesis and pass some of their food to the coral. The corals digest that food and generate ammonium, which in turn provides nutrition for the algae. This helps corals create the calcium carbonate for coral reefs—a foundation that's actually a coral's skeleton.

Coral reefs have different geographical zones. The back reef is closest to shore, where the water is relatively calm and shallow, which causes big fluxes in temperature and salinity. It's also the most exposed to runoff and pollution. Corals here are typically very hardy. The back reef is also habitat—and nursery—to the clams, worms, crustaceans, and fish that form the foundation of a fishery. Too much algae and sediment can smother a reef, and at Oracabessa, a river empties into the middle of the bay. With housing and farming along the riverbanks, we get mud, fertilizer, and human waste on the reef, creating an algae problem.

Next, farther from shore, the narrow crest zone is the highest part of the reef and the most exposed to wave energy. This zone has many corals that grow quickly, if healthy, to constantly repair wave damage. Branching corals here provide vital habitat for fish. But when corals are impacted by climate change and poor water quality, along with over-fishing, they can't recover. The situation has become so bad that elkhorn and stag-horn corals—the two main branching corals in the Caribbean—were officially listed as endangered species in 2014.

Marcia Parish, the sanctuary's coral biologist, says a lot of people fixate on reef restoration. What's more realistic is reef rehabilitation. We can't restore the reef to what it was seventy years ago, but we can help ensure it provides food, security for fish, and coastline protec-tion. We started planting branching cor-als using a process kind of like cloning. You take one piece of living, wild coral, break it in two, and it grows more coral. We started with, maybe, 10 individual pieces; now we have over 3,000 in the nurseries. When they're big enough, we fix pieces to the reef with cement, and the coral overgrows the cement and joins the reef. Ideally, we want to plant coral across the whole sanctuary.

The downside is that there's not a lot of genetic diversity in these corals. A disease or heat stress would affect all of them equally. A disease outbreak a couple of years ago wiped out one of our plots. This is not a perfect science. People are learning constantly and adapting.

When we first started the no-take, no-fishing zone, the first thing we noticed was a lot more smaller fish. The next year, the numbers of fish decreased, but their average size increased. A lot of baby fish got bigger, and predators migrated in to eat those fish—grouper, snapper, tarpon, eventually. The growth in fish biomass—the amount of actual fish in the sanctuary—increased 100 percent the first year, then 200 percent the second, then 500; 1,000. Now we're at a balance of 1,800 percent more biomass than when we started.

The fishermen are very proud. The sanctuary has gotten a lot of attention. Initially, this effort was all the fisher-men's. Now some things don't work out as you want—coral dies, there's poach-ing—but even then, you can double, triple the biomass. These revitalized ecosystems provide a lot of other ser-vices, too, like tourism. Over time, you come to realize, things don't have to be perfect to get results.

HOW DOES A **FLYING FISH** FLY?

Flying fish form the staple diet of just about every predatory fish in the open, or epipelagic, zones of the world's tropical and subtropical oceans—from mackerel and bonito to sailfish and marlin. In the open ocean, little fish have few places to hide, apart from the occasional flotsam and jetsam. But the flying fish family—which includes about sixty-four species, divided into categories of two- and four-wingers—have, over the past 200 million years, developed a unique method of escape. They temporarily leave the sea.

If not for this evolutionary development, enabled by elongated fins and a stiffer, bonier spinal structure, natural selection probably would have eliminated this otherwise unfit piscatorial population.

TAKING FLIGHT

In the 1930s, aeronautical engineers found the glide of flying fish so flawless that they emulated their design in aircraft.

Flying fish first work their tails back and forth to generate a short burst of high speed. Once they break the surface of the water, they spread their pectoral fins, initiating glided flight. After a few more kicks of the tail—essentially walking on the water's surface—they're off.

- Before launch, by reaching speeds upwards of 35 mph underwater, flying fish can stay airborne for up to 40 seconds at a time.

- Despite a maximum altitude of roughly only 6 feet, flying fish can use breezes and updrafts from swells to fly, or glide, impressive distances: between about 160 and 1,300 feet. Experimenting with a wind tunnel, Korean scientists have found flying fish as aerodynamic as some birds.

- Flying fish can change direction or reengage in flight by lowering their tails to the water's surface and thrusting a few more times.

SITTIN' ON THE DOCK OF THE BAY, WATCHIN' THE TIDE . . .

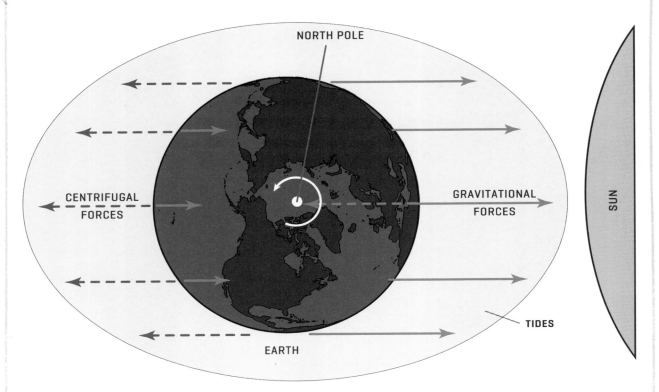

Anyone with time to sit and watch has certainly wondered: What creates the ocean's tides? Is it the sun, the moon, the Earth's rotation? In fact, around four hundred factors influence the Earth's rising and falling tides every day, which is why tide predictions can get complicated.

Way out in the open ocean, the sun's gravity induces about a 6-inch rise in sea level where the Earth and sun are closest. Because its gravity is so much closer to us, the moon, which makes a 27-day-long orbit around the Earth, causes a 12-inch rise. Meanwhile, centrifugal force—generated by the Earth's 67,000-mph orbit around the sun—constantly pulls the ocean away from the Earth on the side opposite from the sun, like a car going around a sharp corner. These opposing forces create a pair of opposing bulges—high tides roughly twelve hours apart on either side of the globe. These bulges circle the Earth as a long, low, endless wave moving at 450 mph. Between the peaks of these waves are the troughs—aka low tides. The "lunar day" is slightly longer because the revolving moon chases the spinning Earth. So the tide cycle follows an approximately twenty-four-hour-and-fifty-minute schedule, making high and low tide occur about fifty minutes later every day.

SPRING, NEAP, AND SEMIDIURNAL TIDES

If the sun and moon are in alignment—during a full moon and a new moon—their gravitational forces combine to create 20 percent higher-than-average "spring" tides (named for the device, not the season). When the sun and moon are at right angles (called quadrature), during the middle of the lunar cycle, their gravities offset and create 20 percent lower-than-average "neap" tides, as the seas spread out more.

Tides hardly change at all in open water near the equator, Eastern Caribbean, and Hawaii. In other places, like the Pacific coast of Panama, England, and Nova Scotia's Bay of Fundy, tides swell from 20 to over 50 feet. These massive surges and recessions make for dangerous currents as they are funneled into bights, bays,

channels, and especially river basins, where they can even cause destructive (though occasionally surfable) waves called "tidal bores."

Worldwide, the most common tides are semidiurnal, two tides of roughly equal heights. Many coastlines, however, see "mixed semidiurnal tides," when each high and low tide varies considerably in height. This is due in part to the tilt of the Earth and a stronger gravitational influence by the sun in larger bodies of water, like the Pacific Ocean. In the Gulf of Mexico, there is typically one tide a day instead of two. In Tahiti, meanwhile, its small tide almost precisely follows the rising and setting of the sun—every day, at the same time.

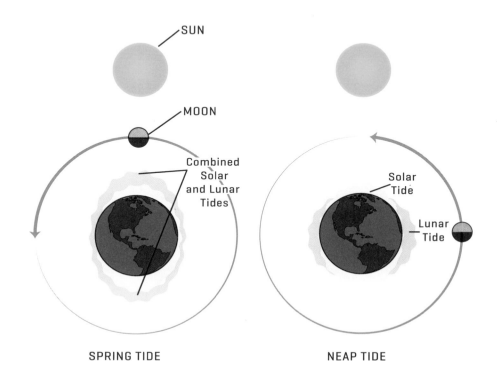

SUN

MOON

Combined Solar and Lunar Tides

Solar Tide

Lunar Tide

SPRING TIDE

NEAP TIDE

BARRIER ISLANDS, DUNES, AND TIDAL MARSHES

AS TOLD BY DR. ORRIN PILKEY
Dr. Orrin Pilkey is the James B. Duke professor emeritus of Earth sciences, Nicholas School of the Environment, Duke University, and one of the most effective coastal advocates the United States has ever seen.

There are around 2,200 barrier islands in the world—on all continents except for Antarctica. That number varies every year as inlets form and close. But the United States has the longest barrier-island coastline in the world—by far—starting from the south shore of Long Island and traveling about 3,000 miles to the Mexican border on the Gulf Coast.

ISLANDS ON THE MOVE

The first thing to know is that barrier islands are the product of a rising sea level. Starting about 18,000 years ago, the Atlantic coastline of the United States extended all the way out to the edge of the continental shelf. At that time, present-day Charleston, South Carolina, was 60 miles inland. Then the ocean began rising around 400 feet to its present level, which flooded the ancient river valleys to form estuaries and marshes. The ridges between the valleys protruded out to sea. Because they stuck out, the ridges got pounded by waves and formed sandy spits. Those spits were broken up by storms and became barrier islands.

During times of rising sea levels, barrier islands migrate toward the mainland at the same time that the mainland shoreline is moving back because of erosion. Big storms will wash sand all the way across a properly functioning barrier island. This simultaneously erodes the island's front-side beaches and widens the back side, leading to what's called "island migration." I think of barrier islands as thinking entities. They know that to survive they have to migrate. And in order to migrate, they have to be fairly thin so that sand crosses the island and widens it.

Core Banks and other islands on North Carolina's Outer Banks are only 100 to 200 yards wide and are in the process of migrating today. Islands like Morris and parts of Folly near Charleston are also actively migrating.

DUNES NEED PLANTS

On barrier islands, dune plants are critical. Without them, the islands would look just like the Sahara, and they'd periodically be completely lost to big storms. South of Cape Hatteras, North Carolina, sea oats stabilize the dunes, and north of Cape Hatteras, the primary dune plant is American beach grass. These plants trap blowing sand, create dunes, and also help build the beach. Interestingly, the way dune grasses grow causes northern and southern barrier islands to look different. American beach grass seeds are washed up by the ocean in lines, so sand dunes form in long lines parallel to shore. Sea oats form clumps. So on southern beaches, you get a dune here and a dune there with a pass in between.

You might say beach plants are always trying to build dunes. When anything blocks the wind, sand accumulates in the lee of the object, and beach grasses will grow there, trapping more sand. On many sandy beaches, clumps of grass form in the lee of garbage, shipwrecks, and wooden dune fences.

Waves and wind both sort sand by grain sizes. Dunes are made up of very fine sand blown by the wind. But the ocean's edge has coarser sand and shell material, which the wind can't pick up. You won't find much actual mud on barrier island beaches unless that mud is a former marsh that's been uncovered as the island migrated.

Some dunes aren't natural, of course. The Outer Banks of North Carolina are so different from how they used to be. In the 1930s and 1940s, the Civilian Conservation Corps piled sand and built fences to form dunes, and they planted shrubs and beach grasses. This created a continuous dune from Nags Head 50 miles all the way down to Ocracoke Island. Before that, there were no beachfront dunes along much of this coast because waves overwashed the islands and kept dunes from forming.

TIDAL MARSHES: FUTURE BARRIER ISLANDS

Tidal marshes are vital for barrier islands and beaches. When I went out on research boats, we took core samples from the seafloor, and occasionally we found submerged salt marsh remnants left behind as barrier islands migrated over them. Today's marshes in the sounds behind barrier islands act as partial buffers for the mainland from landward storm winds. They're also a nursery for a huge variety of marine organisms, while their rotting plants provide nutrients for creatures in estuarine waters.

What's happening today is that many barrier islands don't have healthy beaches or healthy marshes (or mangrove systems) behind them. When you build seawalls, island migration stops. When beach replenishment efforts pump sand from offshore to counter beach erosion, this removes sand for overwashing. As a result, the islands erode from both the front and the back sides. Shackleford Banks in North Carolina, where I've been studying, is losing a combined total of 10 to 20 feet a year on both sides. A deep navigation channel has been dredged at the west end of this east-west trending island. The channel has caused sand loss from the island, leading to serious shoreline erosion. The island is in deep trouble, which is sad, but that's the way it goes.

With a 3-foot sea level rise—which will happen at least by 2100—some beaches will remain along the developed shoreline of the US East Coast, but there will be no way to pump enough sand to replenish them. Eventually people will be forced to leave, and hopefully the islands will migrate like they're supposed to. At the shoreline, nature bats last.

MANGROVE FORESTS:
ESSENTIAL AND ENDANGERED

Mangroves—a tangled mess of roots that weave their way along the intertidal zones of tropical and subtropical regions—once covered roughly three-quarters of the world's tropical coastlines. Mangroves are believed to have originated in Southeast Asia, and today, there are eighty species. Mangroves live in waters exponentially saltier than most other plants can tolerate by extracting freshwater from the tidal saltwater that floods their forests twice daily. Some species even "sweat" salt from their leaves to retain freshwater.

These gnarled aquatic forests are the warm-water nurseries of the sea. They provide shade

and protection for a myriad of creatures, including finfish, crustaceans, mollusks, turtles, and more. In addition, like tidal marshes behind barrier islands, mangrove forests protect coastlines from erosion by taking the brunt of high seas and heavy winds during storms. Mangrove forests are able to spread thanks to their bizarre, spear-shaped seeds. Some seeds drop straight down, anchoring in the sand or mud, inexorably expanding local mangrove habitat—and building shorelines. Other seeds float great distances, exporting mangrove colonies to faraway shores.

Today, mangroves face a myriad of challenges, most of which are, not surprisingly, human induced. Mangrove forests are often cleared for urban development, and mangrove wood is used for construction and fuel. But perhaps the largest destroyer of mangrove forests is shrimp aquaculture. Thailand, the world's foremost provider of farmed shrimp, has lost over 80 percent of its mangroves thanks to clearing for aquaculture.

Heightened awareness and habitat protection as well as restoration are taking place, and in southern Thailand's Trang province, local communities are being given autonomy over their own natural resources with inspiring results. The rest of the world is beginning to follow suit. Consumers can help protect mangroves simply by purchasing sustainably farmed shrimp. For more information, visit Monterey Bay Aquarium's Seafood Watch (www.seafoodwatch.org) or the Aquaculture Stewardship Council (www.asc-aqua.org).

READING THE WEATHER

What's the weather at sea? No sailor, surfer, or angler fails to ask this question or check the skies, often. About the only certainties are that marine weather won't be the same as on land and that it will change. Use this guide to spot a brewing storm and avoid a bad day on the water.

There are two types of weather: localized events and large-scale systems. A large-scale system might be a hurricane or a big cold front, while localized weather includes fog, waterspouts, and afternoon thunderstorms. Pay attention to marine forecasts a day ahead, and remember: In summer, early-day weather is usually calmest.

In general, weather results from the interplay of warm and cold air. These are the basic dynamics:

1. Warm air is lighter than cold.

2. Warm air can hold more moisture than cold.

3. Warm, moist air is lighter than warm, dry air.

4. Warm air rises. As it rises, it expands (like a hot-air balloon).

5. Warmer, rising air has lower barometric pressure than cooler, sinking air.

6. As warm, moist air rises and is cooled, it releases some of its moisture—in the form of rain, snow, or dew on a chilly morning.

7. Air flows from areas of high pressure (which are generally calmer) toward areas of low pressure (generally stormier), which gives big storms that familiar "whirlpool look."

8. The greater the difference in pressure between warm and cold areas, the stronger the wind and weather.

TRACKING CHANGE: USING A BAROMETER

Atmospheric air pressure is measured by a barometer, and changes in barometric readings can indicate if weather is improving or worsening. The lower the barometric reading, the rougher the weather, and falling barometric readings indicate an approaching storm. The severity corresponds to how fast and how far readings fall. In general, check a barometer every hour, and more as weather turns. Conversely, a climbing barometer usually indicates improving weather—though high-pressure areas can still be windy.

There are two types of barometers. A mercurial barometer measures atmospheric pressure against a column of liquid mercury, citing inches. An aneroid barometer reads this pressure in units called millibars—the most common measurement. Curved lines of pressure on weather maps represent millibars. The "standard atmospheric pressure," or a fair-weather day, at sea level is 29.92 inches or 1013.2 millibars.

Of course, to accurately read the weather, you also need to pay attention to temperature, the clouds, and prevailing winds.

ANY WAY THE WIND BLOWS

Like weather, wind comes in local and global varieties. Local sea breezes follow a predictable pattern:

Daytime onshore breeze: In daytime, land heats more rapidly than water. As the warming air over land rises, the cooler air over the ocean flows in to take its place—creating onshore breezes.

Evening offshore breeze: At night, the reverse occurs: Land loses heat more rapidly than the ocean. As land cools, the warmer ocean air rises and is replaced by cooler air flowing from the land—creating offshore breezes. At sea, this can also cause fog.

Meanwhile, the Earth's shape and rotation influence the direction of storms and the spin of air currents. Along the equator (between 0° to 30° north and south), weather systems generally move from east to west. Away from the equator (between 30° and 60° north and south), they move from west to east. This is why Northern Hemisphere weather fronts generally travel west to east and why lower-latitude hurricanes usually travel east to west until they move far enough north to be "turned" by westerly winds.

Another factor is the Coriolis effect, which is created by the Earth's rotation. In the Northern Hemisphere, the Coriolis effect generally turns northward-moving air currents to the right (east) and southward-moving air currents to the left (west), causing storms to spin counterclockwise. In the Southern Hemisphere, this is reversed and storms spin clockwise. However, contrary to rumor, this doesn't affect small-scale whirlpools like toilet bowls.

CLOUDS AND FOG

In essence, clouds provide your weather report. Learn to recognize and read each type:

- **Cumulus:** These big, puffy clouds, often seen in summer, indicate fair weather, but they can develop into cumulonimbus clouds as the day warms.

- **Cumulonimbus:** Aka, thunder heads. These towering columns indicate thunderstorms, and they often have an "anvil top" that points in the direction the storm is moving (since upper-level winds move faster).

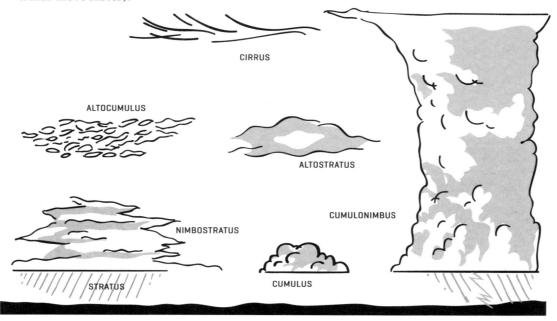

- **Altocumulus:** Smaller, billowy, sometimes wavy individual clouds, moderately high in the sky. In summer, they usually indicate thunderstorms later in the day and, in winter, worsening weather in twelve hours or so.

- **Stratus:** These benign, flat, layered clouds have a curly appearance and are found at 20,000 feet and higher.

- **Nimbostratus:** Form a thick, gray, low-altitude layer. They mean steady rain with a warm or stalled front.

- **Altostratus:** Gray or bluish gray, hazy clouds that cover the sky. Though you can often see a fuzzy sun or moon through them, they mean a front with steady rain or snow is approaching.

- **Cirrus:** Aka, horsetails. These harmless, very high wispy ice clouds can appear up to 50,000 feet.

FOG

Basically a cloud at the Earth's surface, fog is boating's most frequent weather hazard, since it can form within minutes and drop visibility from miles to feet. Fog occurs when moisture-filled air is cooled below its dewpoint, or the point at which air releases its moisture. These conditions favor fog:

- Sooty or dusty air and cool, moist conditions.

- Warm, moist air from land blowing over colder water, which causes advection fog.

- If air temperature is within 10°F of dewpoint at nightfall, fog will form as the air further cools.

- A misty, ill-defined ocean horizon can indicate impending fog.

- Halos around lights at night mean high evening humidity and likely fog.

Don't boat in fog! For advice if you get caught in fog, or any of the storms described in the following, see "Batten Down the Hatches" (page 24).

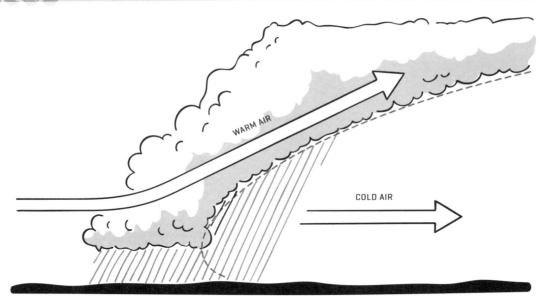

WARM AIR

COLD AIR

An approaching warm front

STORM FORMATION: COLD AND WARM FRONTS

Storms form when moving cold or warm air masses (called fronts) run into each other. A "stationary front" is an unmoving boundary between a warm and a cold air mass. That usually means stable conditions, but stability at the surface can mean instability up higher, creating thick clouds and steady rain.

Cold Fronts: Cold fronts can advance between 10 and 30 miles per hour at the surface (faster in winter) and generate violent storms. The moving colder, denser air plows under the warmer, moister air, which sheds its moisture as it cools (in the form of clouds, rain, and snow). A stormy transition point between cold and warm air masses is called a squall line, and it's marked by gray-black, cumulonimbus clouds and can include heavy winds, lightning, and even tornadoes.

A mariner facing a strong front will initially see winds from one direction (southerly in the Northern Hemisphere), and then as the storm passes, the winds will rotate, becoming perhaps equally as strong, but eventually fading as the front passes.

Warm Fronts: Warm fronts travel slower than cold fronts and hold more moisture. They are signaled by nimbostratus clouds and create gentler storms with drenching rain and sometimes fog.

TYPES OF STORMS

Most storm warning forecasts are issued at least twenty-four hours before conditions. For more on wind and weather signals, see "The Beaufort Wind Scale" (page 82).

THUNDERSTORMS

Ocean and coastal thunderstorms are unpredictable and dangerous. Falling precipitation creates cold down drafts and downpours along the storm's edge while the center still holds rising, warm air. This can lead to a powerful "gust front" or microburst of 100-knot surface winds. Microbursts can occur miles before the storm. Hail builds in size as it circulates through a storm. Frequent lightning along the horizon indicates a likely squall line; the more frequent the lightning, the more violent the storm.

To estimate a storm's distance, time how long it takes for thunder to follow lightning. Sound travels at 1,100 feet per second, so a five-second delay means lightning is about a mile away. To gauge a storm's direction, observe which way the cloud's anvil top points, and remember: North of 30° latitude, thunderstorms generally arrive from the west or northwest.

TORNADOES AND WATERSPOUTS

Tornadoes extend downward from cumulonimbus clouds forming in squall lines and hurricane rain bands. They usually form over land but can move over water. Typically traveling from southwest to northeast, they can be up to 1,000 feet wide with 250-knot winds.

Big, thunderstorm-driven waterspouts are essentially tornadoes at sea, and they can blow up to 175 knots. True waterspouts, however, are funnels that reach from the water toward the sky. They often occur in fair weather at the base of cumulus clouds. More akin to "dust devils," they're between 20 and 200 feet in diameter—dangerous, but not as powerful as tornadoes.

TROPICAL STORMS AND HURRICANES

Called typhoons in Asia and cyclones in the Southern Hemisphere, tropical storms are born from waves of low pressure crossing the ocean during summer and early fall. They are fueled by warm, moist air and an ocean at least 79°F. There are three stages: A depression is defined by winds of less than 34 knots; a tropical storm has winds from 34 to 64 knots; and a hurricane has winds 64 knots and greater. Hurricanes are further broken down into five categories, with category 1 being the weakest and category 5 the strongest.

Tropical weather systems radiate out heavy lines of squalls in what are called rain bands. Meanwhile, hurricane-force winds drive bulging storm surges before them, and the low pressure at the storm's center pulls the water up even higher. Surge is hugely destructive, raising sea levels from 3 to 18 feet.

BECOME AN **OCEAN WARRIOR**

A CHAT WITH SAMANTHA SIEGEL
In 2008, Samantha Siegel launched a relentless six-year campaign to save the famed Angel Oak tree on Johns Island, near Charleston, South Carolina. This ancient live oak is among the largest, and most spectacular, living things east of the Sierra Nevada, and as a college student, Siegel often found a spiritual comfort beneath its magisterial branches.

That year, Siegel learned that a massive home-development project had been approved by Charleston that required burying the maritime forest surrounding the tree in concrete, threatening the oak's vast root system. Despite having no training in environmental action, Siegel led efforts that raised millions of dollars and eventually established a protective park.

"I like to say that I saved the tree," Siegel says, "and the tree saved me."

Then, in 2014, Siegel was hired by the marine conservation group Oceana to help spearhead an effort to prevent offshore oil drilling off the southeastern Atlantic coast. In 2016, after another dogged crusade, Siegel and her allies won, and the drilling proposal was abandoned. As of this printing, her efforts are still succeeding.

A self-made eco-warrior, Siegel shares what she has learned about successful conservation efforts and making a life and a living while saving the ocean:

1. FIND YOUR ISSUE

Once I devoted myself to saving the Angel Oak, I knew I had found my issue. But staying focused can be really hard. You go to your first big meeting and speak up. If you're like me, you get so excited, thinking, *Oh my gosh, I should be speaking up and working on everything.* I care a lot about healthcare, for example, but I can't take on that cause right now.

2. EDUCATE YOURSELF

All I knew when I started the Angel Oak project was, *This is so wrong.* I didn't understand stormwater reports or the environmental laws of the land. But every step of the way, I gathered more scientific and geological evidence that proved me right. It sounds funny, but the tree kept guiding me to new ways to protect it.

3.   SET SMALL BUT ACHIEVABLE GOALS

Start saving the world on your lunch break. During the Angel Oak effort, I worked several jobs. There were so many factors to focus on, but I only had so much time, so I tried to focus on individual goals. First, an online petition. Then a website that urged people to sign up for alerts. Then getting people to a hearing on the development. Then we learned a developer's traffic study was based on a highway that never happened—making their approved projections inaccurate.

My work on the Angel Oak eventually led me to a full-time job with Oceana—which was a dream come true.

With offshore drilling, Oceana first started with public demonstrations of the loud seismic airguns that map deep-sea oil deposits but can kill whales. That was okay, but we ultimately decided a simpler tactic was better: Convince every city council along the coast to sign a resolution against offshore drilling.

4.   ENABLE PEOPLE TO RAISE THEIR OWN VOICES

Facilitate ways for people to raise their own voices: upcoming meetings, social media, letters to the editor, contacting local media. At the "grand tree" meeting, over a hundred people got up and spoke. When local government saw the community involvement, they changed their stance. That was huge.

In the offshore drilling battle, large turnouts at anti-drilling rallies gave local politicians the political cover to vote against drilling. Small victories led to big victories. One town resolution led to another—until 100 percent of our coastal towns were on the record as opposed to drilling.

5. FIND EXPERTS AND ALLIES—EVEN IN UNUSUAL PLACES

I was just this single tree-hugging crusader, but I've developed incredible allies. With the Angel Oak, one local group hired a renowned biologist to do a report that showed development would harm the tree. Another advised me about land acquisition and property rights. An ally in the agency that issued Angel Oak permits offered to feed me information on legal aspects that would hold up the developer.

With offshore drilling, a retired government environmental regulator and other fossil-fuel experts volunteered to help. You need highly educated volunteers to examine reports and provide expert testimony you're simply not qualified to do.

6. FIND THE RIGHT MESSENGER OR A CHAMPION

Sometimes I'm not the right messenger. If you have a potential ally who might not agree with your politics, then find someone that person will be comfortable with to make your argument.

7. DON'T GO AWAY

We had a lot of setbacks and a lot of times when it looked like we wouldn't stop the Angel Oak project or offshore drilling. We just kept going and going and driving every local politician crazy. And eventually, we won. At least for now.

GET INFORMED, GET INVOLVED: SEA SAVIORS

Whether it's plastic pollution, oil exploration, overfishing, endangered creatures, coastal over-development, or all of the above, our oceans and beaches need help in endless ways. To become more informed and involved, take Samantha Siegel's advice (page 185): Name your issue, find your allies, and get cracking. Here are some national and global organizations doing Poseidon's work. They can connect you to local troops in your area.

Surfrider Foundation (www.surfrider.org): One of the nation's strongest networks of local activist-led chapters of surfers, swimmers, and beach lovers.

Natural Resources Defense Council (www.nrdc.org): Specializes in legal challenges to actions and decisions that harm the ocean, with a heavy focus on fisheries and marine mammal protection.

Ocean Conservancy (www.oceanconservancy.org): Lobbies governments to enact legislation to protect the ocean, with a specialty in marine protected areas.

Environmental Defense Fund (www.edf.org): EDF has helped pioneer a global fishing rights program to encourage responsible fishing by all.

Oceana (www.oceana.org): A global organization focused on local issues, like banning bottom trawling in the Bering Sea, ending shark finning in Peru, and stopping offshore oil drilling.

Mission Blue (www.mission-blue.org): Led by "Her Deepness," the legendary scientist Sylvia Earle, Mission Blue aims to increase the protected areas of the ocean by 30 percent by 2030.

Sea Shepherd Conservation Society (www.seashepherd.org): With a simple motto, "If the oceans die, we die," Captain Paul Watson (hero of the TV show *Whale Wars*) isn't afraid of direct confrontation with whalers, illegal fishermen, and poachers. He also combats plastic pollution.

Heal the Bay (www.healthebay.org): Focused on Southern California, Heal the Bay has led the cleanup of storm drains and waterways that pollute the Pacific Ocean with toxic runoff.

Wildcoast (www.wildcoast.net): Wildcoast works to protect the waters and coastline along Mexico's Baja peninsula, including vital gray whale habitat.

Waves for Water (www.wavesforwater.org): In addition to disaster relief, this group works with sailors, surfers, and travelers to bring or send water filters to communities lacking clean water.

Parley for the Oceans (www.parley.tv): Finds direct, innovative market-based solutions to conservation issues, like partnering with Adidas on a shoe with thread made of recycled ocean plastic.

Of all the cephalopods—which also includes squids, cuttlefish, and nautiloids—the octopus is the star, a big-brained, soft-bodied, eight-legged, shape-shifting wonder of nature.

In fact, it's so utterly unique, some scientists consider the octopus a virtual alien. Through a peculiar quirk of evolution, the octopus can use its RNA to tweak its DNA coding to expand the array of proteins its cells produce. In other words, the octopus can literally edit its own genome, though how it and other cephalopods do this is a multi-tentacled mystery.

Native to tropical waters, the octopus family includes some three hundred species. Using sophisticated displays of camouflage, most can quickly change color, shape, and texture to blend in with their surroundings and all but disappear. Improvising as necessary, they can mimic rocks, corals, and the seafloor, and impersonate at least fifteen marine species, including such morphologically diverse creatures as crabs, flounders, sea snakes, lionfish, and sea jellies.

These extreme camo skills—along with a "smoke screen" of black ink to confuse predators—are a matter of life and death, since the octopus lacks armor. Instead, they must be smart to survive, and there's no denying their intelligence. In the lab, with treats as inspiration, octopuses have been observed easily completing mazes and solving mechanical conundrums. And in the wild, they really prove they're among Earth's smartest animals.

Navigating by landmarks, octopuses often explore different hunting grounds, which increases their chances of finding a meal, and on the prowl, they use some pretty cunning tactics. One involves tapping a prey species "on the shoulder" with one tentacle in order to scare it into the waiting arms of the other seven.

Octopuses are known to use found objects—like coconut shells, rocks, and bits of plastic pollution—not just as shelters and tools but also as toys. That's right. Not only can octopuses learn and change their behavior based on environmental feedback (a classic sign of higher intelligence); they also love to play, sometimes shooting jets of water at various flotsam just for fun.

When it comes to the ocean, that's something all species can relate to.

SURVIVAL

TAKE CONTROL WHEN PANIC STRIKES

AS TOLD BY BRIAN KEAULANA
Brian Keaulana is among the most experienced surfers, lifeguards, and water stuntmen on the planet. He's the son of Hawaiian lifeguard legend Buffalo Keaulana.

In the ocean, panic happens—to everybody, from the savviest old sailor to the bravest big-wave surfer to the fittest, most well-trained lifeguard. But there are ways of dealing—mental guidelines for staying cool under pressure and helping others do the same.

Sometimes, would-be helpers can do more harm than good if they panic, too. Whatever your situation, keep cool and focus on helpful tasks. When people feel they're contributing, everyone calms down.

Fear, knowledge, respect: You're way less likely to panic if you know what's going on. What is fear? A lack of knowledge. If you had an abundance of knowledge, how much fear would you have? Understanding your environment crushes fear. When Hawaiians talk about having respect for the ocean, it's another way of saying *educate yourself*.

Beauty and the beast syndrome: People get caught up in the beauty of the ocean, but must understand the dangers. Knowledge and preparation are the first steps. Preplan for a situation; work out the various outcomes. The ocean will throw curveballs, but preplanning helps you not freak out. Before going into unfamiliar water, do some research. Talk to a lifeguard or a local and take time to survey: Who's in the water? If it's all kids, it's probably pretty safe. If no one's out, there might be a good reason.

Be the duck: Whatever the situation, the most important thing is not to lose your head. Even if others are panicking, appear cool, calm, and collected. Be like a duck moving through the water. Up top, ducks appear relaxed. Underwater, they're swimming like mad. Everyone responds to body language and verbal cues, so even if you start to freak out, too, work hard to be calm and keep people focused on solutions.

Breathe: Even in an emergency, take a moment. Pause and tell yourself not to freak out. Breathe and focus on being calm. Even if you're caught in a current, you'll stay alive if you keep your head up and breathe, versus fighting a current and becoming exhausted.

Call for help: Never be too proud to ask for aid or a rescue.

Be aware: Immediately assess the situation. Look around 360 degrees. In an uncontrollable environment, the first thing to assess is the best way to escape. If someone is swept off a cliff into the ocean, gets tunnel vision, and tries to escape by the shortest path, tragedy could result. Rather than climbing back up a wave-smashed lava cliff, the safest, smartest strategy is probably swimming away from the cliff to avoid the waves and seek help. Even in deep water, you're capable of swimming back to safety. Focus on your options and escape the greatest danger. Use that perspective to calm yourself.

Commit: Once you assess, make a decision and go with it. Experience can cover a lot, but sometimes you have to be decisive. The worst thing is to make no decision and waste precious time and energy.

Conserve energy: People who end up in the water often forget it's more important to float than to swim. Roll over on your back and swim calmly.

Turn off another person's panic: Talk to a victim of panic strongly and calmly. This can help override "auditory exclusion," the self-defeating tunnel-vision mind-set. Shift and broaden their attention. Tell them to look at the sky, the clouds, their surroundings, to trust that it's going to be okay. Look where you want to go and follow the swells. Taking one step at a time conquers the mountain.

BEACH FLAG WARNINGS

If a lifeguard is on watch and any restrictions or warnings are in place, they'll probably let you know about it. Here are the standard flag safety ratings and warning system.

Green flag: Low risk. Wind and waves are light, and a lifeguard is on duty. Surf-bathing conditions, but exercise caution.

Yellow flag: Moderate risk. Moderate surf and/or current. Exercise heightened caution. Weak swimmers avoid surfing and swimming.

Red flag: High risk. High hazard, meaning high surf or fierce current. Wise to stay out of the water.

Red over red flag: Water closed to the public. The surf's too high, the current's too strong, or something else is at play, but stay ashore.

Purple flag: Marine creatures present. This could mean jellyfish, siphonophores (like Portuguese man-of-war), stingrays, sea snakes, or other harmful sea creatures. You're allowed in the water, but you've been warned.

Red over yellow flag: Designated swim area indicated by flags atop two poles. Lifeguards are on duty, but swim outside the area at your own risk.

Quartered black-and-white flag: Surfing area. Don't swim or Jet Ski here or you might get heckled—or worse.

Black ball flag: Surfing and other watercraft are prohibited.

Orange windsock flag: Offshore winds. Avoid entering the water with any inflatable, which acts as a sail in high wind and can blow away—even with you in it.

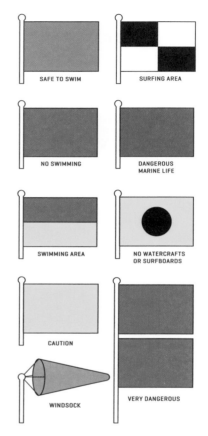

SAFE TO SWIM

SURFING AREA

NO SWIMMING

DANGEROUS MARINE LIFE

SWIMMING AREA

NO WATERCRAFTS OR SURFBOARDS

CAUTION

WINDSOCK

VERY DANGEROUS

SAVE A **DROWNING** SOUL: DROWNING RESCUE

If you encounter a swimmer in distress, first determine if they are conscious or unconscious. Both rescues can be difficult and dangerous but in very different ways. A surfboard or any flotation device can make an excellent rescue tool. Most of all, don't try to be a solo hero. Call or wave for help and tell someone to call 911.

WHAT DOES DROWNING LOOK LIKE?
Drowning swimmers do not flail around, head above water, screaming at the top of their lungs. In fact, they're often so exhausted they're partially submerged, and someone might drown right in front of you if you don't know the signs:

- Head low in the water, mouth at water level

- Head tilted back with mouth open, like they're staring at the sky

- Eyes glassy and empty, unable to focus, or eyes closed

- Hair over forehead or eyes

- Upright in the water, with no evidence of kicking

- Hyperventilating or gasping

- Trying to swim in a particular direction but making no headway

- Trying to roll over on their back

- Moving as if climbing an invisible ladder

ACTIVE DROWNING RESCUE

Panicked swimmers are not only in danger; they can also be dangerous. Desperate for breath, they may climb on top of you and even hold you under in an adrenalized death grip. Bring a flotation device if possible, and approach with extreme caution.

1. If you're without a flotation device, swim beneath the victim and approach from behind; keep their back to you. Say, "I'm here to help, but you have to relax." If the victim grabs or climbs on you, dive down and swim away. Faced with resubmerging, victims often let go. If they don't, push their arms off by the elbows and keep sinking. Surface well away, catch your breath, and try again.

2. Once behind a drowning victim, throw your nondominant arm over their shoulder and chest. Reach for their armpit and slide the crook of your elbow under their chin to stabilize them and get their head out of the water. If they're thrashing, grab the wrist of their free arm with your dominant arm. With your two-handed grip, a hard, painful squeeze of their armpit and wrist—and a calm and reassuring voice—usually helps victims relax enough for you to swim them to shore.

RESCUE WITH A SURFBOARD OR FLOTATION DEVICE

1. Place the floating object between yourself and the victim; extend it to them before you extend yourself. In a calm voice, continually offer reassurance.

2. In a wave zone, fasten the ankle or wrist leash onto the victim to ease recovery amid the surf.

3. Unless you're in immediate danger, allow the victim to rest on the flotation device—catching their breath and gathering their wits—before making for shore.

4. On a short surfboard or bodyboard, have the victim grab the board near the nose, as you swim alongside to stabilize them. On a longboard or SUP, put the victim toward the front of the board and lie behind them with your chest between their legs. Paddle and kick for shore.

PASSIVE DROWNING RESCUE
WITH SURFBOARD

Things get tricky with unconscious swimmers. Most people think drowning means the lungs are filled with water, but it's generally a brain problem from lack of air. It's vital to get breaths into the victim immediately to maintain brain function. If the victim is not breathing, and you're in a safe spot, get air into their lungs as soon as possible. With a surfboard, you can do this in the water before you reach the shore. Tell someone to call 911.

1. Lie across the board and place the back of their neck against the edge of the board. Slide one arm under their armpit, then gently lift their jaw with your hand. With your other hand, pinch the victim's nostrils closed and give five long, steady breaths. Watch for the rise and fall of their chest. Five breaths could take up to a minute. Administer breaths even if you see blood or foaming at the mouth. Then get to shore for proper CPR.

2. To get the victim on the board, flip the board over, fins up. Grab the victim's wrists and pull their head and arms across the board.

3. Next, grab one of their wrists and, with your other hand, the opposite edge of the board, which should be snug under the victim's armpits. In one fast motion, pull hard, lean back, and flip the board, bringing the victim with you so that their chest and body are across the now right-side-up board.

4. Position the victim lengthwise on the board with their head toward the front. On a longboard, paddle the victim from behind as though tandem surfing. On a shortboard, swim alongside.

5. Once you reach the beach, hold the victim from behind, placing both arms under the victim's armpits, while one arm supports their chin and spine. Walk backward, dragging the victim away from surf. Presume that any limp victim, particularly someone who's had a wipeout, also has a spinal-cord injury. Keep their neck in a neutral, aligned position.

6. Lay the victim on their back, but roll them on their side if they vomit—this is vital to keep fluid out of the lungs. Water pouring from a victim's mouth is most likely from the stomach. Never try the Heimlich maneuver or attempt to drain water from victim's lungs. This will actually introduce water *into* the lungs.

7. Begin CPR with five rescue breaths on land. Immediately assess the victim's pulse and breathing afterward. Then begin chest compressions.

8. Keep the victim warm and dry. If they're vomiting, making gurgling sounds, or exhibiting blue lips and fingers, they probably inhaled seawater and may experience "secondary drowning," when some victims exhibit minimal symptoms at first—a cough and a little foam—but can suffocate as their lungs slowly fill with fluid.

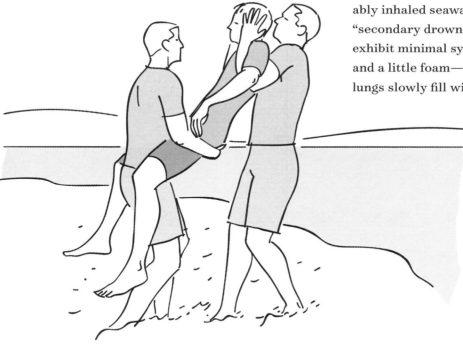

ADMINISTERING C.P.R., A.K.A. CARDIOPULMONARY RESUSCITATION

Cardiopulmonary resuscitation (CPR) is a rescue technique that literally breathes life back into someone who's stopped breathing or whose heart has stopped. In an emergency, commence CPR immediately, even if you're unsure of the techniques. Some help is better than none.

If the victim has a heartbeat but is not breathing, or is only occasionally gasping, initiate mouth-to-mouth breathing. If someone has no heartbeat and isn't breathing, administer chest compressions and rescue breaths. Keep repeating the techniques until the victim's breathing and heartbeat return, trained rescuers arrive, or your surroundings become dangerous. Once the victim is stabilized, get them to the nearest hospital. Anyone who has nearly drowned needs medical treatment.

MOUTH-TO-MOUTH BREATHING

Mouth-to-mouth can expose you to disease, so proceed at your own risk.

1. Lay the victim faceup on a flat surface.

2. Clear the airway of any obstructions.

3. If you're certain there's no neck injury, tilt the victim's head back, gently lift the chin, and look and listen for any breathing.

4. To initiate mouth-to-mouth, pinch their nose and give five rescue breaths. Pause to listen for breathing to return, and repeat if not.

5. If vomiting occurs, turn the victim's mouth to the side and remove any breathing obstruction using a cloth or your finger. If spinal injury is possible, "log roll" the victim over by simultaneously turning their head, neck, and torso to one side, to minimize any twisting of their neck.

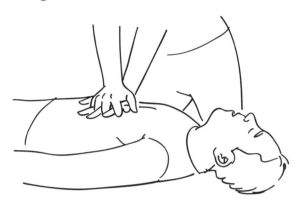

CHEST COMPRESSIONS

With two fingers, feel for the bottom of the chest plate (the sternum). Place the heel of your other hand just above your two fingers. Each chest compression should push down 2 inches, or one-third chest depth. Alternate between thirty rapid chest compressions and then two rescue breaths (tell yourself "thirty then two"), repeating the sequence three times in a minute. Then pause to check for breathing and heartbeat. Continue until the victim revives, trained rescuers arrive, or the surroundings become too dangerous.

PRO TIP: Mouth-to-mouth breathing can obviously transmit diseases, so giving rescue breaths is ultimately up to you. Good first-aid kits contain a rescue "mask" with a one-way valve to prevent transmission. If a kit has one, use it.

Prevent sunburn by covering your skin with sun-blocking fabrics, wide-brimmed hats, sunglasses, and sunblock. Unfortunately, some sunblocks are quite harmful to ocean life—especially delicate coral reefs—so choose your products wisely.

USE SUNBLOCK . . .

1. Broad-spectrum, oxybenzone-free products block both UVA and UVB rays. Choose an SPF rating of 15 or higher. Remember, you'll burn on cloudy days, too.

2. Apply sunblock twenty minutes before sun exposure, so lotion absorbs into your skin. Cover all exposed skin, and apply underneath swimsuit straps, necklaces, bracelets, and sunglasses.

3. "Water-resistant" sunblocks must maintain their SPF after forty minutes of water immersion. "Very water-resistant" sunblocks last twice as long. Reapply generously, roughly every two hours—or more often when swimming, sweating, and toweling off.

. . . WHILE PROTECTING REEFS

Between 8 and 12 million pounds of sunblock enters reef areas annually via swimmers and sewage from cruise ships and cities. The nastiest sunblock chemical is oxybenzone (aka benzophenone-3), which damages, deforms, and stunts the development of coral larvae; makes coral more susceptible to viral infections; and forces coral to expel their zooxanthellae—the little algae that let them photosynthesize. Known as coral bleaching, this often kills coral. Oxybenzone even causes coral larvae to encase itself in its own skeleton.

Further, it's estimated that 90 percent of snorkeling and diving tourists focus on 10 percent of the world's reefs, which means that our most beautiful, diverse reefs are exposed to the highest concentration of deadly chemicals.

To protect reefs, choose eco-friendly sunblocks without oxybenzone, such as those formulated for children and sensitive skin, or those using titanium oxide and zinc oxide, which have not been found to harm corals. Then, use less sunblock by minimizing exposed skin; when snorkeling, wear sun clothes like rash guards.

HOW TO TREAT SUNBURN

If it's too late, here's how to treat sunburn. However, seek medical help immediately if sunburn is accompanied by fever, heat exhaustion, dehydration, shock, nausea, eye pain, severe blisters, clammy skin, dizziness, and rapid pulse or breathing.

- Once you're burned, get out of the sun. Then take frequent cool baths or showers to ease the pain. Keep your skin as wet or moist as possible.

- Apply a natural moisturizer with aloe vera or soy to help trap water next to skin.

- For especially painful areas, apply a thin coat of over-the-counter hydrocortisone cream.

- Aspirin or ibuprofen can reduce swelling, redness, and discomfort. Don't give aspirin to children.

- Sunburn draws bodily fluids to the skin's surface. Drink extra water.

- Blistered skin indicates a second-degree sunburn. An immediate fluid-saline bath and cortisone by mouth may help reduce skin damage and help with itching.

- Protect sunburned skin. Wear protective loose clothing with tightly woven or sun-blocking fabrics.

- Don't treat sunburn with "-caine" products, like benzocaine and lidocaine or with topical Benadryl. All may irritate the skin or cause an allergic reaction.

- Don't use butter, petroleum jelly (Vaseline), or other thick, oil-based products. These can block pores, preventing the escape of sweat and heat—which can lead to infection.

- Similarly, don't pick or peel away at blisters, which also leads to infection.

BAD SEAFOOD AND DEADLY FISH

Mishandling seafood is a frequent, infamous cause of avoidable food poisoning. Why? The bacteria that cause food poisoning grow best on protein—you know, fish meat. Eat what you catch, of course, but make sure what you catch is *safe* and prepared safely.

PREVENTION EQUALS PROTECTION

- Bacteria typically reproduce between 40° and 140°F, so when fishing, keep your cooler, and your catch, below 40°F. Check with a thermometer. Adding salt or saltwater to your ice makes it cooler but melts ice faster.

- Keep knives, surfaces, and hands clean after dealing with raw meats. Wash thoroughly with soap, scrubbing under nails, for twenty seconds using uncomfortably hot water.

- Shellfish can become contaminated by growing in warm, stagnant water, or simply by sitting out too long. Purists might consider it a travesty, but consider steaming shellfish instead of eating raw.

- Ceviche, though technically raw, is usually safe so long as the fish is fresh and the acidic lime juice fully "cooks" the fish. Cut a few cubes of fish to make sure they're white all the way through.

- To dramatically reduce the likelihood of bacterial nasties entering your digestive tract, thoroughly cook foods by heating above 145°F for at least several minutes.

THE "EAT WITH CAUTION" LIST

Sure, people have eaten all of these fish and lived to brag about it, but that doesn't mean you should. Pregnant women and young children should avoid them all.

- Pufferfish are extremely poisonous; avoid unless you're in a restaurant being served by a chef on whose precision you're willing to bet your life.

- Pinktail triggerfish contains palytoxin, which can cause respiratory failure and death.

- Salema porgy (sarpa sarpa) can be mildly to frightfully hallucinogenic.

- Bluefin tuna, king mackerel, billfish, shark, tilefish, and big grouper can all be high in mercury.

- Barracuda and any member of the jack family can carry ciguatera. This nasty illness causes a host of gastrointestinal and neurologic maladies and has no known cure.

- Avoid fish from areas with red or brown tides (see "Red Tides and Algae Blooms," page 256).

OPEN STUFF WITHOUT AN OPENER

No can opener, bar key, or corkscrew? No problem . . .

TIN CAN

Use a knife and stab. Barring that, use a spoon. It takes elbow grease, but beats starving.

1. Wrap your hand in a towel or wear a glove for a better grip. Clasp the spoon against your palm, with your pinky in the dish of the spoon and your thumb against the top of the dish (to control where you apply pressure).

2. Point the tip of the spoon into the top edge of the can and dig back and forth over about an inch. Keep it up till you break through, then puncture more holes, turning as you go.

3. No spoon? Scrape the edge of the lid against a rough surface until you grind away enough to separate the lid from the rim.

GLASS BOTTLE

1. Find anything with an edge of about 90 degrees, set the edge of the cap on it, and give the bottle a swift downward blow with the palm of your hand.

2. Otherwise, grip the bottle just below the cap and pry against your hand, lifting the cap open with a lighter, a tightly folded dollar bill, a key, or any flat piece of metal with an edge.

WINE BOTTLE

1. Carefully whack the bottom of the bottle against a tree or other (ideally vertical) surface that won't shatter the glass. Do this long enough and the cork will ease out enough to grab hold and work it out.

2. No surface suitable for whacking? Slowly and carefully work a knife blade (or thick screw or nail) into the cork at a 45-degree angle. Turn slowly in the direction of the dull back of the blade. The cork will loosen and lift enough to get it out.

THE STING: JELLYFISH DANGERS

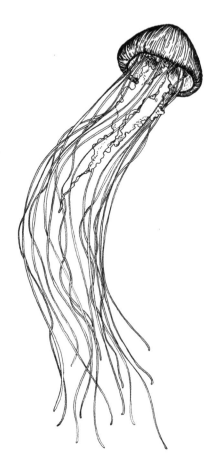

Cnidarians (pronounced "nigh-dare-eeans") include jellyfish, anemones, and corals, and all have stinging cells that contain venom (even tiny immature jellies, aka "sea lice"). *Cnidarian* stings are by far the most common ocean-related, animal-induced injuries, and beyond causing unimaginable pain, some can kill you. However, aside from using vinegar, many popularized "traditional" remedies can be dangerous and worsen stings, so knowing how *not* to treat stings is critical.

Stay vigilant: At beaches, ask lifeguards which types of jellyfish may be present. Jellyfish can be almost invisible in the water, and some are extremely small. Often, you won't see what jellyfish stung you. In crashing waves, you can be stung by a torn-off tentacle.

Prevention: Jellyfish stings are triggered by contact with skin, so even thin fabrics dramatically reduce exposure. Form-fitting wetsuits and Lycra clothing—like rash guards and "swim yoga" pants—are very effective. A "sting suit" is like a body stocking that prevents stings. Two products shown to prevent stings are StingNoMore (developed for the US military) and SafeSea. However, SafeSea is ineffective against deadly box jellyfish, and its efficacy hasn't been clinically tested with the same rigor.

HOW TO TREAT JELLY STINGS

If you're stung by a typical jelly, remain calm, get out of the water, and treat as described.

If someone suffers a severe box jelly, siphonophore, hydroid, or fire coral sting, they may need assistance and CPR. Summon a lifeguard and call 911. If you must rescue someone from the water, cover your own skin, use a rescue board or surfboard, and ID the jellyfish, if possible. If the victim is unconscious, or has labored breathing or heart arrhythmia, begin CPR (page 200). Venom's cardiac effects diminish over time, and lives have been saved after twenty to even forty minutes of CPR.

1. For a typical jelly, first wash the sting site to remove any remaining stingers, ideally using any kind of undiluted vinegar (keep a gallon in your car or boat). Typically, less than 1 percent of stingers discharge on initial contact. Flood the area for at least thirty seconds to "acid-fix" the stinging cells and deactivate unfired stingers. Note that Sting-NoMore has vinegar (and other components) to fully inactivate stingers.

2. If you don't have vinegar, or if the sting is in the eye, flood the site with tolerably hot *freshwater*—washing off the remaining stingers. DO NOT rinse with cool or cold saltwater: This rolls inactive stingers across the skin so they sting again and again. On a boat lacking warm freshwater, use warm/hot saltwater from the boat motor's cooling stream. If any tentacles won't rinse off, soak in hot freshwater or pluck them off gently with tweezers, though this will cause more stinging. Wear gloves if possible.

3. Once all stingers are removed, deactivate the injected venom: Soak the area in tolerably hot freshwater, ideally 110° to 115°F, or use hot packs, for twenty to forty-five minutes. Hot (but not scorching) sand can also help, but only after stingers are removed/deactivated—otherwise, the pressure of the sand will make things worse!

4. To inactivate injected venom even faster, apply StingNoMore cream (rather than hot water). Afterward, use antihistamine and anti-inflammatory creams like hydrocortisone to lessen inflammation.

HOW NOT TO TREAT JELLY STINGS

Despite what you may have heard, NEVER do any of the following:

- Never wash off attached stingers using cool/cold water (fresh or salt), urine, alcohol, ammonia, or bleach. Never treat stings with meat tenderizer, shaving cream, baking soda, or any other folk remedy. Some will increase the level of stinger discharge; none are proven effective.

- Never rub, towel, scrape, or swipe tentacles to remove them. Do not immediately cover or pressure-bandage sting sites. Any pressure can further inject poison into the skin.

- Never apply cold packs or ice.

- Never, ever use an EpiPen, or epinephrine, which could prove fatal. A jellyfish sting is not an allergic reaction.

SPINAL TAP: DON'T STEP ON THAT FISH!

Several sea creatures are notable for having poisonous barbs. Best advice? Watch your step.

Stingrays: Found in semitropical waters, stingrays are easy to step on because they bury themselves in the sand. If startled, they can whip a sharp spine on their tails with lightning speed. Shuffle your feet through the sand to scare them off (this doesn't always work).

Scorpionfish, stonefish, and gurnards: Scorpionfish and stonefish are tropical reef fish that lay nearly motionless, camouflaged among coral. They have an arsenal of very poisonous dorsal spines. Gurnards have a high, spiny dorsal fin and winglike pectoral fins. Avoid walking in their territory.

STINGRAY

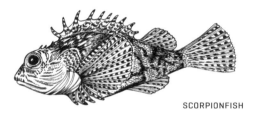

SCORPIONFISH

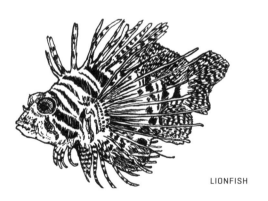

LIONFISH

SEA URCHIN

Lionfish: This invasive but tasty South Pacific species is now present in huge numbers in warm central Atlantic waters. Venom can be delivered even after the fish is dead. Generally, lionfish don't hang out where people walk, but be careful on a tropical sandy beach near a reef. If caught when fishing, carefully snip the spines off immediately, then keep to eat—or toss 'em as lunch for the groupers.

Sea urchins: Sea urchins cling to coral reefs and in rocky crevices. Sharp and brittle, urchin spines can embed in your skin, resulting in multiple, clustered puncture wounds. Spines can be tough to remove. Some urchin species are highly venomous.

TREATING PUNCTURE WOUNDS

1. Soak in hot soapy water (114°F) for ten to fifteen minutes, which deactivates toxic, pain-causing proteins. On a boat, hold the wound in hot saltwater ejected from the motor cooling stream. On a hot beach, use hot (but not scorching) sand.

2. Remove any spines. Clean the wound with soap and warm water, then irrigate with freshwater or a sterile saline solution, not seawater, to remove bacteria. Cold water can reactivate toxins.

3. Elevate the injury above the level of the heart to prevent swelling and reduce pain.

4. Apply an antibiotic ointment like Bacitracin and cover gently with a clean gauze dressing. Seek medical attention.

5. Hot candle wax applied to a wound for at least fifteen minutes is painful but known to provide relief.

"I will have no man in my boat," said Starbuck, "who is not afraid of a whale." By this, he seemed to mean, not only that the most reliable and useful courage was that which arises from the fair estimation of the encountered peril, but that an utterly fearless man is a far more dangerous comrade than a coward.

—from *Moby-Dick*, Herman Melville

DEADLY STRIKES: SEA SNAKES, CONE SNAILS, AND BLUE-RINGED OCTOPUSES

Among the most poisonous creatures on Earth, sea snakes, cone snails, and blue-ringed octopuses are all small, beautiful, and nonaggressive. Sea snakes have teeth so small you might not even realize you've been bitten. But all three can cause paralysis, a coma, or death. The only available antivenin is for sea snakes.

A cone snail's strike causes pain so intense it can cause a heart attack. But sea snake and blue-ringed octopus symptoms usually appear from thirty minutes to four hours after a bite. They include muscle aches, weakness, slurred speech, trouble swallowing, and blurred vision. Seek medical attention immediately.

In the meantime, do the following:

SEA SNAKE

1. Have the victim lie down and remain still. Muscle activity will pump venom toward the heart and into the bloodstream.

2. Use the pressure immobilization technique to prevent venom from spreading to other parts of the body (but *don't* use compression for jellyfish or spiny fish stings).

CONE SNAIL

3. Keep the limb at—not above—the level of the heart.

4. Watch for signs of respiratory paralysis. Be prepared to administer CPR.

5. Do not apply a tourniquet or ice, as these worsen the damage.

6. Do not attempt to cut the skin and suck out venom.

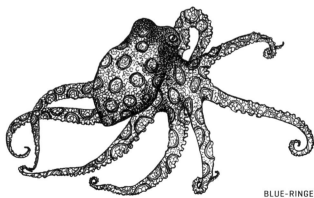

BLUE-RINGED OCTOPUS

PRESSURE IMMOBILIZATION TECHNIQUE

1. Use a broad pressure, Ace-style bandage. Begin wrap from below the bite and work your way toward the torso.

2. Wrap the bandage as far up the limb as you can.

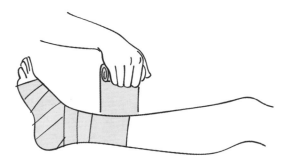
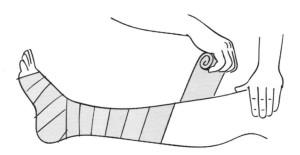

3. Use a wood or other splint to immobilize the limb. Use a new bandage for the splint. Make the limb as immobile as possible.

4. If the bite/strike is on arm, use a sling to immobilize.

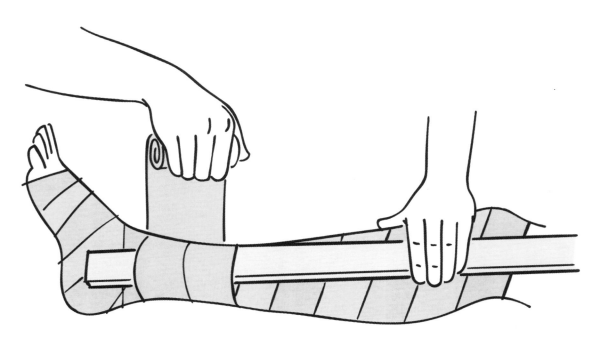

ESCAPE A TSUNAMI

A tsunami is a series of transoceanic waves triggered by an earthquake, volcanic eruption, undersea landslide, or meteor strike. Normal, wind-driven ocean waves reach a maximum speed of about 35 miles an hour, but a tsunami can slosh the entire ocean like a bathtub, with waves running in excess of 600 mph. Depending on your distance from the epicenter, tsunamis appear anywhere from moments to nearly a day after the trigger event.

Ideally, a tsunami warning system—horns, emergency broadcasts, sirens—will alert you to danger. Tsunami warning systems use wave buoys and seismographs to determine wave period and impact location, but seismologists still have no way of knowing how large a tsunami will be. Short of wailing sirens, telltale signs of impending inundation are drastic changes in the waterline or sea level: If the sea suddenly recedes several feet, or the currents become rapidly and dramatically confused, assume a tsunami is coming.

HEAD FOR THE HILLS—OR THE HIGH SEAS

What to do depends on where you are. Are you near high ground? Head for the hills. Take only what you can easily carry—a bottle of water and a cell phone can be indispensable.

In the lowlands with no high ground? Climb the tallest tree and hang on. Note that coconut trees might not support you if you weigh more than 80 pounds. The top of a sturdy concrete building or an automotive overpass can work as well. Anything that's above the rushing water. *Do not stay in a car.*

If you're in a boat at sea, avoid shoals, shallow reefs, seamounts, beaches, and port, where surge effects can become most extreme. However, if you're already close to shore and can get to higher elevation immediately, abandon ship.

Otherwise, make for the deepest water at full throttle. If you're already in deep water, stay put. NOAA recommends finding waters deeper than 200 fathoms (1,300 feet or so), but the deeper the water, the safer you are—and the more likely you won't even feel the exaggerated swells pass beneath you.

SEASICKNESS: THE SEAFARER'S CURSE

Seasickness is common, but why it makes people feel nauseated, dizzy, and disoriented isn't really understood. The prevailing theory is "sensory mismatch," the notion that the brain is getting mixed messages. Sitting on a boat, your muscles are stationary and your eyes see a fairly static view, but the fluids in your ear are sloshing around like you're dancing. This makes you feel wobbly and out of control, causing nausea. In heaving seas, protection from seasickness is crucial—in part to prevent dehydration. Here's how to escape or minimize this ancient seafarer's curse.

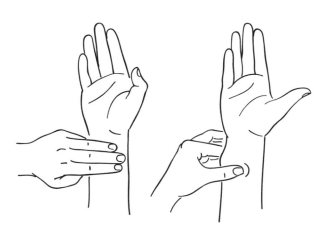

NEI GUANG ACUPRESSURE POINT

- Before boarding, put on a Nei guan pressure-point bracelet. Lacking that, use acupressure on the Nei guan point. It's located three finger breadths below the wrist, on the inner forearm, in between the two tendons. Apply downward pressure, massaging and stimulating the area for four to five seconds.

- An over-the-counter sedative like Dramamine or Bonine can help stabilize the body. But it can make you sleepy.

- On the boat, sip water, keep your eyes on the horizon, and stay on deck. Stay active. Don't focus on the inside of the boat or close your eyes to sleep; this makes it worse.

- Scopolamine patches may help reduce nerve activity in the inner ear.

- Ginger (crystallized or regular) has been used to help digestion and treat nausea for more than 2,000 years.

- Drive the boat. Taking control of the craft engages your muscles, keeping seasickness at bay.

- Move to the center of the boat. As with a seesaw, this is the fulcrum, where the boat rocks least.

- If you can't shake the urge to vomit, sooner is better than later. People often feel better afterward. Sip water to rehydrate.

THE BUG-OUT BAG,
A.K.A. LIFE-RAFT SUPPLIES

The worst has happened. Your boat is sinking. It's time to abandon ship. You already have a life raft, of course, one that meets or exceeds SOLAS (Safety of Life at Sea) requirements. What else do you need? Don't panic, rushing around grabbing random stuff. You prepped a "bug-out bag," right? *Right!?*

Hmm . . . well, if you had remembered, here's what you would have done: Put many (or all) of the items below into labeled, waterproof, sealable plastic bags and containers, and put all that in another waterproof bag, which you labeled in permanent marker with your boat's name and "emergency gear." You pre-tied lanyards to crucial gear and had a hip pack ready for personal items like wallet, passport, money, medications, eyeglasses, and so on.

Next time (if there is a next time), don't forget the bug-out bag!

ESSENTIALS FOR OPEN-OCEAN SURVIVAL

- Portable bilge pump, raft bailer, and sponges (one bagged sponge solely for potable freshwater condensation mop up)

- Sunglasses, sunscreen, extra clothing, towels

- Fishing kit, including hand line, gloves, scoop-style net, and spear gun

- LED-model flashlight, with spare batteries (or solar charged)

- Visual distress signals (page 17) and a whistle

- Survival rations: high-carbohydrate canned and dried foods, plus chocolate, hard candy, dried fruit, shortbread cookies, condensed milk, jams, fruit juice

- Water, one pint per day per person, and a collapsible water cup

- Fillet knife and sharpener, blunt-ended heavy-duty scissors, and a multitool

- Nylon string, trash bags, sealable bags

- First-aid kit (page 222), including seasickness tablets and StingNoMore

GEAR YOU'LL WISH YOU HAD

- Radar reflector

- Telescoping hook for poling tidal shallows, retrieving gear

- Waterproof life-saving signal cards

- Floating PFD cushions to stanch heat loss and increase comfort

- Camelbak or sun shower and hand-held Katadyn emergency desalinator

- Plastic cutting board (to prevent cutting raft)

- Packet of safety pins

- Roll of clear plastic wrap (to make a solar still; see page 246)

- Waterproof logbook with pencils and sharpies

A logbook helped Steven Callahan stay organized and sane during his seventy-six days on a life raft, an adventure he tells in his bestselling book *Adrift*. Pack a copy.

STRANDED: ISLAND SURVIVAL

Boats sink, capsize, and become too damaged to continue, and even the best-equipped life raft is only temporary salvation. No, in this predicament, you need land. Here's how to find some and survive once you reach it.

FINDING AND REACHING LAND

Land heats faster than water, so updrafts from warmer rising air create clouds above islands and landmasses. Look for (and paddle toward) unmoving clouds or ones split or raised into arching "eyebrows." Cloud colors also indicate landscape: darker clouds indicate forests; vivid white means coral and surf; greenish hues signal lagoons; and pinkish could be a dry reef.

Irregular, refracted waves occur as waves hit a landmass. Steep, irregular, and shorter period swells (amid a previously steady, rolling swell) may also indicate a nearby, unseen low island or reef. Head in the direction of the irregular waves, but be alert. You could be heading toward a reef.

Finding land might seem miraculous, but reaching shore without killing yourself is the next trick. Ideally, choose a gently sloping beach during daylight (avoid a night landing), and time your dash through the surf zone for the lull between wave sets. If you're in a life raft or boat, see "Be Shallow-Minded" (page 32). Two more things: If you have a craft, secure yourself to it, but in a way that can be easily released. Then, keep your clothes on through the surf. You'll need their warmth and protection once ashore.

Of course, in addition to surviving, you want to be rescued. See "SOS: Signal for Help" (page 238).

FIRST NIGHT ON SHORE

Priorities depend on your situation. Of course, administer any immediate first aid. Then ask, "What's likely to kill me first—exposure and cold or lack of freshwater?" In the tropics, perhaps seek water first. Break tasks into manageable pieces and complete them one at a time.

Don't underestimate the need for shelter. Hypothermia can kill quickly. Alan Kay, the winner of the History Channel series *Alone*, survived solo for fifty-six days on cold Vancouver Island. He advises: "Get that shelter up enough to get through the first night. The second day, if you're still alive, water, regroup, then improve your shelter."

First-night "shelter" equals dry clothing, a tarp, a sleeping bag, a wetsuit, or a windbreak—from an upturned boat hull or even a hole in the sand. Avoid deadly convection (or ground) hypothermia by creating a thick bed or pad of sticks, leaves, or fronds. Weave wrist-sized branches at the bottom and crisscross with springy branches and leaves so it won't compress.

As Kay says, "Constantly improve your structure. You can never build the walls too thick or have enough grass on your mattress. Just don't spend more energy than you take in. If the juice isn't worth the squeeze, don't do it."

Kay advises: "Clothing is your first line of defense. Survival experts call cotton *death cloth* because once wet, it stays wet. Wet clothing next to your skin creates seven times greater heat loss. Wool maintains its insulation even when wet, and polypropylene wicks away moisture and is fast drying. Make sure your outer layer is windproof, waterproof, and breathable, like Gore-Tex."

Finally, scan the beach for useful flotsam: washed-up plastic containers (for water, fish traps), netting or boat wreckage (cover), and even dried kelp (makes useable cordage).

BUILD A BASIC SHELTER

Over ensuing days, make a durable shelter. Avoid grandiose visions of log cabins. Arguably, the most important aspect is location.

Find the most sheltered, wind-protected area possible and ensure you're not in a storm wash. The debris line on the beach indicates high tide. Be well above it. If freshwater is nearby, position yourself a hundred yards away: Close enough to reach easily, but not so close you attract bugs and other wildlife, contaminate your water with your own waste, or are unable to hear rescuers. If you can, stay near a firewood source, but not along trails—they're likely made by animals.

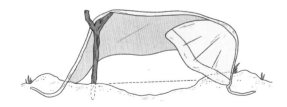

BASIC BOAT HULL SHELTER

SHELTER TIPS

- For a roof and walls, use sturdier driftwood or tree branches for your frame and weave with grasses, ferns, palm fronds, and tough, fresh branches (strong and flexible).

- Lash sticks together with rope or palm fronds, or weave sticks together.

- Leaves = rain protection; turf = insulation. Over time, build up walls as thick as possible, like 2 to 3 feet.

- The steeper the roof pitch, the less it will leak.

- Any fabric—sails, tarps, jackets—will repel rainwater. Fishing nets interwoven with vegetation provide substantial protection.

- Create a "roof inside a roof" for better weather protection.

- Point leaves/fronds "downhill" as you weave them into the roof to better shed water, like roof shingles.

- Dig a culvert around your shelter to divert rainwater.

BEACH NEST WITH GRASS BED

BASIC BOAT HULL SHELTER

On an exposed beach, secure one side of a tarp (or any covering) underneath your hull and support the other side of the tarp with a simple, three-stick setup. Secure tarp against wind by wrapping heavy sand inside tarp.

BEACH NEST WITH GRASS BED

Dig a body-size indentation at the base of a sandy slope. Build a thick nest of dried beach grass inside. Place rocks or logs uphill and downhill of nest. Create a center joist perpendicular to nest and cover with tarp or weave sticks and fronds.

Place upturned boat parallel to shore atop slope (if possible). Support hull with rocks or logs. Use sticks or even a paddle to create a rafter and lay tarp or sticks atop. Weave or lash together with available cordage.

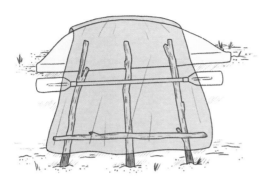

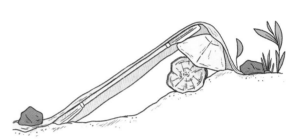

BOAT HULL LEAN-TO

WATER WATER EVERYWHERE— FIND A DROP TO DRINK

If you find freshwater right away, fantastic. However, boil all water if you can. If water holds live creatures, it's likely drinkable. The exception is still or stagnant water covered or filled with floating blue or green algae. Some fatal algal toxins can't be boiled away. Avoid waters surrounded by alkaline mineral deposits or, worse, bones.

If you can't find freshwater, follow these tips. Or build a still to collect freshwater (page 246).

- Seabirds and lizards drink infrequently and won't lead you to water. Mammals will.

- Smaller birds generally fly low and in a straight line at dawn/dusk to water sources.

- Flies stay close to water.

- Follow a line of ants to their water source.

- Bees stay within a few miles of their hive (honey).

- Rainwater often collects at the base of many broad-leafed plant stalks.

- Many flowering species of palm tree contain a potable sap. Bend a stalk downward and slice near the tip of a flowering stem. Collect the sap that drips out. After twelve hours, slice off another inch and repeat.

- Green coconuts are a good source of water (see "Climb a Coconut Tree," page 250).

A BITE TO EAT

Most people have fat reserves that will last at least a week, so food is actually your last priority. See the Fishing chapter for handcrafting fishing tools and fishing techniques. If you can make fire, cook everything you catch, which is the safest approach. When boiled, the rendered oil from fish is highly nutritious.

That said, the number one food rule is don't cook or eat where you sleep—especially on shorelines where food might attract larger predators. Set up a cooking camp at least 100 yards from your sleeping camp, then eat at the shoreline. Leave shells, food residue, and bone fragments in the water. Scrub cooking gear with sand. Literally bathe in campfire smoke to kill residual food smells. Keep nothing food-related in your shelter.

- During low tide, forage for limpets, mussels, seaweed, crabs, clams, oysters, conchs, sea cucumbers, and sand fleas/mole crabs (pull off their digging appendage). In cold water, stick to shallows to avoid falling and freezing.

- Make a simple fish trap from a clear (not opaque) plastic bottle: cut off the top and replace backward. Fish come in seeking shelter and can't get out.

- Crickets, grasshoppers, earthworms, ants, and termites are slow-moving protein. Cook to kill parasites.

- Spear hunt octopus and stingray at night, using a light to attract them. Don't get bit or barbed.

- Red tides can render shellfish poisonous. One clue to a red tide is bioluminescent waves at night, but clear waters can still carry toxins. Crab claw meat does not seem to bear these toxins, but a crab's gut does.

AVOID THE DEATH APPLE

If you're stranded from Florida to northern South America, you might be tempted by the sweet-smelling, tasty manchineel fruit—aka *manzanilla de la muerte* (little apple of death), beach apple, tree of death, or poison guava. Found amid mangroves and coconut trees, manchineel trees bear crab apple–like green or greenish-yellow fruit that, when eaten, can make it impossible to swallow, talk, or breathe. A thick, milky, poisonous sap can ooze from leaves, twigs, and bark, creating burn-like blisters. Smoke from burning manchineel can cause blindness. In short, leave this plant the hell alone.

ISLAND PREDATORS

You may be stranded, but you won't be alone. Survival also means defending yourself from these critters.

Mozzies: Malaria can be a real threat in the tropics. The best defense against mosquitos is campfire smoke (green wood smokes best), thick clothing, and even coating exposed skin with mud.

Crocodiles and alligators: They usually attack from calm, turbid waters without warning. Stay well back from any water's edge, fresh or salty. Look for pressed-down grass and mud "trails," indicating water entry points.

Snakes: Avoid tall grasses, especially in warm weather, and walk only where you can see the ground. Don't reach into crevices or onto ledges you can't see.

Bears: Generally, though attracted to food, bears only attack people when surprised or to protect food or cubs. When encountered, give them plenty of space and back away slowly; don't run. If the bear approaches, stand tall and yell. If it attacks, "play dead" by rolling on your stomach, covering your neck, spreading your legs so the bear can't roll you over. If it starts biting, fight back using any available weapon.

MESSAGE IN A BOTTLE:
A BRIEF HISTORY

If you find yourself stranded or adrift and your only means of communication is an empty bottle and some stationery, don't get your hopes up. But what the hell. A message in a bottle is a poetic gesture that allows you to speak across time and space.

- A traditional wine bottle with a cork is best (don't use plastic and add trash to our seas). Dark glass preserves paper and ink, and cork won't degrade in saltwater.

- Fold your message inward, so the writing won't be bleached by the sun.

- Aim for a predictable current, like the Gulf Stream.

Then, as you wait years for rescue, take comfort knowing your message is part of an illustrious, ancient heritage:

310 BC: Philosopher and oceanographic pioneer Theophrastus launches the first known "message in a bottle" to test his hypothesis that the Atlantic Ocean flows into the Mediterranean Sea (it does).

1500s: Queen Elizabeth I appoints a royal Uncorker of Ocean Bottles, declaring any unauthorized opening of such a bottle a capital crime.

1784: Shipwrecked treasure-hunting Japanese sailor Chunosuke Matsuyama sends a message that's discovered in 1935 on the shores of the village he was born in.

1877: British journalist John Sands alerts mainland authorities to a shipwrecked Australian crew on the remote Scottish island of St. Kilda using a native-derived "mailboat." St. Kildans learned to send letters from Scotland to Norway in wooden canisters, floated by sheepskin balloons, by releasing them in a westerly wind.

1875: British ship's steward Van Hoydek and cabin boy Henry Trusillo release twenty-four bottled messages into the Bay of Biscay, reporting the murder of their captain and officers by mutineers. French authorities receive the message and capture the ship.

1800s: The US Coast and Geodetic Survey begins dispatching bottles as a means of gathering data on ocean currents.

2018: A message in a bottle is found along Florida's Atlantic Coast that was released in the 1980s by schoolchildren from Forfal, Scotland, who were studying pirates.

ULTIMATE MARITIME FIRST-AID KIT

Here are all the things you need to handle almost any emergency, including both hardware and software (medications). Perhaps the first and most important item, however, is a card with your personal and medical information: emergency numbers, health insurance, allergies, and vaccination history.

If you're in charge of a group trip, have people bring their own basics. This avoids people rifling through the main first-aid kit taking items you'll need in an emergency.

HARDWARE: THE ESSENTIALS

- Soap
- Six latex or vinyl gloves
- Rubbing alcohol
- Vinegar
- Elastic wrap or Ace bandage
- Quarter-inch Steri-Strips and wound-closure Benzoin tincture
- Adhesive, waterproof bandages (Band-Aids), variety of sizes, and sterile gauze pads
- Unbreakable oral thermometer (and extra battery)
- Tweezers and razor blades
- Strike-anywhere matches and/or disposable lighter
- Headlamp (with extra batteries)
- Applicators (cotton Q-tips) and tongue depressors
- Unbreakable compact mirror

HARDWARE YOU DIDN'T KNOW YOU NEED

- Water filtration straw or pump
- Duct tape
- A multitool with scissors and pliers
- Plastic eyedropper
- Safety pins, various sizes
- Pen and notepad (to record meds used, and so on)
- Condoms (also store water well)
- Combat application tourniquet (page 224)

SOFTWARE: ESSENTIAL MEDICATIONS

Keep track of expiration dates on meds and components.

- Aspirin, acetaminophen/Tylenol, and ibuprofen/Advil

- Melatonin, 3 mg tablets (for sleep/prevent jet lag)

- Antacid tablets

- Bismuth subsalicylate (Pepto-Bismol; for diarrhea, nausea)

- Loperamide (Imodium) capsules (acute diarrhea)

- Laxative pills

- Diphenhydramine (Benadryl) tablets and cream

- Antibiotic ointment (Bacitracin, Polysporin)

- Antifungal cream (Micatin, Tinactin)

- Pseudoephedrine (Sudafed)

- Eye drops

- Oil of cloves (Eugenol; for tooth pain or mouth sores)

SOFTWARE: ADVANCED MEDS

These meds are far better at treating injuries and illness, but many require a prescription. Tell your doctor that you're building a serious medical kit to be ready for anything. Most will help you. Ensure that any narcotics are kept in a legal container with your name on it, or ask for a doctor's note on letterhead stating that you're allowed to carry such medications. Always check the legality of drugs in your intended port of call; don't let meds land you in a foreign jail.

- Cephalexin (Keflex), 500 mg tablets (general infections)

- Doxycycline, 100 mg tablets (general infections; use if allergic to Keflex or penicillin)

- Ciprofloxacin (Cipro) 500 mg tablets (for diarrhea, urinary tract infections)

- Sulfacetamide sodium 10 percent eyedrops (eye infections)

- Antibiotic ear drops (Otobiotic; painful ear infections)

- Vicodin (hydrocodone 5 mg/acetaminophen 500 mg; for severe pain)

- 1% silver sulfadiazine cream (Silvadene; for burns, skin infections)

- 1% lindane lotion (Kwell; for crabs/lice)

- Fluconazole (Diflucan), 150 mg tablets (for vaginal yeast infection)

- Injectable epinephrine (Ana-Kit, EpiPen; for allergic/anaphylactic reactions; *not for jellyfish stings*)

- Malaria prophylaxis (discuss proper drug with doctor)

THE DEEPEST CUT:
TREAT A LACERATION

Here's what to do if someone gets a serious cut, particularly if proper medical care is hours or days away.

Stop the bleeding: Most bleeding can be controlled with direct pressure. Apply solid pressure over the length of the cut. If a wound is spurting blood at the same rate as a heartbeat, this indicates a severed artery, and steady compression is critical. You must exceed the internal pressure with external pressure. Hold clean fabric—or whatever you have, like a towel or T-shirt—while applying nonstop direct pressure for as long as it takes to stop bleeding. If it's still dripping, it's still bleeding, and if it drips through one bandage, apply one on top and maintain pressure. Remember, removing a bandage can rip away the clots that have formed. If pressure fails to stop the bleeding or it's spurting badly, you must apply a tourniquet.

Apply a tourniquet: A tourniquet cuts off blood circulation to a limb, and once applied, it must remain in place until the victim reaches a medical facility (removal can cause shock). The most effective is a combat application tourniquet (CAT). To improvise one, wrap a long strip of cloth at least a half inch wide (not shoestring or wire) one or more times above but not over the wound (ideally, above elbow or knee). Wrap over clothing to protect skin. Tie a half knot, place a rigid stick on the knot, then tie another knot to bind the stick. Twist the stick until bleeding stops, then immobilize the stick so it doesn't loosen.

Clean the cut: With bleeding stopped, use a gallon or more of clean, freshwater to flush the wound—aim a solid forceful stream, high volume and high pressure. Minor bleeding is normal. Do not use hydrogen peroxide, alcohol, or lime juice; these can kill good tissue that helps the healing process. Inspect the wound and clean out any remaining foreign matter, which can cause infection.

Apply antibiotic and bandage: After cleaning, apply Bacitracin or other antibiotic dressing, gauze, and a bandage. In most cases, leave the cut open and unsutured, especially for the first few days, when infection is most likely; this is particularly important for deep wounds, puncture wounds, and animal bites. Closing the skin over the wound can seal in an infection. Clean and repack the wound daily. Cover rash-like wounds at night with a layer of antibiotic ointment but leave uncovered to allow a protective scab to form. During the day, use nonstick bandages and aloe vera gel to speed healing and ease pain.

Seal for swimming: If you still want to surf, dive, or swim after being wounded, and the wound is very clean, you might seal it closed with either a flexible glue called Dermabond, old-fashioned Steri-Strips, or even Band-Aids. In each case, apply at roughly quarter-inch intervals.

Blood and sharks: If you're actively bleeding, stay out of the water, to avoid infection as much as sharks. If you're not actively bleeding, swimming is probably fine. For instance, there is no scientific evidence that women who are menstruating are any less safe or more likely to be attacked by sharks than men or nonmenstruating women. Nor do sharks seem particularly attracted to human blood. That said, a possible correlation has never been studied in any meaningful way.

Recognize infections: Five percent of lacerations will become infected from bacteria. Telltale signs include warmth, swelling, spreading redness, tenderness, and a yellowish, smelly discharge. If infection occurs, seek professional medical care immediately. If that's not possible, reopen the wound, irrigate it, and take antibiotics. Soak the wound in warm water twice a day and pack it inside with sterile gauze to keep it open and allow drainage. Note that antibiotics differ for marine bacteria. If you're unsure of the nature of a potential infection, take both cephalexin and doxycycline (Levaquin), which is effective on both terrestrial and marine bacteria.

COLD SHOCK AND HYPOTHERMIA

Cold shock happens when you jump (or fall) into a frigid ocean. Stay long enough, and you develop hypothermia, when your body's core temperature falls to 95°F or cooler. Any lengthy exposure to chilly, windy, and wet ocean weather can bring on hypothermia, but when submerged in water, the body loses heat twenty-five to even thirty times faster than in air. Thus, with startling quickness, a cold swimmer can progress from simple shivering to pain and numbness of the extremities, compromised muscle and vital organ function, confusion due to a cooling brain, and death.

HOW LONG CAN YOU LAST?

WATER TEMPERATURE	EXPECTED TIME BEFORE EXHAUSTION OR UNCONSCIOUSNESS	EXPECTED TIME OF SURVIVAL
32.5°F / 0.3°C	< 15 minutes	45 minutes
32.5°–40°F / 0.3°–4.4°C	15–30 minutes	30–90 minutes
40°–50°F / 3.3°–10°C	30–60 minutes	1–3 hours
50°–60°F / 10°–15.6°C	1–2 hours	1–6 hours
60°–70°F / 15.6°–21.1°C	2–7 hours	2–40 hours
70°–80°F / 21.1°–26.7°C	3–12 hours	3 hours–indefinite
> 80°F / >26.7°C	Indefinite	Indefinite

HITTING THE WATER: COLD SHOCK

Things get dangerous with rapid cold-water immersion. This can strike in water as warm as 77°F, but it's debilitating when the temperature drops below 59°F.

Typically, with cold shock, you involuntarily gasp and can hyperventilate. If your head is submerged, you'll inhale water, and it's tough to swim and breathe in a controlled way. You may also feel pain and numbness in the extremities, as if you're immediately hypothermic (but you're not—yet).

Cold water can also induce conflicting autonomous responses. The sympathetic nervous system may respond with a heart-racing fight-or-flight panic, while the "mammalian dive reflex"—triggered by cold water on the face and water pressure against the chest—tells the parasympathetic nervous system to slow down in preparation for a low-oxygen dunking. The heart slows and blood vessels constrict in the limbs to conserve oxygen, diverting it to the heart and brain. These two competing impulses can potentially cause fatal heart arrhythmia.

HUDDLE WITH OTHERS
FOR WARMTH

SURVIVING IN COLD WATER

If you experience cold shock, keep your head above water and try to relax. Control over your breathing and muscles will return in a minute or so. Have someone throw a PFD (if you're not wearing one), and get out of the water as quickly as possible.

If that's not possible (say, your boat capsized), climb onto anything that floats. Being exposed to air may *feel* colder but it's *not*. Rose outlived Jack in *Titanic* because she climbed onto a door. Act quickly before you lose full use of your hands. Turn a capsized boat over and climb in; if you can't, climb on top—you'll be far easier to spot.

If immediate rescue isn't possible, don't swim or flail around, which accelerates heat loss, and can cut survival time in half. Instead, huddle with others for warmth and support. If alone, use the "heat escape lessening position" or HELP: Hold your knees to your chest to protect your trunk and clasp your arms around your calves. Do not submerge your head, and do your best to keep wave splash off your face.

HELP: HEAT ESCAPE
LESSENING POSITION

TREATING HYPOTHERMIA

Your body and brain's electrochemical metabolic reactions function optimally at 98.6°F. Mild hypothermia happens when the core body temperature falls between 97° and 93°F. Symptoms include uncontrollable shivering, cold hands and feet, numbness and/or pain in limbs, loss of dexterity, and clumsiness.

Never give alcohol or caffeine to a hypothermia victim. Both increase blood flow to extremities, including the skin, robbing the body of heat.

MILD TO MODERATE HYPOTHERMIA

1. Lay the victim on side or back. Wrap the victim in warm, dry clothes and blankets; leave on a wetsuit, but towel dry. Stay out of wind.

2. Give warm (not hot), sweet drinks and simple carbohydrates (bananas, raisins, fruit juice) to generate metabolic heat.

3. Actively warm the victim. Put in a warm room (like a car), or use direct body-to-body contact. Wrapping a hypothermia victim in a blanket doesn't add heat; victims generate insufficient heat to rewarm themselves. Wrap a blanket around you and the victim to conserve the heat you are supplying.

4. If possible, put the victim in a warm-water shower or bath—around 105° to 110°F, or comfortable enough to remain in. Direct warm water to body core, and *keep arms and legs clear of water*. Heating the extremities causes cold blood to flow to the body core, further cooling the core. This can prove fatal.

5. Apply hot, wet towels or blankets (115°F) to the victim's head, neck, groin, chest, and abdomen. Do not warm or massage arms or legs.

6. Keep the victim warm for several hours, with head and neck covered; shivering to rewarm is fine. Mild exercise can help generate heat.

MODERATE TO CRITICAL HYPOTHERMIA

When body temperatures drop between 93° to 82°F, the risk of death increases quickly. Symptoms of critical hypothermia can appear confusing: uncontrollable, violent shivering can suddenly stop completely; victims may act dazed, drunk, and/or irrational; and victims may even appear dead when they might still be saved.

In such cases, immediate medical help is crucial. Lay victims down, elevate their feet, and wrap them in warm blankets. Handle victims gently—rough handling can cause cardiac arrest—and plan immediate medical evacuation. If a victim is unconscious and appears dead, tilt their head back, as with CPR, to open the airway. Look, listen, and feel for breathing and pulse for two minutes. If you're certain they're not breathing and have no pulse, initiate CPR (page 200). Above all, don't give up. Many people, especially children, have been saved when it seemed that all was lost.

COLD-PROOF YOURSELF: WIM HOF'S BREATH TECHNIQUE

Is it possible to mitigate the cold-shock response and ward off hypothermia in frigid conditions? Dutch fitness guru Wim Hof has developed a controlled, meditational breathing regime that he says taps into the ancient wisdom gained by Tibetan monks, Native Americans, and prehistoric humans, whose lives revolved around surviving cold.

Hof's method has gained converts among extreme athletes such as surfer Laird Hamilton, who says:

I tell people, if you have a car and want to make it go faster, what you need to do is shove more air into the engine. The body's no different. If you want to rev up your system or deal with more stress, you oxygenate. Stoke the fire and get it rumbling. There's a basic science around Wim Hof's breath work that helps you deal with cold. There's no doubt you can ward off hypothermia. I've done fifteen minutes in ice in my tub. I do it five times a week. The reason you have that reaction of cold shock is that the body is aware of the danger, and it's our way to get you out of there. But once you start taking ice baths on a regular basis, you don't get that shock anymore. It just goes away.

Here's a simplified version of Hof's method. Practice with a friend at first, in case you pass out. An empty stomach will maximize O_2 inhalation.

1. Assume a meditative seated pose or lie on your back. Relax.

2. Take thirty power breaths: Imagine you're inflating a balloon. Close your eyes. Inhale forcefully and deeply through the nose or mouth and exhale through the mouth in a steady rhythm. You may feel a bit dizzy, your ears may ring, and your hands and feet may feel prickly or tingly.

3. The breath hold: After thirty breaths, take another relaxed but deep, slow breath that fills your lungs. Exhale fully, and then hold your breath until you start to feel diaphragm spasms (see "Unleash Your Inner Seal," page 233).

4. Recovery: Inhale deeply with your diaphragm to completely fill your abdomen and chest. When full, hold your breath for ten seconds, then exhale slowly.

5. Repeat steps 1 to 4 three times.

6. During step 3, the long breath hold, do pushups or yoga poses to gauge the strength the breathing method gives you.

7. After the breathing routine, take a cold shower. Breathe slowly, relax, and limit exposure to fifteen to thirty seconds. Gradually, over several weeks, increase your cold showers to three to five minutes. Eventually, immerse your whole body (except your head) in a cold-water bath (or swim in cold water). Finally, when you feel well-acclimated, submerge your head, too.

TOO HOT: HYPERTHERMIA AND HEAT STROKE

Hyperthermia (or heat illness) occurs when your body can't shed excess heat fast enough. In hot weather, heat exhaustion can be triggered by exertion coupled with dehydration and/or high humidity, preventing cooling sweat from evaporating. Dehydration also impairs heat transfer from blood to skin. Victims can quickly become incapacitated and disoriented, not even realizing anything is wrong. Deadly heat stroke can follow.

Dehydration is possible long before thirst and even if you rehydrate enough to quench your thirst. Drinking alcohol on a hot day makes dehydration worse, since metabolizing alcohol generally removes more liquid from the body than it provides. Also avoid caffeine.

RECOGNIZING AND TREATING HEAT EXHAUSTION

The symptoms of heat exhaustion include feeling overheated, lightheaded, dizzy, and uncomfortable. A victim may hyperventilate or feel "pins and needles." Stronger signs are cramps, nausea, vomiting, and dark urine.

To treat someone, get them breeze, shade, and liquid. Have them relax or lie down away from the heat source, and even strip down to underwear. Drink lots of cool liquid, which removes more heat than pouring it over skin. To rehydrate, mix a half teaspoon salt and five teaspoons sugar in a liter of water. Gatorade and other sports drinks work as well. Fairly clear urine signals recovery, but stay out of the heat for a day.

HEAT STROKE

In addition to the symptoms for heat exhaustion, heat stroke can be signaled by diarrhea, a collapse into unconsciousness, a very high temperature like 112°F—above the ability of many thermometers to even register—and the ceasing of sweating (though a person may still be covered with residual sweat).

Heat stroke is life-threatening, so seek immediate medical help. Treat like heat exhaustion, but even more urgently: Remove all clothing, have victim lay down with slightly elevated legs, and keep skin wet and cool. If someone is unconscious, continue treatments until consciousness returns, then rehydrate with cool fluids.

UNLEASH YOUR INNER SEAL:
INCREASE YOUR LUNG CAPACITY

There may come a time when you are forced underwater for longer than planned. Surfers can be held down by waves; free-diving spearfishers may fight with a catch. How will you survive? By not panicking and by increasing your lung capacity on dry land first. (Thanks to South African free-diving guru Hanli Prinsloo for the wisdom.)

DIAPHRAGM CONTRACTIONS AND THE MAMMALIAN DIVE RESPONSE

Humans are unconscious breathers. We breath reflexively. When rising CO_2 levels in the body signal the need for more oxygen, the diaphragm contracts automatically. The trigger to breathe is so uncomfortable that, when it's denied, we often panic. But despite that initial trigger, we have more oxygen than we think.

The mammalian dive response occurs when we submerge in water: heart rate slows, causing vessels in the limbs to constrict, and the spleen releases its stores of oxygenated hemoglobin. The trick to holding your breath longer underwater is learning not to panic and resisting those contractions to get the most out of your stored O_2.

PRACTICE HOLDING YOUR BREATH

A panicked brain consumes tremendous stores of oxygen, so if nothing else, learning to relax underwater can save your life. This practice helps you discover and push your limits by acclimating you to the generally awful sensations during long breath holds. Practice these techniques on land first, and *never* practice underwater without supervision from a qualified free-diving professional.

STEP 1: "THE BREATHE UP"

Increase your oxygen intake with three-stage belly breathing. Practice lying on your back, arms at your sides or on your chest.

- Inhale over a slow eight count through pursed lips, visualizing filling three spaces: stomach, chest, shoulders.

- Start with your stomach, expanding as you inhale. Think Buddha belly.

- Next inhale into your chest, expanding your ribcage to its fullest.

- Next inhale into your shoulders, expanding your upper chest.

- Exhale slowly through pursed lips over a ten count. Pursed lips create a slight pressure in the lungs that better oxygenates the blood.

STEP 2: "THE BREATH HOLD"

Repeat step 1 two or three times, and after a final exhale, relax and perform these three inhalations over thirty seconds.

1. Inhale and hold your breath until you reach the "trigger point," when you become uncomfortable and your body says, *It's time to breathe*.

2. Exhale and take a deep inhale. Hold this breath beyond the trigger point until your diaphragm spasms and contracts. Hold for a few seconds longer; this will be terribly uncomfortable.

3. Exhale and deeply inhale a third time. Hold your breath through the contractions and resist the urge to exhale as long as possible. Exhale before you black out, but know that if you do black out, you'll start breathing again, which is why you should be lying down.

STRETCHING YOUR LUNGS

The following stretches expand lung capacity by increasing the flexibility of the intercostal muscles that line your ribcage. This is free-diving champion Hanli Prinsloo's regimen, and using it, her lung capacity has swelled from 4 to 6 liters.

Be careful not to fully inflate your lungs, which can put too much pressure on your thoracic cavity, causing you to blackout. Aim for about 80 percent of lung capacity. Practice these stretches from a kneeling position, back bolt upright. For each, inhale, hold the breath, and stretch, only exhaling once you feel discomfort in your diaphragm.

- **Overhead stretch:** Lift arms straight overhead, one palm atop the other. Keep shoulders away from ears, lift and stretch arms upward, chest out, chin in.

- **Behind-the-back stretch:** Interlace the fingers behind the back, opening your chest to the front.

- **Overhead, side to side:** Keep one hand on the ground and slowly reach the other hand over the head to the side. Exhale as you lower the overhead arm, and repeat on the other side.

"MAYDAY! MAYDAY!"—DISTRESS, URGENCY, AND SAFETY CALLS

There are standard procedures for making emergency radio calls and hailing any vessels or organizations that might provide help. Call the US Coast Guard on channel 16 VHF-FM (156.8 MHz).

Remember, for rescuers to find you, providing latitude and longitude is essential, especially when no shore landmarks are visible (see "Where Am I?," page 76). If landmarks are visible, describe your relation to them. Always have a compass aboard and a dedicated GPS unit—and no, smartphones don't suffice, though they can help. For nonvoice emergency signaling, see "SOS: Signal for Help" (page 238).

1. Turn on VHF radio and select channel 16 (156.8 MHz).

2. Press and hold the Transmit button.

3. Clearly and calmly repeat the appropriate radio call, such as, "Mayday, mayday, mayday."

4. Clearly and calmly hail and identify yourself. For example: "US Coast Guard, US Coast Guard, US Coast Guard, this is the [type of vessel] S.S. *Minnow*, S.S. *Minnow*." Repetition is key.

5. Briefly provide additional information. Describe your vessel, your coordinates and/or map location, the exact nature of your emergency, and the number of people on board.

6. Release the Transmit button.

7. Wait ten seconds. If you receive no response, repeat your call.

TYPES OF RADIO CALLS

The four types of emergency calls—distress, urgency, safety, and quiet—all use phrases derived from French.

Distress: Say "mayday," from the French *venez m'aider*, or "come help me." Only to be spoken over VHF radio by a vessel in need of immediate emergency assistance due to sinking, burning, a serious injury, and so on. Nonemergency mayday calls are subject to hefty fines and prosecution.

Urgency: Say "pan-pan," from the French *panne*, or "breakdown." Signifies that a vessel is incapacitated in some way and, while not facing "grave and immediate danger," is in need of relatively urgent assistance.

Safety: Say "secure-it-ay," from the French *securité*. Used to request that the Coast Guard—or any nearby vessels potentially capable of rendering aid—stand by to deliver assistance in light of any navigational or weather hazards that might lie ahead.

Quiet: Say "seelonce," from the French *silence*. Used in the phrases "seelonce distress" and "seelonce mayday" to hush all radio transmissions other than those originating from the vessel in distress, the Coast Guard, or any other vessels providing assistance during an emergency. Regular working traffic may resume only after someone broadcasts "seelonce feenee" (from the French *silence fini*, for "silence finished").

RADIO LINGO

Despite Hollywood's insistence to the contrary, it makes no sense for a radio operator to say, "Over and out." You might as well say, "It's your turn to talk, but I'm not listening."

"Over": End of transmission, response expected

"Out": End of transmission, no response expected

"Roger": Transmission received

"Wilco": Will comply with your transmission

"This is": Name and call sign immediately follow

"Figures": Numbers follow

"Speak slower": Can't understand you

"Say again": Repeat

"Words twice": Can't understand you; repeat every phrase

"I spell": Phonetic alphabet spelling of a name follows

"Wait": Stand by

"Wait out": I'll call you back

"Affirmative": Correct

"Negative": No

S.O.S.: SIGNAL FOR HELP

In an emergency, you can signal for help in many ways besides shouting *"Mayday!"* into a radio. For all non-radio communication, SOS (for "save our souls") is the standard call, and it's signaled by almost any sequence of threes—three horn blasts, three light flashes, three shots, three puffs of smoke. The general rule is to wait one minute between sets of three signals. Here are some common signaling methods, in addition to using semaphores and Morse code to communicate.

Beach blazes and symbols: On a beach, burn anything petroleum-based—including tires and plastic—to signal for help. If there's a high hill with a 360-degree vantage, signal from there. Green plant matter produces lots of signal smoke and repels bugs. And/or, arrange beach debris into a big X (at least 10 feet across) to mark your spot. Create a series of big arrows pointing in your direction. A triangle of equidistant fires is a universal rescue signal. Fires have been seen from 50 miles away during rescue situations. However, preserve batteries and lantern fuel; use them only to signal when potential rescuers approach. Have fire spots ready, just in case.

Whistle: Survival life jackets—particularly those on ships—have a whistle. Keep one on your boat key ring. Since the late nineteenth century, the Acme Thunderer has been a solid choice, but today's gold standard is the 130-decibel Storm Safety Whistle. It can even be heard from 50 feet *underwater*.

Air horn: Standard compressed air units produce a shockingly loud blast and also meet US Coast Guard requirements. All boats must have a horn/sound maker on board.

Bell: If your vessel is between 40 and 65 feet, it must have a power whistle *and* an old-school bell on board.

White flag: A white flag—or a white or brightly colored tarp or shirt—is a universally understood distress signal. Wave in a figure eight. If no flag is available, wave extended arms up and down slowly.

Cyalume sticks: These long-lasting glow sticks can be seen from far away at night.

Pyrotechnics: Boats should always carry three USCG-approved pyros in a watertight container. Use with care; they emit a molten goo that can burn you and destroy a life raft. With rocket-type pyrotechnics, look away and brace yourself for launch.

Meteor tube and 12-gauge pistol: These shoot parachuted fireballs to 500 feet that, at night, are visible 21 miles over the horizon.

Hand flare: These generally burn brightly for a couple of minutes; best at nighttime.

Smoke flare: Deploy downwind for daytime signaling in low-wind conditions; be careful not to melt a life raft.

SOLAS flares: SOLAS (Safety of Life at Sea) flares are a huge step up from standard USCG-approved flares. Thirty times brighter and lava hot, they're for serious crises, are waterproof, and don't spray molten material. Rocket-propelled models shoot up to 1,000 feet, burn for forty seconds, and are visible for nearly 40 miles over the horizon.

Distress flag and rescue streamer: An orange flag with a black square and circle is the universal distress flag. This See/Rescue Streamer features a long, floating, bright-orange streamer that can be seen very well from the air. Some models even feature infrared reflective materials visible to night-vision equipment.

Electronics: Though far less visible than pyrotechnics and not USCG-approved, electronic signaling devices like LEDs and laser pointers might save your neck. Don't point any light at a rescuer at night; this can blind someone in night-vision goggles.

Signal mirror: Mirrors have been detected as far away as 45 miles and by aircraft at 10,000 feet. A used CD or DVD can work, too. Point constantly at any potential rescuer until seen.

Rescue sausage: Also known as a surface marker buoy, these stand up out of the water vertically for easy spotting.

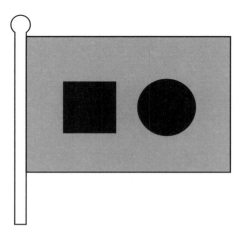

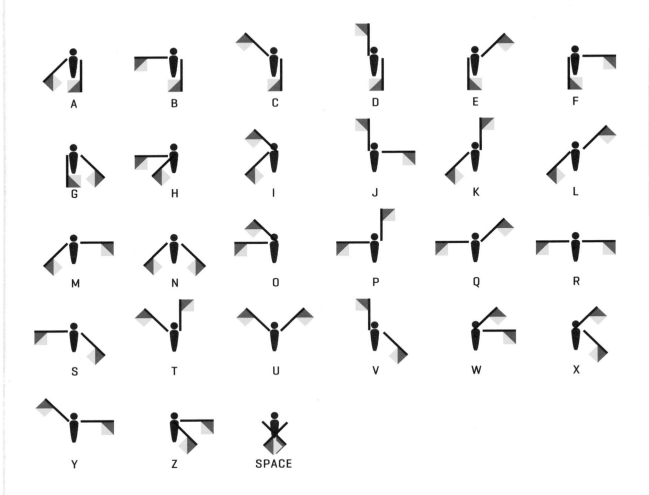

SEMAPHORE

Semaphore is a visual communication system using two flags on short staffs held in each hand: Use "Oscar" (red-and-yellow) flags at sea and "Papa" (blue-and-white) flags on land. Semaphore was the primary means of conveying information across water during the nineteenth century. While no longer popular, semaphore still works for emergency communication; just memorize "SOS." To use semaphore at night, replace flags with glow sticks.

A	▪ ▬		N	▬ ▪
B	▬ ▪ ▪ ▪		O	▬ ▬ ▬
C	▬ ▪ ▬ ▪		P	▪ ▬ ▬ ▪
D	▬ ▪ ▪		Q	▬ ▬ ▪ ▬
E	▪		R	▪ ▬ ▪
F	▪ ▪ ▬ ▪		S	▪ ▪ ▪
G	▬ ▬ ▪		T	▬
H	▪ ▪ ▪ ▪		U	▪ ▪ ▬
I	▪ ▪		V	▪ ▪ ▪ ▬
J	▪ ▬ ▬ ▬		W	▪ ▬ ▬
K	▬ ▪ ▬		X	▬ ▪ ▪ ▬
L	▪ ▬ ▪ ▪		Y	▬ ▪ ▬ ▬
M	▬ ▬		Z	▬ ▬ ▪ ▪

MORSE CODE

Morse code reproduces the Latin alphabet and ten numbers to communicate, using light or sound in a series of short and long tones. Although the US Coast Guard quit using Morse code in the mid-1990s, some vessels still send messages in Morse code through commercial relay stations when voice transmissions can't get through. At minimum, memorize "SOS."

ABANDONING SHIP AND BOARDING A LIFE RAFT

No one, including the captain, wants to go down with the ship. These techniques apply especially when abandoning giant boats like cruise ships.

JUMPING INTO THE WATER—ESPECIALLY FROM HIGH UP

1. Always wear a life vest, and tighten it very securely before jumping. If you have a wetsuit, wear it if you can.

2. Consider your location on the boat, and get as close to the water as you can before jumping. Chances of survival are greatest for drops of less than 30 feet. But don't jump where the ship might roll on top of you. If it's rolling, the bow or stern are the safest places to be—and to escape.

3. Keep your shoes on to protect to your feet.

4. Before jumping, pinch your nose and cover your mouth with your left hand. Reach across your left arm with your right and grab your PFD securely at the arm hole. Keep your arms crossed at your chest, with your elbows in tight. Adopt this position even without a PFD.

5. Don't dive. Step out into the air, keeping eyes open and looking straight ahead (not up or down) to prevent tumbling. Enter the water as straight as possible; as you fall, cross your legs, slightly bend your knees, and hold tight. From a big height, the surface impact can dislocate joints.

6. Once in the water, quickly swim away from the ship to avoid entanglement in any rigging and to escape any vortex from the sinking ship.

7. If you have to jump into flaming water, do not wear a PFD. First, throw the PFD clear of the flames, then jump and swim underwater as far away as possible before resurfacing. Then retrieve the PFD.

8. If there's no life raft, lash together anything floating: coolers, life rings, soda bottles, cushions. People can even be lashed and huddle together, but don't huddle in a circle in heavy seas. Those facing into the waves will be at risk from drowning from wave splash.

9. No PFD? Improvise one: Once in the water, tie the ends of long pants into a knot and flop air into the waist or inflate with your lungs. Inflate plastic bags, shirts sleeves, or anything to help you float.

MANNING THE LIFE RAFT

With luck, you won't have to jump into the water. All large commercial vessels have prepared life rafts and trained crew. Captains of offshore boats should also have a life raft, a prepared bug-out bag (page 213), and a plan. When you're sinking is no time to practice.

When preparing to deploy your raft, increase the sinking boat's buoyancy and float time by pumping out live wells and emptying attached coolers or watertight compartments. One crew member should deploy the life raft, and another strong crew member should be the first person onboard to assist everyone else. If possible, load the raft directly from the boat to keep everyone out of the water. Roll onto the raft—don't step or jump—and maintain a low center of gravity.

To board someone from the water, have one person assist from a very low position (to avoid going overboard), while other passengers sit on the opposite side to keep the raft from flipping.

Once everyone is aboard, pay out plenty of line and decide whether to cut the raft free of the mothership. If it hasn't completely sunk, the boat may float for a while—even indefinitely if it has a foam-infused hull. Remaining tethered helps maintain your position and visibility to rescuers. If it's safe enough, you can also return to the ship to salvage more gear. However, be ready to cut the line and deploy a sea anchor should the big boat sink.

Seasickness is dangerous and demoralizing. Dole out seasickness medications early. If you feel queasy, look outside the raft. If someone is sick, clean up quickly to maintain sanity and morale and to prevent a cascade of vomiting.

Next, see to first aid, review supplies, and assign lookouts. Remove wet clothing, cushion the seawater-chilled floor to prevent hypothermia, and always beware of anything sharp—knives, fish hooks, the fins of caught fish—that could puncture the raft. Vent the raft regularly to purge carbon dioxide, too.

Remember: Believing you're going to survive is key to ensuring you *will* survive. Each person needs to keep busy, stay positive, and be decisive. Inaction is perilous. Bail water, watch for rescuers, catch a fish, patch a sail, keep a log of events and supplies, and so on. Think of loved ones. Prayer and meditation not only slow metabolism, they replace fear and anxiety with hope.

SURVIVAL HYDRATION

The human body is about 65 percent water. After warmth, hydration is the first priority for survival at sea or on an island. In a warm ocean environment, surrounded by and breathing water vapor, you'll last six to seven days without water—perhaps longer. However, do everything you can to maximize your water intake, ration wisely, and collect freshwater.

- Consume no water in the first twenty-four hours. The water already in your body is sufficient.

- After that, if freshwater is readily available, the general requirement is 1 quart (roughly 1 liter) per day. At minimum, drink 4 to 8 ounces per day, if possible.

- Sip water slowly, regardless of thirst.

- Sun exposure quadruples water loss through skin. Seek any shade and cooling breeze.

- Wet clothing to slow sweat loss.

- Engage in little to no hot daytime activity.

- If foul-tasting freshwater is too gross to keep down, or someone is too sick to swallow, hydrate via enema. A SunShower- or Camelbak-type hydration bag can do the job.

NEVER DRINK SEAWATER OR URINE

Seawater contains a higher concentration of salt (3 percent) than your blood (0.9 percent). Drinking seawater will overwhelm your kidneys, pull water from your cells, and kill you after locking you in the grip of horrible madness. Meanwhile, dehydration will concentrate salts, electrolytes, and acids in urine, making urine perhaps even worse to drink than seawater. Contrary to myth, no tablets can desalinate seawater.

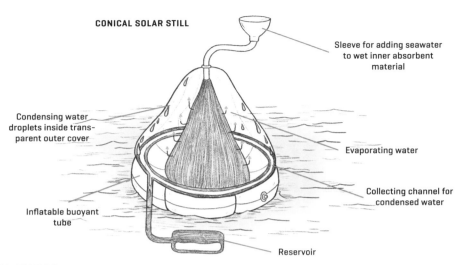

CONICAL SOLAR STILL

Sleeve for adding seawater to wet inner absorbent material

Condensing water droplets inside transparent outer cover

Evaporating water

Collecting channel for condensed water

Inflatable buoyant tube

Reservoir

COLLECT FRESHWATER

Solar stills: A solar still features a sealed plastic membrane surrounding a seawater-saturated material like a towel or shirt. When sunlight passes through the membrane and heats the fabric, pure water evaporates and condenses on the wall of the membrane and drips into a reservoir. It's exceedingly difficult in a life raft at sea to devise and use a solar still. Buy an ocean-survival still as part of your life-raft equipment.

To make an emergency still: Cap a plastic bottle and cut an even circle around the bottom. On the bottom, fold the plastic inward to form a gutter a couple inches high. Place this over a smaller can or cup of seawater or, better, a seawater-soaked fabric. Ensure that the seawater stays out of the gutters. Set the still on a flat surface in the sun, minimizing gaps at the bottom. Pure water will condense on the bottle sides and run into the gutters. Invert the bottle, remove cap, and drink. Or, seal a plastic bag around a leafy, sun-exposed tree branch; transpiring leaves will create fresh water condensation.

Reverse osmosis: Far better than stills are small, hand-operated "reverse osmosis" pumps. These pump seawater through a high-pressure membrane that separates water from salt. The gold standard is the "survivor" model by Katadyn.

Rainwater: On a life raft or disabled boat, salt will encrust everything. Keep containers sealed and deploy anything that can collect rainwater when weather approaches. Use rain jackets, tarps, and trash bags to guide rainwater into containers. In a hard rain, rinse the salt off your body and watercraft.

Sea ice: The longer seawater remains frozen, the more salt molecules are squeezed out from below. Old, deep-blue sea ice is mostly freshwater. Newly formed sea ice, generally whiter and flaky, is not. Icebergs, formed from glaciers, are freshwater.

LIFE-RAFT CUISINE

After a few days in a life raft at sea, you'll become hungry as well as thirsty. In survival situations, a person needs between 600 and 1,400 calories per day (compared to an average nonsurvival intake of 2,400), and carbohydrates are ideal sources of quick energy. Sugary sweets, cookies, sweetened oatmeal, and granola bars also conserve water by reducing the body's need to metabolize its own muscle and fat for energy. High-calorie survival biscuits are ideal. You packed some, right?

On the other hand, digesting protein (fish) can actually make you more dehydrated. Digesting meat requires considerable metabolic water and energy. But eventually, you may need to catch, kill, and eat animals, some of which you never would outside of a life-or-death emergency. Assuming you have survival fishing gear, here are the best options:

Dorado: Also known as mahi-mahi, or dolphin fish, dorado loiter beneath life rafts and bump survivors from below. If you hook one, prepare for a massive fight that could compromise your raft. Thinly filleted, their dense meat dries well for later. They'll hit nearly any bait or lure and can be speared.

Flying fish: Can be caught at night with a raised tarp. Shine a light behind the tarp, and fish will fly toward it, hit the tarp, and land in the boat. Tasty and make excellent bait for larger fish.

Triggerfish: Very tough hide, but tasty flesh. Spear or catch on a smaller hook with cut bait or lure.

Tuna: Flesh rots quickly and doesn't dry well. Eat immediately. Catch by casting far from raft and reel in lure as if trolling. Tuna don't often hit cut bait.

Wahoo: Excellent eating, but dangerously sharp teeth, snout, and fins. Kill or disable before landing and beware of their jump. Fish with trolling lure or bait and a wire leader.

Sharks: Sharks like to rub against things. Their skin is very rough and can damage a life raft. If your raft has anything dangling, a shark might bite it. This includes your raft's CO_2 inflation canister and the indentation your body makes in an underinflated raft. To run sharks off, hit them with a paddle or poke with a spear (but don't lose your tools).

If you hook a shark by mistake, let it go. If on purpose, kill before bringing aboard; shove a paddle in the mouth and stab in the eye. Urea in a dead shark's blood quickly turns to ammonia, fouling the meat, so immediately behead, invert, bleed out, and eat. Livers of open-ocean sharks are nutritious.

Remoras and pilot fish: These follow sharks, will take cut bait, and are edible and safe to land.

Birds: Can be caught with a line, bait, and hook like fish. Wait for a bird to swallow small baited hook and set the barb. They'll also land on your raft if you're very still. Grab by the feet and snap the neck.

Sea turtles: Understand, the only morally defensible reason to kill a sea turtle is for absolute survival. However, if captured, they can be kept for weeks upside down without dying, but they will bite you and your raft. Don't eat turtle organs, especially the liver, which can be poisonous.

Barnacles: These will form after a few weeks on your raft. Lever off your raft carefully. Throw a line over to be sure you can get back aboard. Eat everything, even the shell.

Seaweed: Many are edible, including sargassum, commonly found floating in the open ocean.

SEEING STARS

In 1969, big-wave surfer Greg Noll survived a drop down a titanic wave that would be considered the biggest ever ridden for the next twenty-five years. Lesser known is the fact that Noll is one of the most experienced mariners you'll ever meet.

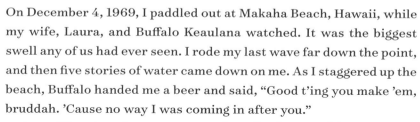

On December 4, 1969, I paddled out at Makaha Beach, Hawaii, while my wife, Laura, and Buffalo Keaulana watched. It was the biggest swell any of us had ever seen. I rode my last wave far down the point, and then five stories of water came down on me. As I staggered up the beach, Buffalo handed me a beer and said, "Good t'ing you make 'em, bruddah. 'Cause no way I was coming in after you."

I was like, okay, for twenty years here I've been waiting to catch a wave bigger than anything ever ridden. That happened. And then what? By the time another twenty years rolls around, I might be in a wheelchair. Usually, I'm stoked at the end of a good day of surfing, but it took me days to get out of that zone. I just went home with Laura. Here's this eager, overly adrenalized monster, and all of a sudden it's over. The pressure was off.

After that I began to focus on fishing—and boats. We moved to Northern California. I've owned three boats, including a 65-footer, and have spent years on the Pacific, from Vancouver Island to southern Baja, in search of fish, shrimp, and crabs. I've survived a lot of hairy situations. Even at eighty, I still scare Laura out on the water. My philosophy is simple: Know the risks, keep your head, and pray for just enough luck.

If I could tell you one thing, the most important is don't ruffle your feathers. Because no matter the situation—whether it's surfing, diving, boat's sinking—stop and think. What can I hang on to? Can I get a call out before the electronics go? If you're surfing and get the crap kicked out of you and don't think you're gonna make it, just don't get excited. If you blow up, you're done.

The most underrated situation that people ignore, especially in Hawaii, is currents. If you don't know the currents, you're gonna be in deep shit. If it was a big day and I didn't know a place well, I'd spend twenty to thirty minutes watching the waves and the current. It's so important.

At Waimea, I went through stages the years I surfed there. I held my breath to the point where you start seeing red, and then you pop up and think, I was really close to drowning. Then, as I started surfing bigger waves, it'd go from red to a bluish color. And I thought, *That's it*. Then it went from red to blue to stars. I never figured out what was beyond that.

CLIMB A COCONUT TREE

Coconuts mean food and water. Legend has it that falling coconuts kill roughly 150 people a year, but despite the aerial hazard, it's not as difficult as you might think to harvest this staple of tropical island life.

1. Palm trees are ringed with ridges that provide decent hand- and footholds. Find the shortest, most slanted tree with the largest, ripest coconuts (mostly green but turning a yellowish brown).

2. Take your shoes, rings, and bracelets off. Make sure your feet are clean. Sand and grit will chew them up, and you'll lose traction.

3. Make a loop of sturdy rope or cloth. Twist the loop into a figure eight and put your feet through each end so that the ends circle your feet, over the tops and under the arches. Splay your feet out to hold the loop in place and keep it tight; grip the tree as best you can with your toes.

4. Place one hand on the back of the tree and your other hand slightly lower on the front. This grip provides leverage as your feet move.

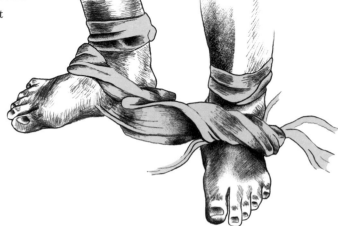

5. While pulling with your upper hand and pushing with the lower, hop up to place your feet around the trunk and lift yourself up the tree. Sort of mimic a frog, with knees bent. Practice at the base before venturing higher, then use the same gripping-and-hopping technique to ascend the trunk.

6. Once coconuts are within reach, twist the fruits until they loosen and fall.

7. To descend, lower your hands one by one and let your feet slide down the trunk. Tender feet may get a bit torn up, but this is the easiest and safest way down.

To open a coconut, a machete or sturdy spike is imperative, though sometimes you can break the shell open against a tree, rock, coral, and so on. In a survival situation, never drink and toss the husk without also eating the high-fiber, fatty-acid rich flesh inside.

NAUTICAL LORE:
THE PIRATE CODE

The seventeenth century is called the Golden Age of Piracy, as if that were a good thing. But if you had the choice, would you submit to the oppression and cruelty of the British Royal Navy or seek out the thrills of a lawless but more democratic adventure? Pirates, of course, chose the latter. Swashbucklers suffered less work and enjoyed more reward—plus their rum was better.

Pirate's articles kept the peace. Sometimes they offered surprising protections, like making sexual assault of a woman punishable by death. All crew members were required to sign the code (sometimes in blood), swearing on the Bible, an axe, a rum bottle, or whatever was at hand that they would abide by it.

The piratical documents that survived that golden age reveal a strange seafaring society that, despite its infamous shortcomings, was fairly honorable. These excerpts—from the 1724 pirate code from Captain John Philips, of the *Revenge*, and the 1721 code of Bartholomew "Black Bart" Roberts of the *Royal Fortune*—are classic examples."

"The code is more what you'd call
'guidelines' than actual rules."

Captain Barbosa, *Pirates of the Caribbean*

I. *Every man shall have an equal vote in affairs of moment. He shall have an equal title to the fresh provisions or strong liquors at any time seized.*

II. *The captain and quartermaster shall each receive two shares of a prize, the master gunner and boatswain one and one-half shares, all other officers one and one-quarter, and private gentlemen of fortune one share each.*

III. *Every man shall be called fairly in turn by the list on board of prizes. But if he defrauds the company to the value of even one dollar of plate, jewels, or money, he shall be marooned. If any man rob another, he shall have his nose and ears slit, and be put ashore where he shall be sure to encounter hardships.*

IV. *That man shall snap his Arms, or smoke Tobacco in the Hold, without a Cap to his Pipe, or carry a Candle lighted without a Lanthorn, shall receive Moses' Law (that is, 40 stripes lacking one) on the bare Back.*

V. *None shall game for money either with dice or cards on board ship.*

VI. *Each man shall keep his piece, cutlass, and pistols at all times clean and ready for action.*

VII. *If any man shall offer to run away, or keep any Secret from the Company, he shall be marooned with one Bottle of Powder, one Bottle of Water, one small Arm, and Shot.*

VIII. *If at any time you meet with a prudent Woman, that Man that offers to meddle with her, without her Consent, shall suffer present Death.*

IX. *None shall strike another on board the ship, but every man's quarrel shall be ended onshore by sword or pistol.*

X. *Every man who shall become a cripple or lose a limb in the service shall have eight hundred pieces of eight from the common stock and for lesser hurts proportionately.*

XI. *The musicians shall have rest on the Sabbath Day only by right. On all other days by favor only.*

SURVIVING KIDNAPPING AND DANGEROUS PORTS OF CALL:

A CHAT WITH MICHAEL SCOTT MOORE

In early 2012, journalist, author, and surfer Michael Scott Moore visited Somalia to write a story on Somali pirates. However, he was double-crossed by his Somali guards and captured by a brutal pirate gang, who held him captive for over two and a half years, along with a pair of poor Seychelles fishermen. Moore endured grinding solitude, hunger strikes, beatings, and strange, random acts of torture and of kindness at the hands of his captors. Then, after 976 days of bad tuna, stale bread, fetid water, and the occasional cup of mango juice, Moore was suddenly flown back to the life he knew. Chris Dixon spoke to Moore about his ordeal, which he describes in his 2018 book, *The Desert and the Sea*.

EVALUATE DANGEROUS PLACES

How do you decide if a place is too damn dangerous? Well, there are no rules. That's the problem. But you have to sit down and really think about it. Consider the risks. Kidnapping on land—all pirates can do that. If you're in a pirate gang, and you decide kidnapping is your business, kidnapping on land can actually be easier and safer than water.

In the place you are visiting, how accustomed are they to seeing people from another country—or a rich country? That makes a big difference. But you also need to know if there's any animus against foreigners. If there's an Al Qaeda element, for example, you have to be careful about where you go. That said, learning a place firsthand is the best way to figure how to blend in. Go to the area first and get to know it before you do anything dangerous. I thought I was doing that. I certainly wasn't new to East Africa when I went to Somalia. But this was my first time in Somalia.

KEEP A LOW ONLINE AND PUBLIC PROFILE

How prominent are you on the internet? Before Somalia, I did prune my website a little bit because my first novel was a ghost story with a Jewish ghost, and there's a huge problem with anti-Semitism in Somalia. So I decided to take that off and a couple of other details I didn't want pirates to learn if they looked me up. But there was only so much I could do about scrubbing myself from the internet. I didn't do anything formal, but maybe in the end I should have. Because they did look me up and found an interview I did with the *New York Times* about my book *Sweetness and Blood*, and they found my picture. I certainly didn't post to Facebook from Somalia. That would be really stupid.

I tried to maintain as low a profile as I could when I was there. Which meant don't flag the attention of Somali officials, so to speak, when I landed. I also traveled on my German passport rather than my American one. The problem in part is that a place like that—it's such a closed society that any outsider sticks out, a white person especially. You simply have to choose your guides and your security extremely well. We were careful about it, but in the end, we didn't do it well enough.

DON'T RELY ON GOVERNMENT HELP

I'm sure if I'd gone to the State Department and told them I was going to Somalia, they would have said don't go. Because they had a very sensible policy of saying don't go to Somalia. It's not a bad thing if officials know where you are before you go and do something a little bit dangerous. But there's not much the State Department can do, either. In extreme situations, the best they can do is reach out to another government. But most of the time, you get in trouble like I did, either the government itself is irrational—as in the case of, say, you get arrested in Iran and thrown in prison—or you're not dealing with a government at all. Now your government will put somebody on your case and start a file. They'll keep track of it. But let's say you go surfing around Indonesia, wind up too close to the Philippines, and end up getting kidnapped by Abu Sayyaf. There's just not much the government can do in situations like that.

BE STRONG THROUGH HUNGER AND PANIC

When I did a hunger strike—I did several, but the first one—the thing I was not prepared for was the visceral panic that the body goes through once you stop eating. Even after a few hours of missing a meal, your body rebels. Your mind has to be ready for that. What did I actually do? It was a question of detaching myself emotionally from what was going on. And that was really, really difficult. Because you're vested in ways that you don't realize. The tendency to panic and become apocalyptic about the situation you're in is sometimes more dangerous than the situation itself. It's the panic of the unexpected I'm talking about. Until you've actually been there, you just don't know how to navigate something like that.

BAD WATER: RED TIDES AND ALGAE BLOOMS

Red tides and toxic algae blooms create, in essence, poisonous conditions for fish and humans, and exposure—whether in the air, in the water, or in the fish you eat—can lead to illness and a host of physical problems. Avoid the water whenever these tides are present, and avoid fish you fear might be infected. Learn to recognize the signs.

Red or brown tides are caused by exploding populations of photosynthetic phytoplankton, called *Gymnodinium breve*, which turn the ocean reddish and murky. Some species bioluminesce when disturbed, giving nighttime waves an eerie blue glow. These harmful algal blooms (HABs) often happen after rain dumps nitrate- and phosphate-rich pollution and fertilizer-laden runoff into the ocean, supercharging algal feeding and breeding.

HABs suffocate fish by clogging gills. The bacteria that then consume dying phytoplankton also deplete marine oxygen, resulting in massive fish kills. Certain phytoplankton can release potent neurotoxins. These accumulate in the bodies of fish and shellfish, and toxins can even be aerosolized by wind and waves.

Blue-green algae blooms are similar, but they're generally neon to dull green to yellow-brown—resembling mats of awful smelling paint on the water. They're most often associated with warm freshwater that's laden with nitrogen and phosphorus from agriculture and leaking sewage or septic systems. Cyanobacteria toxins, called microcystins, can affect the skin, lungs, nervous system, and liver. They're shunted into marine estuaries—particularly in Florida—during storm flooding and can cause massive fish kills, while sickening mammals and birds.

Symptoms of bloom exposure vary, usually beginning within hours and lasting a few days. Swallowing the toxin can cause abdominal pain, vomiting, and neurologic effects. Airborne, they cause watery eyes, a sore throat, and a wicked cough. People with preexisting lung problems can be badly affected. Some swimmers can have skin reactions.

In animals, related toxins can cause severe disease, such as excessive salivation, weakness, staggered walking, difficulty breathing, convulsions, or even death. If you suspect exposure, contact a poison control center and see a doctor.

"Water, water, every where,
And all the boards did shrink;
Water, water, every where,
Nor any drop to drink."

—from *The Rime of the Ancient Mariner*,
Samuel Taylor Coleridge

SCUBA
AND
SNORKELING

GETTING SCHOOLED

AS TOLD BY MORGAN MOCHESTER
Morgan Mochester is a PADI-certified open-water diving instructor from
Charleston, SC.

FULL OPEN-WATER CERTIFICATION COURSE

If you're going to dive seriously, get fully certified in a multiday
open-water course. Diving is a risk-inherent sport and lots of law-
yers are involved. That means PADI instructors are held to the
same exact standards whether you're in the Caribbean, Germany,
or Japan. It's like going to a Starbucks.

During a diving course, we review the same things over and
over, using manuals, videos, and personal instruction. So whether
you're an auditory, visual, or hands-on learner, everything you
need to know should be nailed into your head by the end. That's
so important in an emergency, when you don't have time to think.

SHORT RESORT DIVE COURSES

Discover Scuba is the PADI-certified short dive course given at
resorts, but not all resorts offer a certified course. If not, and in
general, evaluate a resort's offerings for yourself. First, look at
online reviews. At the resort, pay attention to how the people
present themselves, especially in places like the Caribbean or
Thailand. When there's a crew, is everyone wearing the same
uniform? Are people walking around not giving you that customer-
service feel? Ask yourself, *Do these people seem more interested
in taking care of themselves or taking care of me? Do I feel safe
having them take me underwater?* Remember, no one can tell you
to do a dive. At any time and any point, you can say, "Hey guys,
I can't do this." It's your life. Also—actually read the medical
statement you're required to sign. It asks important questions.

If you're a beginner, throw resort staff some loaded questions.
In PADI-certified short courses, the maximum safe depth we will
take you is 30 feet, so ask, "Can we go down to 60 feet?" Or get to
know a couple of the local dive spots and say, "I heard about this
statue at 70 feet—can we check it out?" If they say yes, then say,
"See you later."

Evaluate the resort's equipment. Is there sun cracking on the rubber hoses? Bend them to check. There's 3,000 pounds per square inch flowing through that hose. Turn on the tank and hit the regulator mouthpiece button. If it keeps free-flowing air when you release, and they have to tap it to stop, get a different rig. That free flow is a failsafe so if something goes wrong, the regulator fails in the open position so you can still get air.

Finally, bring your own mask, snorkel, fins, and wetsuit boots. Do you want a snorkel that's been in other people's mouths? Would you rent someone else's sneakers? The mask is one of the most important pieces of equipment. Buy one before diving and test it. I tell customers buying masks, even if it's just snorkeling, we can do most of your fitting in the store, but the real test is when you jump in the water. That's where you figure out if something's bothering you. After twenty minutes, you're going to find out if a mask is not right. If you wait until you're scuba diving and are 60 feet down, you can't do anything about it until you reach the surface.

MY BODY LIES UNDER THE SEA: PRESSURE DROP

Everything is different underwater. That's the draw and danger of snorkeling, free diving, and scuba, which stands for "self-contained underwater breathing apparatus." Here's what to expect when you're submerged in the deep blue ocean:

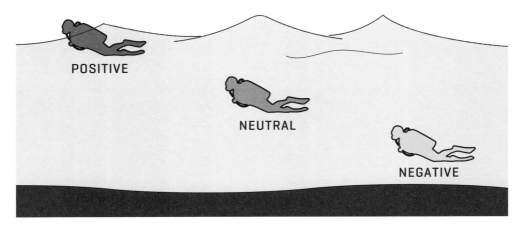

- **Magnification:** Through your mask, light refraction will magnify the world by about 33 percent. Objects look larger and closer than they are.

- **Colors:** Water absorbs wavelengths of sunlight. The deeper you go, the less color you see. Reds disappear first.

- **Sound:** Sound travels four times faster in water than air, making it tough to discern a sound's direction. You can make your voice heard by screaming, but unless you're wearing a special mask, talking's impossible. To get a diver's attention, bang your tank with a steel object like a wrench or dive knife.

- **Temperature:** Snorkelers enjoy warmer surface waters, but just below the surface, water can be dramatically, unexpectedly colder. The depth where water temperature drops sharply is called the thermocline. Since cold water can sap heat from your body at twenty times the rate of air, divers often wear wetsuits.

- **Buoyancy:** Snorkelers float because their lungs are filled with air; divers sink because dive belts weigh them down. However, like a submarine, divers can hover in the sea, becoming neutrally buoyant, by varying the amount of air in their lungs, the weight on a dive belt, and the air in an inflatable buoyancy compensation device (BCD).

PRESSURE DROP

Pressurized liquids don't compress. Pressurized gases do. Thus, the pressure changes wrought by descending are felt only in spaces that are filled with gas: your ears, sinuses, diving mask, and to a degree, your lungs. Water is eight hundred times denser than air. At a depth of 33 feet, the pressure on your body ratchets up to twice that at sea level. By 99 feet, it's four atmospheres. In diving terminology, one atmosphere is known as a *bar* or an *ata*.

Divers must continually equalize the pressure of air in their bodies as they change elevation. At four atmospheres, or 99 feet, it takes four times as much air to fill a space as at sea level. As you descend, gas-filled spaces compress as the gas becomes more dense. As you ascend, those spaces expand and become less dense. This explains why divers get "squeezed" descending and why they must exhale air as they rise. Rise too rapidly and air can over-expand, damaging a scuba diver's lungs. Thus, while ascending, always slowly exhale a steady stream of bubbles—such as by saying "ahhhh" as you rise.

DEPTH	PRESSURE	AIR VOLUME	AIR DENSITY	
0m/0ft	1 bar/ATA	1	x 1	
10m/33ft	2 bar/ATA	1/2	x 2	
20m/66ft	3 bar/ATA	1/3	x 3	
30m/99ft	4 bar/ATA	1/4	x 4	

Air becomes more dense and takes less volume as you go deeper, so you need more air to fill your lungs.

AVOID THE SQUEEZE: EQUALIZE

As you descend, the air pressure in your eardrums, sinuses, and even diving mask becomes lower than the external water pressure, and you feel uncomfortably, even painfully *squeezed*.

As on an airplane, you can "equalize" ear and sinus pressure by opening the eustachian tubes between your mouth and your inner ear. Try swallowing several times or jutting out your jaw, shuffling it from side to side. Also pinch your nose and contract your diaphragm as if blowing, but don't exhale. Equalize slowly and steadily, and don't overpressurize your head. If your mask presses painfully against your face, simply exhale through your nose to equalize it.

When ascending, a pressure imbalance is called a *reverse block*. Again, ascend slowly and equalize pressure as you go.

If you have a cold or congestion, equalizing may be impossible. Predive decongestants can help. Finally, very rarely, air trapped in a tooth filling will compress painfully. If this happens, or anytime equalizing efforts don't work, abort the dive.

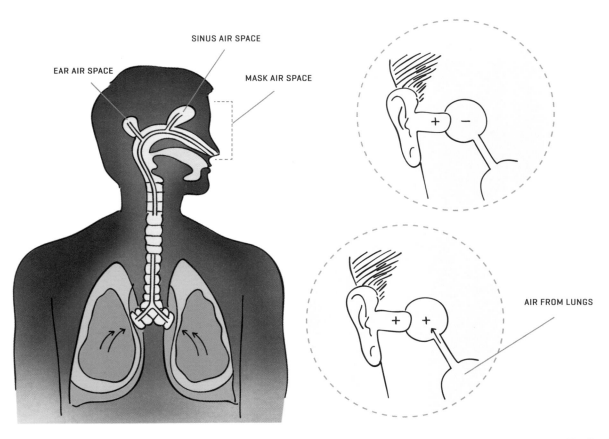

SINUS AIR SPACE

EAR AIR SPACE

MASK AIR SPACE

AIR FROM LUNGS

SNORKELING AND SCUBA GEAR

Here's the skinny on essential scuba gear: Get a mask, snorkel, fins, BCD, wetsuit, and scuba tank. When it's time to shop, ask yourself: *What is my life worth?* Don't skimp.

Take care of your gear with that same question in mind. Always rinse dive gear with copious amounts of freshwater after every use, dry well, and store out of the sun. Clear silicone on snorkels and mask skirts often becomes a bit opaque, but if kept out of the sun, they will retain suppleness for years. Neoprene (wetsuit) rubber left in contact with your snorkel or other gear may cause discoloration. See "Wetsuit Care" (page 101).

SNORKEL

A snorkel is necessary even for scuba diving. You'll use it waiting for the boat in rougher water or cruising shallows when you don't need your tank. Also, after a tiring dive, it saves energy, since you won't need to raise your head to breathe.

- Find a wide-tube model that permits heavier breathing.

- A splashguard at the top prevents water from entering snorkel.

- A flexible tube at the base allows snorkel to easily drop out of the way for scuba or swimming.

- A purge valve at the base makes it easy to expel water.

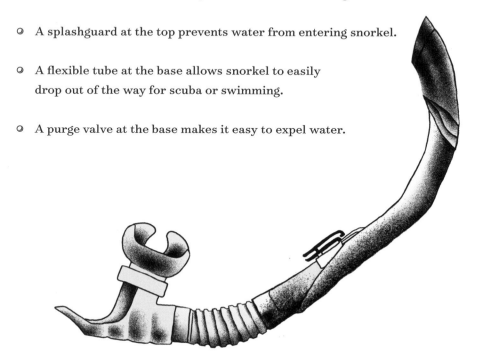

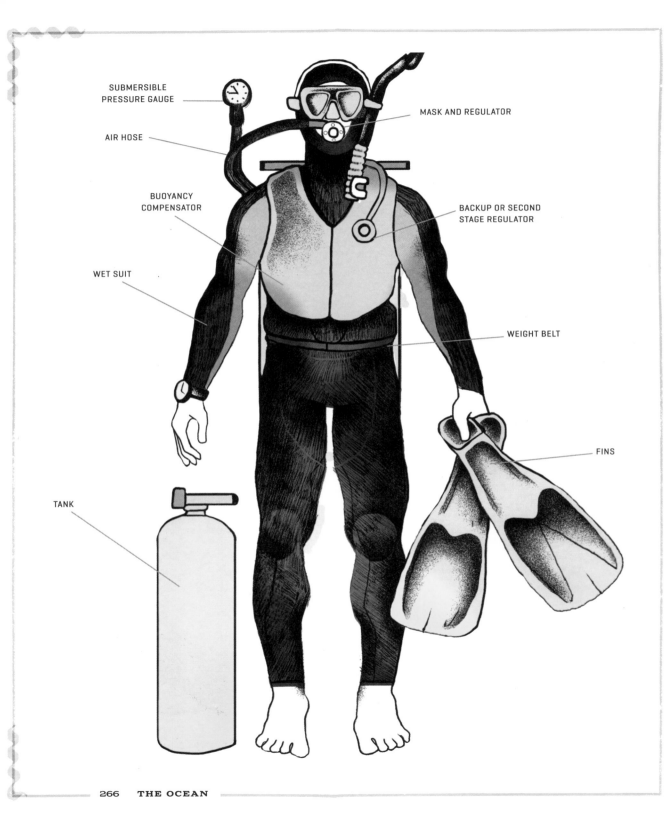

SUBMERSIBLE
PRESSURE GAUGE

MASK AND REGULATOR

AIR HOSE

BUOYANCY
COMPENSATOR

BACKUP OR SECOND
STAGE REGULATOR

WET SUIT

WEIGHT BELT

FINS

TANK

DIVING WETSUITS

Basically, the thicker the wetsuit, the warmer you'll be. For a description of how suits are made, see "Wetsuit 101" (page 98). Surfing and diving wetsuits differ and aren't really interchangeable. First, most diving suits have a front zipper, since you're wearing a tank on your back. Then, the neoprene is much stiffer to resist compression. Softer, squishier surfing wetsuits compress as you descend and lose their ability to insulate. Buy specific suits for each activity.

Like surfing wetsuits, the best diving suits have glued and blind-stitched rubber. Look for a mix of "compressing" neoprene at mobility points, stiff rubber for body panels, and wearproof surfaces at knees and shoulders.

Smooth skin suits are more fragile, but this material protects better from wind when out of water. To avoid seepage, most dive suits have waterproof zippers (some lined inside) and rubber O-ring seals at the ankles, wrists, and neck.

To work well, the suit should fit snugly. "Airspace" in the suit will fill with water, making movement cumbersome and costing metabolic energy to warm up.

Choosing the right thickness is key. Consider your own metabolism and where and how deep you plan to dive. Diving is a fairly low-intensity activity, so you get cold more easily. Always get booties, gloves, and a hood. To pick the right suit, visit a dive shop. Here's a general guide to diving wetsuit thickness.

WATER TEMPERATURE	BODY COVERAGE (neoprene thickness in mm)
Bathwater, 85°F and up	Bathing suit to 1-mm or 2-mm "shorty" springsuit or long-sleeve top
Tropical, 80°–84°F	1-mm to 2-mm fullsuit
Cool, 73°–79°F	4/3-mm to 5-mm fullsuit
Chilly, 66°–72°F	5/4-mm fullsuit
Cold, 50°–65°F	8/7-mm semidry to 7-mm wetsuit
Wicked Cold, 49°F and below	8/7-mm semidry or drysuit

MASK

Since our air-bound eyes can't see clearly in water like a fish's eyes, a diving mask creates an air pocket so we can see. Before using a new mask, gently clean the interior with toothpaste and a cotton ball or other nonabrasive cloth to clear the invisible silicone coating and enable the mask's antifog properties to work. When buying, consider these issues:

- The mask must completely surround your nose, and the nose pocket should be easy to finger squeeze for equalizing. Masks with a clear silicone rubber skirt let in more light and are less "claustrophobic." Black silicone masks keep down glare and may be better for shallow diving and snorkeling.

- Ensure a good fit and seal by getting your hair out of the way, pressing the mask against your face, and inhaling through your nose. If air gets in, try another. If the dive shop allows, test it in the water.

- Ensure mask lens is tempered glass, which is very strong and won't shatter into splinters.

- Masks should fit close to the face. Less air space facilitates equalizing.

- Ensure a comfortable, easy-to-adjust strap that won't pull hair.

- A one-way purge valve makes it easy to clear water by exhaling through your nose.

- Some masks are tinted to help bring out muted underwater colors.

- For prescription masks, order from your local dive shop.

FINS

Fins provide propulsion, and a well-fitted pair can make snorkeling and scuba a low-effort affair. There are two basic fits—shoe and adjustable strap. Most divers choose strap models because they can be worn with wetsuit booties and tailor fit. Slip-on shoe-type models are used in warmer water areas. Recently, in addition to "split blade" fins that increase maneuverability, shortened versions are increasingly popular. Abbreviated fins don't generate the thrust of long fins, but they're great for snorkeling and easy to pack. Long, carbon-fiber fins are best for free diving.

BUOYANCY COMPENSATION DEVICE

For scuba, a reliable buoyancy compensation device is essential gear. It holds your tank and works similarly to a blow-up life jacket on airplanes. You fill it using your tank and regulator or an oral blow-up valve; tugging a valve string deflates it. BCDs not only keep you neutrally buoyant underwater, they allow you to rest at the surface or make an emergency ascent. When washing your BCD after use, also rinse the inflation hose and bladder. Then leave some air in the BCD to maintain the integrity of the bladder.

SCUBA TANKS, VALVES, AND REGULATORS

Tanks generally come in 8-, 10-, and 12-liter capacities. They must be tested regularly for structural integrity because they carry a small roomful of air and bear up to 4,500 pounds per square inch (320 bar) of pressure. Your valve assembly will attach to a submersible pressure gauge (SPG) that indicates how much air is left.

In addition to ensuring your valve is tightly attached to your tank, always check that the rubber O-ring that seals the pressure gauge and regulator is in good shape. The valve on your tank should turn smoothly with very little effort. If there are "chinks" in the turn or difficulty, have it serviced professionally or don't use it.

Tanks are very strong, but keep them secured when hauling. Always keep them out of the hot sun. Before use, check the tank for any surface cracks or rust and check beneath the rubber boot to ensure it's not corroded.

The regulator is a complicated little device that reduces the high-pressure air in your tank to a pressure you can breathe. Through a specialized two-stage valve system, it also delivers the right amount of air based on your depth. The regulator holds your SPG and primary and secondary air sources—mouthpieces that open and release air when you inhale and close when you exhale. The second mouthpiece, or "alternate air source," is for emergencies, such as sharing air with another diver. It's literally your lifeline, so be sure yours is operating properly and maintained regularly. Always ensure the regulator is clear of sand or any obstructions, and rinse thoroughly after each use.

OTHER SNORKELING AND DIVE GEAR

- A rinsable mesh carry bag for all your gear.

- For your mask: antifog lotion and a soft cloth.

- Weight system—either on a belt or on your BCD.

- Dive computer and compass.

- A dive-specific knife with a sheath.

- A good underwater watch with a stopwatch (digital) or a rotating timer bezel (analog).

- A depth gauge.

- A whistle to call for help.

- "Diver down" signals or flags.

- For snorkelers, a snorkeling vest. Bright colored and typically inflated by mouth, these are excellent life-saving devices. Also consider inflatable rescue and marker buoys held in an unobtrusive, line-secured belt.

- Collecting bags (see "Rules for Found Objects," page 288).

- Underwater slate or subsea chalkboard for communication.

- Vinegar and/or jellyfish sting protective lotion (see page 206).

PLAN THE DIVE, DIVE THE PLAN

Every time you scuba dive, or even snorkel far from shore, follow the buddy system. This means staying close together and always knowing where your buddy is. It also means agreeing on a plan before diving and checking all equipment—using a predive PADI-approved checklist.

Of course, if you're scuba diving, we assume you've already taken a PADI (Professional Association of Diving Instructors) or NAUI (National Association of Underwater Instructors) open-water scuba course. If you haven't, see "Getting Schooled" (page 260). This book can guide you in the basics, but it's no substitute for certified, instructor-led scuba training.

If you've had such a course, you know how to calculate the length of a planned dive: by dividing the air in your tank by your depth. That is (per "Pressure Drop," (page 263), at 33 feet (2 bar), you consume twice the amount of air as at the surface; at 66 feet (3 bar), it's three times. Thus, if a 12-liter scuba tank could last ninety minutes at the surface, it would run low around forty-five minutes at a depth of 33 feet and last around thirty minutes at 66 feet.

In addition, keep in mind:

⊘ The most basic rule of diving is to plan the dive, then dive the plan. Don't improvise.

⊘ Before you dive, inspect, label, and, oh yeah, triple-check your gear.

⊘ Know the tide and weather forecast; if conditions seem sketchy, pick a different site or don't dive.

⊘ Even when snorkeling, establish the physical boundaries of your excursion, your route, and the in and out points.

⊘ Review hand signals (page 276) and discuss plans for potential problems and emergency scenarios.

⊘ If launching from a boat, familiarize yourself with getting in and out of the boat (page 272), and anticipate seasickness.

⊘ Finally, alert someone to where you're going and when you'll be back; see "Make a Float Plan" (page 22).

GETTING IN, OUT, AND AROUND

Entering and exiting the water while wearing your gear takes practice. Always check that everything is securely fastened and other divers/obstructions are clear.

From the beach: Walking forward in fins is very tough out of the water and nearly impossible in it. Don your fins at the water's edge. Then walk slowly backward until you're deep enough to swim. Reverse for exit. If it's very rough or rocky, wear booties and put on your fins when you're in deep-enough water.

From a boat—giant stride: Stand facing the water on a stable platform. If scuba diving, ensure the BCD is half-inflated. Before stepping, place one palm on the regulator/snorkel, with finger-tips on your mask, while the other hand secures the mask strap or BCD at your abdomen. Take a big step straight off with legs spread wide, and make a strong scissor kick as you hit to stay near the surface.

From a boat—back roll: Best for low gunwale boats or boats that are rocking. Sit on the edge of the boat amidships. Half-inflate the BCD and put the regulator in your mouth. As with the giant stride, hold the regulator/snorkel/mask with one hand, while the other hand secures the mask strap. Cross your ankles, tuck in your chin, and roll backward into the water.

Clear your mask of water: If your mask has a purge valve, simply exhale. Otherwise, take a deep breath, look up, press the mask against your forehead while gently lifting it away from your lower face, and exhale strongly. It takes practice, but a solid exhale can purge almost all the water.

The fin kick: To swim efficiently with fins, point your feet and don't bend your knees too much. Most of your kick should come from your hips and thighs, through the range of motion. The power stroke is down; the resting stroke is up. Keep your arms at your sides to reduce drag, and don't hurry, which burns through air and energy.

DIVING HAND SIGNALS

These are the commonly accepted hand signals used by PADI.
Review them with fellow divers before every dive.

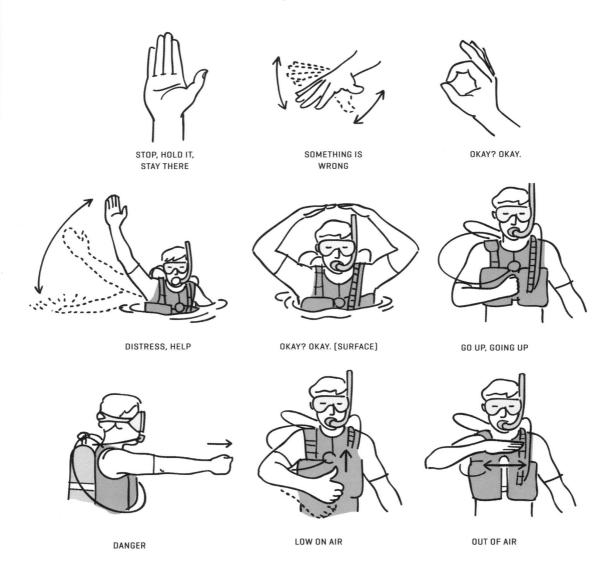

STOP, HOLD IT,
STAY THERE

SOMETHING IS
WRONG

OKAY? OKAY.

DISTRESS, HELP

OKAY? OKAY. (SURFACE)

GO UP, GOING UP

DANGER

LOW ON AIR

OUT OF AIR

LEVEL OFF, THIS DEPTH

HOLD HANDS

OKAY? OKAY. (ONE HAND)

EARS NOT CLEARING

GO DOWN,
GOING DOWN

YOU LEAD,
I'LL FOLLOW

GET WITH YOUR
BUDDY

BUDDY BREATHE OR
SHARE AIR

I AM COLD

DIVE DANGERS

Humans don't belong underwater. That's why so much can go wrong on a dive. This covers the most common issues—exhaustion and cramps, breathing issues, visibility and currents, and the dreaded bends—but take a PADI diving course and see the Survival section for more advice.

TIRED DIVERS, CRAMPS, AND PANIC

Divers can tire more quickly than expected, and the unusual muscle movements of dive swimming, dehydration, cold, and overexertion can cause debilitating cramps. This combo can lead to anxiety and panic, which shortens breath, using precious oxygen.

If you cramp up, signal your dive buddy immediately. Stop, relax, breathe deeply, and massage the cramped muscle. Stretch a calf muscle by pulling the tip of your fin toward you. Once the cramp releases, continue slowly and gingerly.

If a cramp happens to your dive buddy, calm and relax them; help them reestablish breathing control. If necessary, assist the diver back to shore or the boat by having them establish buoyancy and lie on their back. From that position, you can push them from their feet or tow them from the back of their BCD.

BREATHING TECHNIQUES: EASY DOES IT

Breathing hard through a snorkel or regulator can lead to overexertion, and if breathing feels restrictive, it can cause panic. Prevent this with the following:

- Breathe and swim slowly and steadily to avoid fatigue.

- If you feel tired, stop and rest. Hold something for support if available.

- On the surface, inflate your BCD, become buoyant, then relax.

- A little water in your snorkel or regulator is normal. To purge water, inhale slowly, using your tongue to keep from swallowing the water, then give a strong exhale.

- Take slower, fuller breaths because the snorkel tube and regulator can pool carbon dioxide–laden air. Deep breaths ensure you purge the CO_2.

- If you accidentally inhale water and gag or cough, stay calm and breathe through your mouth. Take hold of your snorkel or regulator and cough into it to clear your lungs and breathing apparatus.

VISIBILITY AND CURRENTS

Visibility can change quickly and is affected by many things: currents, waves, shore runoff, plankton blooms, and your own movements stirring up sediment. When visibility is poor, keep your buddy close or dive another day. If you suddenly lose visibility and feel disoriented, keep calm and grab a fixed object or your buddy's hand. Follow your bubbles to the surface; sometimes water is clear a few feet up. Be aware that clear water can impair distance judgment; be cautious diving near obstructions and jumping in.

Currents can change rapidly. They're typically stronger at the surface and weaken with depth, but not always. The general rule is to avoid swimming against the current because you'll quickly tire. If you're diving somewhere with a mild current, begin your dive by swimming against the current, so you will naturally be carried back to your starting point.

If you're caught in a current stronger than you can swim, don't fight it or panic. The current may be localized. Swim perpendicularly to its direction to escape its grip. If it's clear you can't escape it, inflate your BCD or snorkeling vest, get to the surface, and blow a whistle or wave your arms to attract attention. Remain calm. You can often find a current-free route back to shore even if swept far from your starting point.

Surge is the undulating motion of waves undersea. It can sweep you back and forth, and typically weakens as you go deeper. Avoid diving around rock outcroppings and through narrow areas, since surge can bash you against rocks or stuff you in a hole.

Be particularly careful at embayments. When substantial waves or surge push water in, that water tends to escape along the edges of the embayment (though surface water appears calm). Snorkeling an unfamiliar spot? Size it up, ask a local, and see "Shorebreak, Rip Currents, and Rogue Waves" (page 104).

THE BENDS AND A.G.E.: DECOMPRESSION ILLNESS

Diving can bring on two types of acute illness. The first is called decompression sickness (DCS), also known as the bends. DCS happens when bubbles effervesce from the blood, usually due to a too-rapid ascent, and enter body tissue. The second is arterial gas embolism (AGE). AGE happens when bubbles enter the lung or blood circulation and travel through the arteries. These bubbles can block blood flow to vessels.

DCS generally arises due to long, deep dives, cold water, heavy exertion at depth, and rapid ascents. But it can happen to anyone. Divers can follow a proper plan and still be afflicted—even from shallow dives. When you breathe at depth and pressure, inert nitrogen molecules are forced into your body tissues, but they remain dissolved and "in solution." When you ascend, the pressure decreases and the nitrogen can come "out of solution," essentially fizzing in your blood like bubbles leaving an opened bottle of soda. In extreme cases, rapid ascents can affect the spinal cord and brain, causing paralysis or brain damage.

If a diver displays any of the symptoms that follow, assume they need emergency treatment. A hyperbaric chamber may be required, and quick treatment can reverse what might otherwise become severe, lifelong debilitation or death. Seek local emergency help first, then contact the Divers Alert Network (www.diversalertnetwork.org), who can refer you to the nearest specialist.

SYMPTOMS AND SIGNS OF D.C.S. AND A.G.E.

These usually appear between fifteen minutes and twelve hours after diving.

- Unusual fatigue or weakness

- Itchy skin and blotchy skin rash

- Pain in joints, muscles, legs, arms, or torso

- Dizziness, vertigo, ringing in the ears, blurred vision

- Numbness, tingling, paralysis

- Shortness of breath, inability to breathe, chest pain

- Difficulty urinating

- Confusion, disorientation, or amnesia

- Tremors, convulsions, staggering

- Coughing up blood or bloody froth

- Collapse, unconsciousness

CREATURES AND CORAL:
LEAVE NOTHING BUT BUBBLES

If you find an animal in distress, see what you can do to help it, but generally don't feed or interfere with sea creatures you encounter underwater. You can alter their natural behavior—especially by feeding them. This can be a big problem. For instance, in Florida, some operations take divers out to feed sharks; this, in effect, teaches certain sharks to associate humans with food. Obviously, that's bad on many levels. The following guidelines reflect PADI advice. See also "Swimming with Sharks" (page 282).

○ Treat all animals, including corals, with respect. Don't tease or intentionally disturb them. Touching some corals—even gently—can result in a nasty, painful sting, or it can kill the fragile polyps whose limestone skeletons create the reef in the first place.

○ Be cautious in extremely murky water, and watch where you put your hands. Potentially aggressive animals could mistake you—or your hands—for prey. Avoid diving in unclear waters with known dangerous predators or poisonous fish.

○ Remove shiny, dangling jewelry, which can resemble baitfish or other small prey. Barracuda are said to be attracted to such objects, though they may simply be curious. Barracuda have an unnerving tendency to follow humans, but actual barracuda attacks are even more rare than shark attacks.

○ Remove speared fish from the water immediately.

○ Wear gloves and an exposure suit to avoid stings and cuts.

○ Maintain neutral buoyancy and stay off the bottom.

○ Move slowly and carefully.

○ Avoid contact with unfamiliar animals.

SWIMMING WITH SHARKS

If you swim in the ocean, you've had a close encounter with a shark. You simply didn't know it. Sharks frequent coral reefs, seal colonies, and sandy beaches. Despite that, you are eighty times more likely to be struck by lightning than attacked by a shark. Bees, dogs, and falling flowerpots kill more humans in America every year than sharks do globally. More humans are annually bitten *by humans* on the New York City subway.

But fear rarely listens to facts. Plus, snorkeling and diving does increase the chances of a shark encounter. You're swimming where sharks live.

METHODS FOR AVOIDING SHARKS

First, most species pose little to no threat. In terms of human attacks, the "big three" are bulls, tigers, and great whites. Bulls and tigers prefer warmer water. Great whites colder water.

As for shark repellents: some work by electromagnetically interrupting the exquisitely tuned electrical field receptors in a shark's snout, and some smell like dead shark, which sharks appear to hate. Early research suggests repellents can work on curious, slow-moving sharks, but not reliably. An agitated shark may well ignore them. However, if a repellent makes you feel better, or smell worse, go for it, just don't depend on it.

- Sharks are most active at dawn, dusk, and night. Swim near shore, during the day, around other swimmers.

- Erratic motion attracts sharks. Don't splash excessively, and keep dogs out of the water.

- Avoid murky or effluent-tainted water.

- Sharks feed on schools of baitfish like mullet, so avoid baitfish schools; look for fish jumping at the surface and for dive-bombing seabirds.

- Dolphins and porpoises don't necessarily keep away sharks. These species are often found together.

- Don't assume a fresh or brackish nearshore river has no sharks. Bull sharks can survive in freshwater and sometimes journey up the Mississippi River.

- Avoid waters where fishermen are actively catching fish or cleaning them.

- Though evidence of a shark's attraction to actual human blood is inconclusive, get out of the water if you're bleeding.

- Sharks frequent steep drop-off areas and deeper stretches along beaches between shallow sandbars.

- Jewelry and shiny objects that evoke fish scales can attract sharks. Sharks also see contrasting colors well. Hide your farmer's tan and avoid neon clothing.

- Great white sharks eat black sea lions, which humans in black wetsuits can resemble. Pick a different wetsuit color: blue, camouflaged, painted, or black-and-white zebra stripe (which might actually discourage great whites). Check out Shark Attack Mitigation Systems wetsuits.

- If you're spearfishing and a shark becomes interested in your catch, leave it.

- If you're diving near a cliff face, kelp forest, or the seafloor, get right up next to them to interfere with a shark's normal feeding behavior.

FENDING OFF A SHARK ATTACK

Sharks indicate agitation and potential aggressiveness when their normal, slow-moving swimming style changes to a faster, zig-zagging pattern or when swimming with pectoral (side) fins pointed down, snouts up, and backs arched (called "hunching"). They may also rub their bellies along the seafloor. If you see this behavior, swim smoothly away, backward if possible, avoiding sudden movements and always watching the shark. Keep your dive buddy close to expand your visual field and help fend off the shark.

In the vast majority of attacks, a shark bites a human by mistake, immediately realizes its mistake, releases, and disappears. In a genuine attack, the shark rushes from beneath at tremendous speed, leaving little chance for any defensive maneuver. Still, you can try.

- Use any equipment—like a spear, knife, or pole—to hit the shark, aiming for the snout. The shark will likely return, so retreat immediately.

- Some advise yelling at an attacking shark. Why not? You'll probably be hollering, anyway.

- Punching a shark in its sensitive snout is sound advice, but "punching" underwater is terribly difficult. You might have more luck gouging the eyes and tearing at the sensitive gills with your fingers or anything sharp. Bottom line: Fight like hell.

SPEARFISHING AND FREE DIVING

BY MARK HEALEY
Mark Healey is a renowned big-wave surfer, free diver, and spearfisher who regularly spends four minutes underwater on one breath. He is one of the most accomplished watermen on Earth.

The difference between snorkeling and free diving is the difference between wakesurfing in a Texas lake and surfing in the ocean. That wakesurfer doesn't know how to read waves, handle underwater thrashings, or deal with changing conditions.

SPEARFISHING AND FREE-DIVING EQUIPMENT
The foundation is a free-diving mask. Remember, the mask is just another air-filled cavity. You want to equalize the mask with as little air as possible, since you only have the air in your lungs. So you want a low-volume mask with the glass close to your face.

Also, clean the invisible silicone coating off a new mask. If you just use soap, it'll fog like crazy. Use toothpaste and keep washing and scrubbing until you get it all out.

Free-dive fins are longer and use a different kicking technique than body-boarding or snorkel fins. Don't drive with your knees. Whip the fin's long blade in a snapping motion mostly using your hips. Use the wave of motion so one wave snaps off the tip while you're already loading up another wave. Kicking too hard can overload the fins—the blade bends too much and never gets that snap. With the correct technique, you get twice the propulsion for half the oxygen.

The wetsuit is crucial. A lot of people come to Hawaii and say, "Oh, it's tropical, I'll be fine without a wetsuit." No. Even if you wear a 3/2-mm surfing wetsuit, due to the compression of neoprene at depth, you'll be freezing in half an hour. In free diving, you're trying to cheat and conserve oxygen any way you can. You're limiting your movement, and your metabolism slows due to the mammalian dive reflex, so you get colder. If the water's below 98.6 degrees, you can eventually get hypothermia.

I use a two-piece free-diving wetsuit: a farmer john style under a hooded long-sleeve top. From waist to chest, that gives almost 7 mm of neoprene. Don't just cram in your bare leg, since the suit might rip. Lube yourself up first. I keep a bottle of nontoxic hair conditioner mixed with water.

As for a snorkel, I like a basic J-shape with a purge valve at the bottom and an open top. A water-blocking valve adds drag; plus, the snorkel needs to fill with water so it won't be buoyant.

Spearfishers, of course, need a spear. I learned with a pole spear. We call them "three prongs" in Hawaii, but they're also known as "Hawaiian slings." I think they're the best way to learn because you have to use it very close to the fish. It can be frustrating at first, but you've got to work your way up—learn fish behavior. Walk before you run. When you're ready for a speargun, don't start with anything longer than 120 cm. For slower-moving fish in lower visibility water (like lingcod in Northern California), you probably only need a 90-cm gun.

Finally, you need a weight belt—to stay neutrally buoyant, as in scuba—and a good dive knife, in case you need to cut a line in an emergency or dispatch a struggling fish.

LEARNING TO FREE DIVE

At first, practice holding your breath in a pool or another controlled environment, and always have a partner—because you don't know your limits (see "Unleash Your Inner Seal," page 233). Not knowing your limits can create anxiety, which doesn't help. On the other hand, you'll also probably surprise yourself with how long you can stay under, which is intoxicating. It's such a great feeling when you push past those barriers. That's a really dangerous point, too, because you're like, *Now I'm really gonna push myself.* Then you black out and die.

In the ocean, dive with a partner and have a plan. Ideally, you want a partner who's more experienced than you. It happens all the time: Two beginners in the water. One blacks out. The other goes down for them and blacks out, too. Then you've got two dead people. I've seen cases where you end up with three dead people.

Make sure you don't weight yourself too heavily starting out. At depth, the air in your body compresses, reducing your buoyancy. So at 30 feet, that weight will feel twice as heavy, making it a lot harder to come up and reach oxygen. Also don't go too deep. Beginning free divers do this a lot—they see a fish and chase after it past the point of ear discomfort. This can really mess up your ears. If you feel ear discomfort, go back up, start again, and equalize before your ears get uncomfortable.

SPEARFISHING TECHNIQUES

Always check local fish regulations and methods allowed. In some areas, spearguns are forbidden. You must use pole spears. Always spearfish with a partner, and use a buoy-and-tagline setup. The buoy marks your location for those on the surface, and you can tie your gun to the line.

EXPECT THE UNEXPECTED

Spearfishing is not like free diving, where you go to the bottom and come right back up. Spearfishing means dealing with wild animals. You have no idea what's going to happen, and you can easily lose track of time.

When you face an animal, your adrenaline is pumping. But your spear line could wrap around the fish or a shark might want your catch. Or more likely, you don't get a great shot. You shoot the fish in the guts, and since too much pressure on the line will rip out the spear, you baby the fish while reeling it in and burn crucial oxygen at depth. Or it's something mundane like ascending slowly for a cool photo—and you come up too slowly. The end result is the same. You run out of gas and drown.

That's why you don't chase fish. Everybody does this at first, but fish can stay underwater longer and swim faster. The entire foundation of spearfishing is getting the fish's curiosity or using the element of surprise.

KNOW YOUR DINNER AND SHOOT SMART

Get to know the fish you're hunting—their motivation and diet. Is it carnivorous, herbivorous? Is it feeding, mating? Realize that most fish that taste good to us also taste good to other predators. Usually, the slowest, dumbest-looking fish is not the best tasting. An exception is lionfish (see "Spinal Tap," page 207).

When taking the shot, only shoot at half the distance you can hit in a controlled environment. Where you aim depends to a degree on the fish, but generally anywhere in the head and gill plate works. If you draw a straight line back from its eyeball to the tail—that's the spinal line.

Remember, the mask will make things look slightly bigger and closer than they actually are. It takes time for your brain to adjust. Refraction only comes into play if you're throwing a spear from land (see "Pole a Boat and Gig a Flounder," page 332).

PAY YOUR TAXES AND HONOR THY FISH

If a predator wants your fish, you have to decide whether to defend it. If you fight, show aggression. Show dominance. Maybe nudge the predator with your gun. They'll usually give you space. But *never* actually spear a shark or any fish if it comes for your fish. If a shark has already bitten your fish, it's game over and you gotta pay your taxes. The shark's commitment to get your prey is quadrupled. Let the shark have the fish.

Honor thy fish means eat what you catch, which is important for a lot of reasons. First, have an ice-filled cooler ready and a game plan for caring for your fish, which makes the quality that much better. Spearfishing is the most selective way to harvest fish from the ocean. It's an incredible experience. But do it ethically. Unless you find that a caught fish is poisonous or diseased, eat it. No matter how bad it tastes. When you hold that fish in high regard and appreciate what it's given up for you, it makes the entire experience far more meaningful.

RULES FOR FOUND OBJECTS

Every diver and snorkeler has felt the temptation to take a souvenir from the sea. But should you? What's legal, ethical, sustainable—and safe—and what isn't? Here, pioneering underwater archaeologist and treasure hunter E. Lee Spence lays down the law.

BOTTOM LINE

The laws vary from state to state, country to country, and even beach to beach. If you're metal detecting, most states and towns generally allow you to keep objects you find above the mean low-water mark, but they may not. If you're on a state beach, archaeological site, or national seashore, metal detecting is probably illegal, and your metal detector might be confiscated. If you find the skull of a turtle and take it home, you might be breaking the law if it's an endangered species. Depending on the national seashore, it may even be illegal to collect fossilized shark teeth.

DIVING A SHIPWRECK OR OTHER UNDERWATER SITE

The general rule here is to leave everything alone, no matter what the country or jurisdiction. If you find something of genuine value, leave it alone until you do some research. Say, for example, you stumble on an uncharted shipwreck. You need to know whether the site has already been claimed, where exactly it lies (in international or national waters), and whether its losses were ever paid out by an insurance company. If so, the company might have a legal claim to *your* find.

COASTAL CONCERNS

Along some coastlines, the possibility of finding live ammunition from long-ago battles or naval exercises is very real. Leave ammunition alone, unless you're an expert at disarmament, metallurgy, and electrolysis. If you remove ordinance from water, the saltwater inside will evaporate, leaving expanding salts and creating a rapidly disintegrating and potentially explosive chunk of iron.

HOW TO BECOME A *NATIONAL GEOGRAPHIC* PHOTOGRAPHER

AS TOLD BY BRIAN SKERRY
Brian Skerry is a diver and *National Geographic* staff photographer who's also published ten books. He's been named Rolex's Explorer of the Year and is president and chairman of the Boston Sea Rovers.

I started out wanting to be an ocean explorer. I had no idea that would evolve into twenty years as a *National Geographic* photographer, doing twenty-eight stories, including four covers, along with everything else. There's no way in any universe I could have predicted that. I think I'm a bit of an anomaly.

EXPLORING THE OCEAN—WITH A CAMERA

I came from a working-class background in a little inland town called Uxbridge, Massachusetts. I worked in textile mills after football practice. Life was good, but I wasn't taking exotic vacations to the Bahamas. We went to local beaches and visited relatives in Newport News. The sixties were a magical time for ocean exploration—*National Geographic*, *Popular Science*, and all this stuff on TV: Cousteau, *Sea Hunt*, *Voyage to the Bottom of the Sea*, and definitely *Flipper*. I fantasized about being a game warden in Florida and having a friendly pet dolphin; out in boats, diving for sunken treasure. Man, that was the life.

When I was fifteen, I had a friend whose parents had scuba gear. I remember strapping on a tank and putting that regulator in my mouth in the shallow end—maybe 3 feet deep. I submerged my head and remember the sensation of being able to breathe. It was life-altering.

I dove in New England at local beaches, lakes, and quarries—cutting my teeth on cold-water diving. Then I attended a dive conference called the Boston Sea Rovers that had all kinds of luminaries: Jacques Cousteau and Stan Waterman, Bob Ballard and Eugenie Clark. I went with Marsha, my girlfriend— now my wife of thirty years. As photographers and filmmakers presented their work, I had an epiphany: *This is how I'll explore the ocean—with a camera.*

MY EVEREST

In the early eighties, a lot of older divers took me under their wing. I also started working unpaid for a charter boat. The captain was this cigar-smoking, blue-collar guy who drank coffee all day. I'd lay on my back, grinding the hull for painting. It was miserable. But I was learning to load gear, set anchor, run the boat, navigation, all that. I was also photographing constantly, including

German U-boats with human remains inside, and made twelve dives, two hundred feet down, to the *Andrea Doria*.

My first editorial break came in 1984, when I teamed up with a writer for the *Boston Globe*. The first story I wrote and had pictures published was for *Skin Diver* magazine in 1985. I sold stock photography to *Esquire, Sports Illustrated*, and *Men's Journal*, and did speaking engagements. Still, I spent more on those trips than I was making. So I also had a real job with a packaging company. I hated it. I remember saying to myself, *It would just be so easy to give up this crazy foolish dream*. You wake up every day and your heart is racing because you want something that may never happen. But I couldn't forget it. Working as a *National Geographic* photographer was my Everest.

My first wildlife trip out of the country wasn't until 1994—the Norwegian Arctic, photographing orca—all on my own nickel. Then it snowballed: manatees in Florida, great white sharks in California. I wrote my first book, *Complete Wreck Diving*, in 1995. Then my first quantum break came with my first *National Geographic* assignment in 1998.

MAKING A LIVING—WITH A CAMERA

My advice to emerging photographers? Take a very practical approach, while being driven by passion and love. You'll need it because this job is all about work. Someone recently asked me, "What do you do for a vacation?" I realized my last vacation was to the Grand Canyon in 1993. I do these *National Geographic* expeditions where my family can go along on the boat while I teach photography. Anybody who really wants this has to put away a bit of the romance. It's essentially a nonstop, 365-days-a-year pursuit. I work every single day in some fashion. Maybe that's just my personality, but it's also necessary.

Emerging photographers need a strategy. Where do you ultimately want to be? If the final step is a successful audience with the director of photography at *National Geographic*, you need to build a kick-ass portfolio. Start out with personal projects that have repeatability. Emulate photographers you admire, but ultimately develop your own style. Learn to shoot journalistically, too. Sure, you need spectacular natural history photos, but you also need storytelling pictures. Maybe that's working with scientists, conservationists, or fishermen. Maybe it's paying dues assisting an established photographer. A single personal project like that may take a year.

Edit yourself harshly. If you come up with thirty or forty pictures, and if you can write—or team up with someone who can write—you can create a package to shop to local magazines or newspapers, something attractive to a busy editor.

In time, you'll learn how to sell that package while honing your photography and interpersonal skills. To navigate this field, you must work with a wide spectrum of people, from PhDs to high school dropouts. Being a great editorial photographer is not only about making great pictures, but diplomacy, problem solving, and getting people to trust you.

If you stay true to that plan—and, say, sell five coverages to smaller titles—then you take the five best images from each and create a twenty-five-image portfolio. Finally, you go to meet the DP of *National Geographic* and say: *This is what I've done for the last five years.* If you've done it right, you can show that storytelling narrative, that journalistic style, along with beautiful pictures that, hopefully, do something a little different. Before that meeting, also ask yourself: *What kind of stories do I want to do? What is the voice I want to speak with, and what do I want to tell people?* Photo editors are not only looking for great photographers, but experts in their field who can bring them good ideas.

An unfortunate reality is that the big print media are in decline. The *National Geographic*s of this world don't have the budgets they used to. Photographers need multiple streams of income: speaking engagements, working for a bunch of magazines. NGOs and conservation organizations need good photography.

There's the old saying, *Follow your heart and the money will follow.* That's a little Pollyannaish, but it's the truth. At my speaking engagements, people come up and say, "Your passion is infectious." I've been doing this for forty years, and I get burned out lugging twenty cases of equipment around the world. But when I'm talking about it, it still fires me up. If you have that passion, it *will* open doors.

One thing I worry about, though: A lot of young people expect success immediately. It took me decades to get that first assignment with *National Geographic*. Yes, you can do it younger, but there are few real shortcuts. You have to maintain that proper spirit and attitude.

Also, I've heard stories about photojournalists who are passionate about conservation, but they're willing to make stuff up. They tell a very different story than the reality because it fits a narrative they want to project. If a journalist does that and gets caught, it ruins it for everybody. A lot of forces on the other side don't want us to tell the truth. And if they can cite one example where someone faked something, it gives people the ammunition to say, "Everything's faked."

Follow your dream, your heart, and your passion. Be ambitious as hell. But play by the rules.

A BRIEF HISTORY OF TIME—
UNDERWATER

Whether for food, treasure, or sheer enjoyment, humans have been attempting to return to the sea from which we sprang for as long as there have been humans. Here's a brief history of our evolution into submariners—and our re-evolution into an aquatic species.

300 million years BC Early ancestors of the *Argyroneta aquatica,* or diving bell spider, learn to weave a tightly bound web that can entrap air, thus allowing the spider to live its entire life underwater.

2500+ BC Pottery and other artifacts indicate divers are pursuing pearls from ancient Meso-potamia to China. Polynesians and Hawaiians ingeniously craft diving goggles from polished tortoise shell and air-filled bamboo rings.

1000 BC Homer writes of diving tuna-sponge fishermen who use rocks to plummet over a hun-dred feet. They fill their ears and nose with oil to help mitigate the pressure effects on their ears and sinuses.

500–300 BC Greek sculptor and diver Scyllias and his daughter, Cyana, become paid treasure divers by Persian ruler Xerxes. When Xerxes betrays the pair, taking them hostage, they escape by swim-ming underwater using reed snorkels.

Athenian and Spartan combat divers drill holes in enemy ships and clear obstructions, while professional salvage divers ply major Mediterranean ports. Aristotle describes divers using diving bells supplied by tubes so that "they can draw air from above the water, and thus may remain a long time under the sea."

Alexander the Great makes remarkable dives in a partially glass-enclosed diving bell, once remarking, "The world is damned and lost. The large and powerful fish devour the small fry."

AD 1480–1518 In his Codex Arundel, Leonardo DaVinci includes a spooky illustration of a leather diving mask, supplied with surface air from a bellows via a series of bamboo pipes. It's not known if such a device was ever built.

1535 The first reported successful deployment of Guglielmo de Lorena's single-diver diving bell at Lake Nema, outside Rome, Italy. Diver Francesco de Marchi writes: "From the waist up, it felt as if one was in a hot oven, but from the elbows down one felt a great cold."

1637 Chinese pearl divers use a reinforced breathing tube and sealed leather mask that feeds air from the surface.

1685 New Englander William Phips successfully deploys one of the first diving bells to recover a tremendous Spanish treasure (worth $42 million today) in the Caribbean Sea.

1715 English salvager John Lethbridge invents a tapered, bellows-supplied barrel that allows a diver to work with his arms free.

1825 Briton William James creates perhaps the first self-contained underwater breathing apparatus (or SCUBA). The diver's helmet is supplied with compressed air via a cast-iron belt tank.

1828 After rescuing a barn full of horses from a fire by stuffing a fire brigade's water hose up a medieval armor helmet and pumping in air instead of water, Englishman John Deane and his brother, Charles, invent "Deane's Patent Diving Dress"—a hose-fed underwater helmet with multiple viewing ports and undersea suit to keep a diver warm. Failure to keep the helmet upright could drown its inhabitant.

1831 American Charles Condert, attempting to invent his own scuba system, drowns testing it—becoming the world's first known scuba fatality.

1837 German inventor Augustus Siebe updates Deane's invention as the "Siebe Improved Diving Dress." This becomes the template for deep-sea diving suits for several generations.

1839 The "buddy system" is introduced by British salvage operator Charles William Pasley, saving countless lives. Salvage diving becomes big, dangerous business. Occasionally, the horrendous suction from a broken air hose causes so much of a deep-diver's body to be sucked and stuffed into his helmet that it takes the place of a coffin.

1864 Frenchmen Benoit Rouquayrol and Auguste Denayrouze invent a deep-sea reservoir system that allows a diver to temporarily roam the seafloor without his hoses. This system helps inspire Jules Verne's *Twenty Thousand Leagues under the Sea*.

1876 English diver Henry Fleuss creates a remarkable scuba system that supplies pure oxygen and scrubs exhaled carbon dioxide. Later versions allow dives of two-plus hours.

1878 Frenchman Paul Bert publishes *La Pression Barométrique*. His study of the effects of altitude and depth makes revolutionary suggestions about the nature of decompression sickness and recommends gradual ascent to combat its effects.

1900–1907 Augustus Siebe's "recompression chamber" is first used to treat "divers' palsey," aka the bends. Briton J. S. Haldene authors the first set of tables that help divers ascend at a proper rate.

1918 Three Japanese inventors—Riichi Watanichi, Kanezo Ogushi, and Kyuhachi Katao—devise the "peerless respirator," a groundbreaking system that looks remarkably like a modern scuba system. Air flow from back-mounted tanks is triggered by squeezing a valve with your teeth.

1943 Frenchmen Jacques Cousteau and Emil Gagnan revolutionize diving with the creation of the "aqua-lung." The system employs a backpack-mounted high-pressure tank and respirator to precisely meter and deliver air by simple, natural inhalation. The Aqua-Lung makes the undersea kingdom accessible to the world. Modern scuba setups today still use the same basic technology.

FISHING

HOW SMART IS A FISH?

BY CULUM BROWN

Dr. Culum Brown is a professor at Macquarie University and assistant editor of the *Journal of Fish Biology*. He is one of the world's leading experts on fish biology and cognition.

How smart is a fish? Smarter than you'd think.

The human expectation of fish intelligence, learning, and memory is extremely low, but there's basically no scientific reason to separate fish from other animals. Their brain structure is the same. Even the evolutionary history of humans is mostly a story about fish. We're basically made up of fish genes with a few little tweaks. We have this silly-looking cortex slopped over the top of our brain, and the cortex is a great thing, but a lot of its functions are stolen from other parts of the brain—parts that fish have.

We're up to 35,000 or so fish species, with 150 to 200 new ones discovered every year, and all the tests we've done show they're basically just as smart as any other animal. They're complex social creatures. Their spatial learning and memory capabilities are as good. Their cognitive retention rates somewhere between rats and dogs. They clearly have preferences for certain individuals. Researchers at Bimini Sharklab have found shark social networks.

Fish are renowned for schooling—they not only learn things by themselves but from others. There's social learning that accumulates across generations. This cultural transmission of information is most often about movement and migration: Where's the most appropriate place to mate, feed, lay eggs? With overfishing, such as with cod, a kind of cultural loss occurs that is just so bad for a species—and for its recovery.

There are fascinating examples of social complexity between species, too. Take grouper and moray eels. Morays hunt the coral crevices hoping to snare any hiding fish. Grouper, on the other hand, tend to cruise over the top of a reef and grab anything in the open. If a grouper is feeding, fish hide in the coral. If a moray's hunting, fish come out.

So the grouper shakes his head to signal to the moray, *Let's go catch some fish*. Grouper actually have preferred partners—a "best mate" moray they've had success with. When they get together and coordinate, no place is safe, and their kill rate goes up massively.

The very survival of the cleaner wrasse fish depends on being socially savvy. They hang out at coral outcroppings, and they control and defend their cleaning stations from other cleaner fish. They have thousands of social encounters a day. Generally, another fish comes up and does a "clean me" display: They flare gills and fins and wriggle from side to side. Then the wrasse comes out, takes off parasites, and cleans teeth. They always prioritize the transient strangers, recognizing, *This is not a fish I see very often, so the chances of it waiting around for me are slim*. The regular fish already like to be cleaned by that fish, so they're willing to wait in line.

The other thing cleaners do, occasionally, is take a little bite out of a client. Experiments have shown they'd rather have a bit of tasty fish than the mucous, detritus, and parasites they usually get. The client then swims off, but the cleaner, as a mode of reconciliation, chases after the fish and does this fanning motion along the back of the client, like a back massage. This seems to placate them, and they come back to be cleaned.

That interaction led these researchers to put a back-rubbing mechanism in a fish tank. It turns out that, given the option, fish will give themselves a daily back rub. If you measure cortisols or the stress hormones in their blood—the same hormones humans have—the ones getting back rubs are less stressed.

Fish use tools as well. Fish fan and squirt water to uncover things quite a lot. Archer fish even manipulate water to shoot down bugs. A colleague of mine, Scott Gardner, was diving in the right place at the right time and heard this tap, tap, tap noise. A tuskfish with a massive clam in its mouth had positioned itself between these pyramid-shaped rocks and was smashing the daylights out of the clam. Obviously, this wasn't the first time the animal had done this, but it was the first time a fish had been documented using a tool. After we published that, two weeks later, a guy in California calls with video of the same behavior by another species of tuskfish—and since then, we've seen fantastic examples of lots of fish doing similar things all over the world.

We know, too, that fish can feel pain. About five people in the world argue against this fact—and it only takes a few dissenters to cast doubt in the public mind. Their argument is really basic: Essentially, in humans, pain is mostly processed in the cerebral cortex. Since fish have no cerebral cortex, they must not feel pain. But almost all animals lack a human-like cerebral cortex, and yet we know many animals feel pain. Humans also use their cortex to process visual information. Are we suggesting that other animals can't see because they don't have a cortex? It's just a stupid argument.

I don't know why we have this tendency to separate fish from other animals. I think part of the reason is a phylogenetic difference. Fish are unfamiliar. People say it's also because we don't hear them cry out in distress. But if you stick a hydrophone underwater, you hear a dawn and dusk chorus like with birds on land. To understand the aquatic environment, you have to spend time underwater, in their world.

TEN ESSENTIAL FISHING KNOTS

You really need only a handful of knots for fishing, such as these ten crucial, classic ones. Some lingo: "Tag end" simply means the end of the line. "Lubricate" means to wet with water or saliva; never use anything petroleum-based, like WD-40, since it can repel fish and degrade your line.

1. **Arbor knot:** For tying any line to any spool.

   a. Wrap line around spool.

   b. Using tag end of line, tie an overhand knot around running end.

   c. Tie a second overhand knot at the end of the tag end.

   d. Lubricate, cinch over spool, and trim tag.

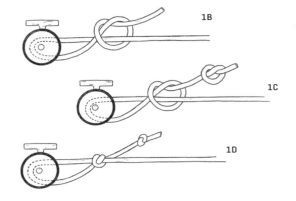

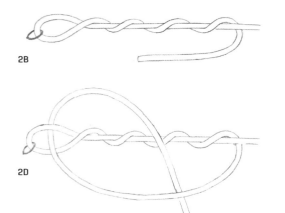

2. **Improved clinch knot:** For attaching monofilament or fluorocarbon fishing line to swivel or hook.

   a. Send tag end of fishing line through hook eyelet.

   b. Twist around running end three to seven times (heavier lines use fewer twists).

   c. Return tag end through loop at eyelet.

   d. Send tag end back through last loop made.

   e. Lubricate and cinch down using thumbnail and forefinger.

3. **Palomar knot:** For attaching braid, mono-filament, or fluorocarbon fishing line to swivel or hook.

a. Double line on itself, making a loop.

b. Send loop through hook or swivel eyelet.

c. Tie overhand knot in loop.

d. Pass running end (loop) over hook shank and tip.

e. Pull line back over eyelet.

f. Lubricate and cinch down above eyelet.

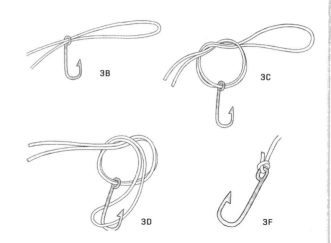

5. **Albright knot:** For adjoining two lines of different diameter.

a. Form a loop in thicker line.

b. Pass one end of thinner line through loop; tidily wrap it around itself about ten times.

c. Pass loop back through original loop over thicker line.

d. Lubricate and pull tight.

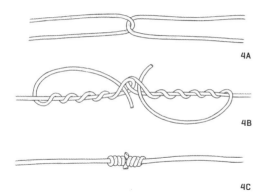

4. **Blood knot:** For adjoining two lines of similar diameter. This pairs two improved clinch knots.

a. Overlap the ends of both lines, so each has a tag end of about 4 inches.

b. On each line, make a clinch knot: Wrap each tag end five times around its own line, and send tag end through loop with other line.

c. Lubricate lines and pull in opposite directions, cinching down until tight.

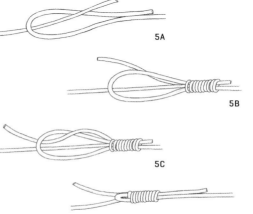

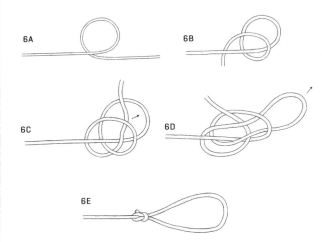

6. Perfection loop: For light or slippery line, and for lures or flies that require more "action."

a. Form a small closed loop.

b. Form a larger loop over top of original.

c. Place tag end between two loops (under large loop, over small).

d. Pull large loop through by reaching through small loop.

e. Lubricate and pull all four "legs"—both loops, running and tag ends—tight.

7. J knot: For splicing lines (like a main line to leader), especially to monofilament.

a. Lay main line and leader (or backing) parallel, overlapping about 12 inches.

b. Form an overhand knot, pulling leader through loop.

c. Send line and leader through backside of loop, pulling leader through again.

d. Repeat entire process twice.

e. Lubricate, cinch, and trim all four ends.

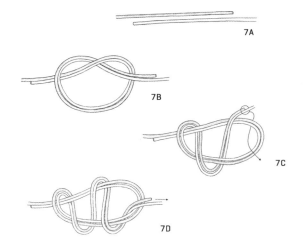

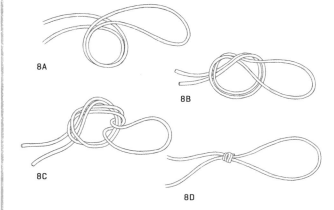

8. Double surgeon's loop: For tying a loop in a line or leader of a snelled hook.

a. Double line over itself.

b. Tie double overhand knot.

c. Bring double loop through first knot to make a second overhand knot.

d. Lubricate, cinch, and trim tag end.

9. **Snell knot:** For tying a hook to main line or leader; especially useful for thicker lines.

a. Pass tag end through hook eyelet.

b. Make a small loop and wrap tag end around hook and inside loop five times.

c. Pass tag end through loop.

d. Lubricate, pull tight, and trim end.

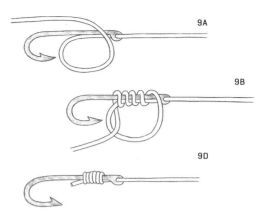

10. **Rapala knot:** For tying a lure or fly to a line, especially for "freer" or looser action.

a. Tie overhand knot about 5 inches from tag end of line, leaving loose.

b. Insert tag end through hook eyelet.

c. Run tag end back through loop.

d. Make at least three twists in line above loop (more twists for lighter line).

e. Pass tag end through original loop.

f. Pass tag end through last loop formed.

g. Lubricate, cinch, and trim.

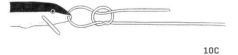

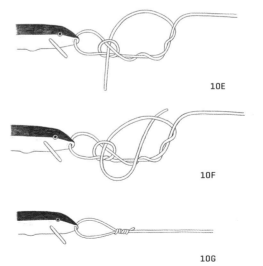

YOUR TACKLE BOX:
THE "MUST-HAVE" GEAR LIST

A well-supplied tackle box, which includes repair tools, is the difference between a day spent fishing and a day spent cursing. What follows isn't a list of every fish hook, fly, sinker, swivel, spinner, and float you need. Gather a healthy assortment of terminal tackle: all the various stuff you tie to the end of your line. Also, make sure your gear is saltwater-specific; otherwise, it'll rust faster than you can say *Titanic*.

What follows is the stuff you only discover you need after the cursing starts. Before each item, just say silently or out loud, "Oh crap, I need . . ."

- A metal file for sharpening rusted or dulled hooks.

- Stainless-steel needle-nose pliers: for countless reasons—not least of which for turning fish loose in the best possible shape—but absolutely for changing out hooks and any vital, unexpected reel repair.

- A wire crimper, a leader with crimping sleeves, and a small spool of stainless-steel wire—for salvaging, with a little ingenuity, any piece of tackle, especially crumbling lures and unraveling flies.

- Extra rod tips and guides, since these break all the time. Make sure they fit your rod.

- Thread for holding lures and flies together. Thread also helps stabilize a replacement rod tip or guide (along with head cement).

- A small bag of extra feathers to create a makeshift jigtail or fix an unraveling fly.

- Head cement (or nail polish) to glue thread, lines, and flies. While a bottle of clear nail polish is comparable, head cement will outlast polish, and most fly-fishing stores sell it.

- Black nail polish for replacing the worn-off eyes on a favorite lure after a thousand casts.

- Reel grease for a suddenly balky reel. The more strain you put on dirty or under-lubricated gears, the worse they can get.

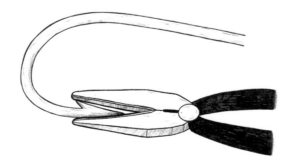

CATCH A FISH WITH A HANDLINE

Along with spearfishing (page 284), fishing by handline is one of the oldest methods of outwitting aquatic creatures. Handlining is the ultimate purist's pursuit. The gear is rudimentary, compact, and always ready: snelled hooks, sinkers, swivels, and a few fishing lines.

Gear up: A "snelled" hook is tied to keep the hook from spinning and to keep the line from weakening at the point where it's tied (see "Ten Essential Fishing Knots," page 300). In addition, you need a spool or spindle for your fishing line. Use a handlining "yo-yo"—a circular plastic spool specifically created for the pursuit—or a kite spool or even an empty water bottle. Generally, you need about a hundred feet of line of varying test strength and various hook sizes, depending on your quarry, plus your standard leaders and weights. If you're after sharp-toothed fish like barracuda, use a wire leader so the fish doesn't chew through your line. If casting across jagged rocks, use heavier, thicker line to withstand scrapes.

Cast: First, make sure your line is ready to "run" or unravel freely. A yo-yo spool has a gradually sloping "freespooling" edge on one side that allows this. Place the yo-yo spool on the ground with this edge facing upward or hold it in your hand facing outward. The yo-yo spool's other edge is designed to hold the line in place during retrieval and recoiling. With any other type of spindle, unspool your outgoing line and let it rest on the pier, dock, or deck before casting so that it is clear to run freely.

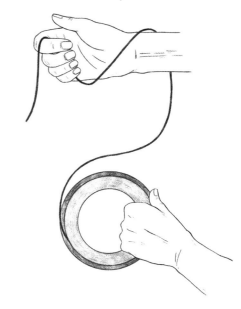

Casting is a bit like throwing a rope or lasso. Hold the line a foot or two from the weight at the end. To generate momentum, swing the line horizontally overhead or vertically at your side. When ready, let go while simultaneously thrusting your arm in the direction you want to throw the bait. Avoid a trip to the emergency room by practicing first with rubber weights in an open area.

Set the hook: Protect your line-retrieval hand with a thick glove or a wrapped handkerchief (or protect both hands). Hold the line firmly and wait until you sense tension on the line from a biting fish, then yank the line vertically to set the hook into the upper corner of the fish's jaw (the best place to hook a fish by any method). Now it's pure tug-of-war. Tailor the pressure on the line to how the fish reacts: where it swims, how hard it fights, and whether it might be making for a rock or a hole.

Reel it in: Finesse the fish toward the boat by reeling in the line hand over hand, carefully dropping the retrieved line into a cleared area or a bucket. Retrieving a handline can be messy and even dangerous, especially in confined spaces like boats. Always keep the line clear of legs and feet, and be ready to let go, especially when fighting larger fish, lest you become entangled and even dragged into the drink. You wouldn't be the first.

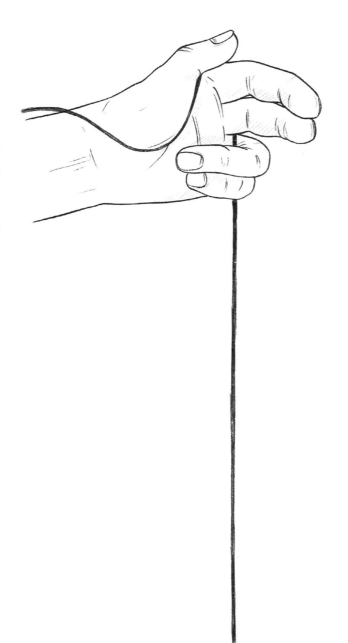

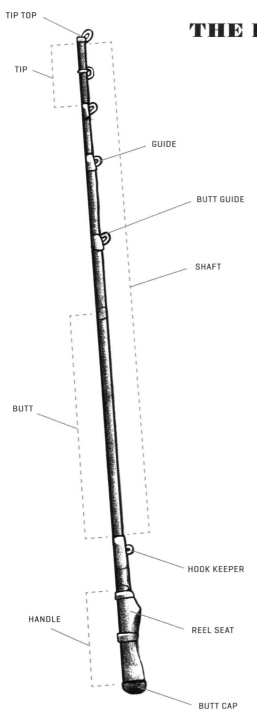

TIP TOP

TIP

GUIDE

BUTT GUIDE

SHAFT

BUTT

HOOK KEEPER

HANDLE

REEL SEAT

BUTT CAP

FIRST-TIME ANGLERS:
THE ROD, THE REEL, THE CAST

Fishing with a rod and reel is easy. But casting technique still takes hours of hands-on practice to do well.

When it comes to choosing the best rod-and-reel setup, the first question is always: What are you trying to catch? For fish under 8 pounds, get what's called "light tackle." This generally means a lightweight rod with a line whose "test" strength will support an 8-pound fish without breaking. For bigger fish, choose "heavy tackle" that's rated for the size of your quarry. See also "On and Off the Hook" (page 311).

Also consider your goal. Heavier tackle and bigger, barbed hooks improve your chances of successfully landing your fish. But lighter tackle and smaller, barbless hooks cause far less injury to fish and help ensure their survival upon release. We strongly recommend barbless hooks for this reason.

A ROD IS A FANCY POLE

The variety of test strengths and materials aside, a rod is a fancy pole.

Get a natural-cork handle, which transmits the slightest hint of a fish's bite. In the handle is the reel seat, or where you mount the reel. The shaft is lined with guide loops that keep the line straight; the final one is, indeed, actually called the "tip top." A recommended option is a "hook keeper" loop near the handle, to attach the hook for safety and transport.

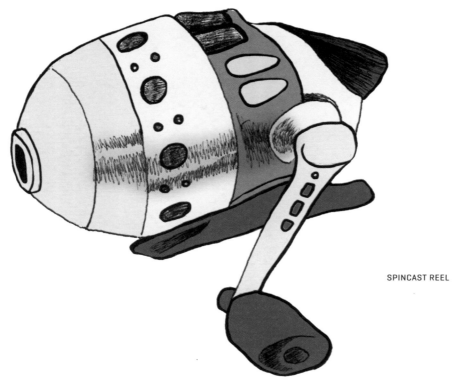

SPINCAST REEL

REEL TIME: THREE CHOICES

Beginning anglers need only concern themselves with three basic reels. All are easy to deploy.

THE SPINCAST REEL

The easiest reel of all, the spincast is also known as a closed-face reel because the spool of line is fully covered. Zebco's original, famed 33 Spincaster (first sold in 1954) is still a favorite because of its dead-simple operation and revolutionary ability to prevent line-entangling back-lashes (when the line lands in the water but the spool keeps unwinding). Plus, the Spincaster's thumb-actuated button permits one-handed casts with a flick of the wrist.

THE SPINNING REEL

Unlike the other reels, the spinning reel has a stationary spool, and a roller rotates around it to wind the line. Originally developed to cure back-lash, spinning reels are great for long-distance casting and light-line fishing. Because reel and guides are at the bottom of the rod, it's easy to detect minute movements from fish bites. Drag adjustment—for fighting your fish—is easy using a simple knob. The classic reel is the Mitchell 300, whose descendants are still available today.

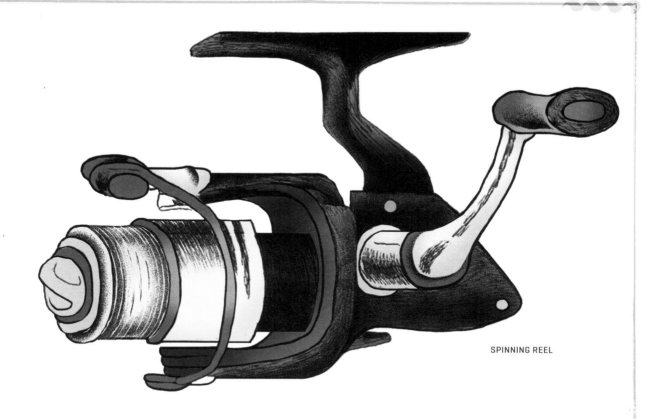

SPINNING REEL

THE BAITCAST REEL

Around since the 1800s, the baitcast reel is the oldest design. It's a favorite of fishing purists due to its relative simplicity, the distance of its casts (if hurled properly and with finesse), and its ability to spool huge amounts of line—crucial for long fights with big fish (e.g., Quint in *Jaws*). To prevent backlashes during casting, you adjust the tension of the reel with a tension knob and modulate the feed of the unspooling line using thumb pressure.

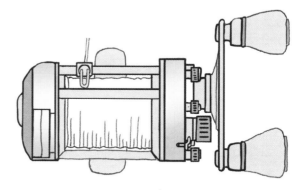

BAITCAST REEL

THE CAST

Like casting a fly, mastery of these reels is an art. But if fish are directly below, just drop your line. See also "Types of Bait" (page 318).

Casting a spincast reel: First, in all cases, let about a foot of line hang from the rod tip. Turn your wrist sideways to maximize your range of motion, with your elbow just above 45 degrees. Then flick your wrist forward while pushing the button. It's that easy.

Casting a spinning reel: Flip the handle on the roller and loop the line over your index finger. Cast with both hands for more heft and control: The hand holding the line is at the reel foot, so put the other at the handle base. To cast, release the line from your index finger just as you cast the rod; timing is everything. When the lure and line reach their destination, flip the roller and start reeling to take slack out of the line.

Casting a baitcast reel: Start with your rod reeled in. Raise the rod and tighten the tension spool on the right side of the reel (reel facing upward) by spinning clockwise so that the bait does not fall to the ground when the thumb button reel lock is released. Now loosen the tension spool just until the bait falls slowly to the ground with the button released. Next tighten up the brake on the left side of the reel to nearly the tightest setting. This will prevent a "birds nest" or backlash in the line. You can fine-tune the braking after your first few casts.

The cast. Push down the "release button" (in most cases this will be thumb-actuated) and place your thumb gently on the spool to keep the line from unspooling. Don't whip the rod as you would with a spincast or spinning reel, but make a smooth cast with your whole arm. A sidearm cast is usually best. As the rod reaches the end of the cast, release your thumb just enough to let the line unspool and feather the unspooling line gently with your thumb until the lure hits the water to prevent backlash. Lock the spool to reel it in. (On some baitcast reels this will happen as soon as you start reeling.)

ON AND OFF THE HOOK: SALTWATER **FISHING HOOKS**

When choosing saltwater hooks, consider size, gauge, metal, shape, and barb.

Size: Hook sizes are based on the space between the point and the shank. But the number scale is strange: A medium-size 1 hook is about 1.25 inches long, and higher numbers, up to 32, indicate smaller hooks. Bigger hooks, above size 1, use /0. So size 1/0 ("one-aught") is around 1.5 inches long; these go up to 9/0 for the biggest fish.

Also consider shank length. Long-shanked hooks are best for sharp-toothed fish like mackerel, which can cut fishing line. Use short-shank hooks for smaller, "soft-mouth" fish like trout or whiting.

Gauge, or thickness: Similarly, use thin-gauge hooks for fragile bait like shrimp (so they move more naturally) or to catch smaller fish (to pierce the mouth more easily). Use thicker hooks for toothier, tougher fish.

Metal: Regular carbon steel hooks flex better than stainless and salt water will eventually rust them away should your fish escape while still hooked.

J HOOK   CIRCLE HOOK

Shape: Most anglers use the standard J hook, but when fully swallowed, these damage a fish's innards when removed. Mortality studies suggest it's better to leave in a deeply embedded hook than remove it yourself—fish usually find a way to eject it. Circle hooks are less damaging to fish and are popular with catch-and-release fishing. The hook's circular design keeps it from lodging in a fish's stomach or throat, while still hooking the fish's mouth. To work properly, circle hooks must be tied with a snell knot (page 303).

Barbless hooks: Removing barbed hooks can injure fish so badly they die even when released. Consider using barbless for all fishing. Either buy or create your own by crimping the barb with needle-nose pliers and filing down the rough bits.

REMOVING A HOOK FROM YOUR FLESH

Not only are barbless hooks kinder to fish, they slide out easily if you accidentally hook yourself. If a barbed hook catches you . . .

Advance and cut: If possible, push the hook forward till the barb emerges from your skin and snip it off with wire cutters. Then slide the now-unbarbed end back out.

Tie and pull: Otherwise, steel yourself. Tie line onto the hook's bend, press the shaft against the skin, and yank hard, so it exits the entry wound. Commitment is key. Then clean the wound really well (see "The Deepest Cut," page 224).

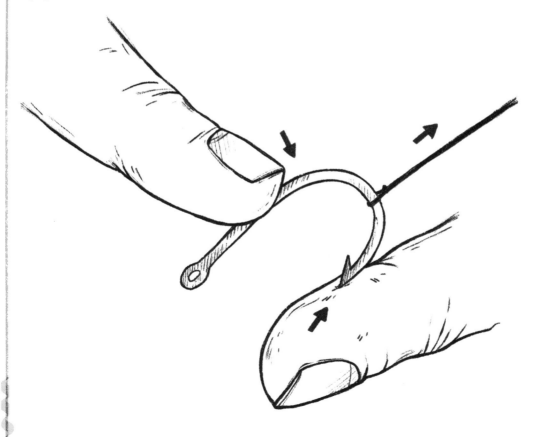

D.I.Y. ANGLER: MAKE A FISH HOOK

All fishing equipment can be improvised. String or wire can substitute for line, and bamboo or branches for a pole. Flexible dogwood or willow saplings are best, about 1 inch in diameter and 5 feet long; if you have time, soak the sapling in saltwater for a day to make it more durable.

Fish hooks must be sharp, but almost any hardened material can work. Shell hooks are ancient and formidable, if labor intensive to craft. Here are four much easier methods:

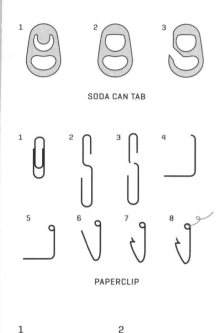

SODA CAN TAB

PAPERCLIP

GORGE HOOK

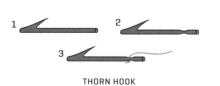

THORN HOOK

1. **Soda can tab:** Using pliers or wire cutters, cut two parallel 45 degree angles into one section of the tab, so it resembles a J hook. Cut a sharp hook. Tie line to the tab's other closed section.

2. **Paper clip:** Open and cut or break the paper clip in half so the metal forms a J shape. Curl or bend the tip of the longer "shank" to form an eyelet to attach the line. Cut the end of the "hook" at a 45-degree angle to make a sharp tip. Or, open a safety pin and use that.

3. **Gorge hook:** Like a tiny javelin, this simple, ancient design is an unbent shard, sharpened on both ends, and tied by line in the middle. You can use a fat splinter, needle, even a toothpick. Cut a groove in the middle of the shaft so the line will stay in place. The fish must swallow the entire assembly, so don't make it too long, and wait to set the hook to ensure the bait is swallowed. Be aware: This hook *always kills the fish,* so only use when you must.

4. **Thorn hook:** Small fish can even be caught with a thorn hook. Leave about an inch of stem for the shank; on the end, cut a groove to wrap the line or cordage around. Or whittle a small piece of wood into the same shape.

SALTWATER FLY-FISHING: A PRIMER WITH JIMBO MEADOR

In the ocean, most people use a traditional, baitcasting rod and reel. That's fine, but sometimes tedious: Cast, lose your bait, reel in, rehook new bait, repeat. The lightning-quick action of a fly rod lets you cast over and over to a precise spot—once you perfect your technique. Second, casting a fly rod, contrary to popular mystique, is terribly fun, remarkably easy, and highly addictive. So we asked fly-fishing expert Jimbo Meador to share his advice on this lifetime pursuit.

YOUR ROD

A good beginner saltwater fly rig is an eight or nine-weight, 9-foot rod with a spool of "weight forward" floating line on the reel. This line is thick and heavy along its first 30 to 40 feet and tapers to a thinner width "running line" after that. The weighted line replaces the weighted lure or lead at the end of the traditional rod and reel. In short, the line is the weight. The fly is just along for the ride.

With a simple fly cast, you basically perform two casts. The first is a sort of "windup" back-cast, and the second is the forward cast that releases the line. Key to both is smooth acceleration, a straight line, and an abrupt halt at the end of the cast. This halt flexes the rod tip and gives an energetic snap to the line, unfurling the line and propelling it forward. If you don't stop abruptly, the line will continue around in an arc and not land where you want.

3

4

THE PERFECT CAST IN SIX STEPS

Two things: Keep your casting wrist locked straight, not bent, which helps the rod stop abruptly. A good reminder is putting the end of the rod handle in your shirt sleeve. Also, these instructions are for an overhand cast, but you can cast horizontally using the same exact motion.

1. Strip out the weighted segment of line from the tip so that it's as far out as you want to cast—20 to 30 feet.

2. Begin with your rod pointing toward but not touching the ground. Hold the rod above the spool and grip the line with your index finger to prevent additional line from unspooling.

3. Draw the rod up and backward, accelerating smoothly until it's around 45 degrees over your shoulder (roughly between nine and twelve o'clock). Watch the rod's progress and halt the cast abruptly to set line in motion.

4. Pause briefly, then cast the rod forward, accelerating smoothly to set the line in forward motion.

5. Halt the cast abruptly at eye level and point the rod tip toward where you want the fly to go.

6. Slowly lower the rod toward the water, but don't touch the water.

Repeat, over and over, to put the fly in a better spot. If you get a bite, smoothly lift the rod upward and yank back on the line to set the hook, and then strip and/or reel in the line.

SEVEN SALTWATER FLIES

In fly-fishing, it's shocking that a bunch of feathers tied together around a hook can look enough like a squid or an anchovy to fool a hungry fish. But something happens to those feathers beneath the sea's surface: They dance, reacting to the slightest push of current or wave and taking on a life of their own. Provided the fly angler has timed and placed the cast just right, they can be irresistible.

The one attribute that defines fly-fishing is obsessive meticulousness. There's merit in this—part of being a good angler is preparation, and nothing is more essential to fly-fishing than flies. Anglers typically have boxes and boxes of flies—many of which may never even hit the water.

There are thousands of saltwater fly patterns designed to emulate every species of prey, but these seven might be the only ones you'll ever need.

1. **The Clouser Minnow:** This baitfish imitator is designed to suspend in the water column between "strips" of your fly line. The clouser minnow comes across to a salmon or a snapper as anything from baitfish—like a sardine or menhaden (or "moss bunker")—to a squid or even a small eel. Arguably as old as saltwater fly-fishing itself, this may be the single-most-popular saltwater fly in America, if not the world. Works weightless or with tungsten or bead chain eyes.

2. **Lefty's Deceiver:** Designed by pioneering saltwater fly fisherman Bernard "Lefty" Kreh, Lefty's deceiver is another baitfish imitator that works well with a weighted head—popularly with tungsten "dumbbell" eyes. Fish a weightless black pattern for nighttime outings. Counterintuitively, black is the easiest color for fish to see at night, especially looking up toward dock lights, stars, or the moon. Oftentimes, a fish can't even see a white fly at night.

3. **The Crazy Charlie:** Invented by Andros Island native Charlie Smith—the first Bahamian to own a bonefishing lodge—the "crazy Charlie" is a favorite fly on the sandflats; no fly box is without one between Abaco Island and Ascension Bay. It's a handy fly to learn to tie; work up a half dozen colors and that's all you need for a successful day.

CLOUSER MINNOW

LEFTY'S DECEIVER

CRAZY CHARLIE

CHERNOBYL CRAB

SEADUCER

4. **The Chernobyl Crab:** Fish on the flats—be they mud or sand—primarily key in on crustaceans. The crazy Charlie is designed to imitate shrimp, while other flies imitate crabs, but the Chernobyl crab, as the name might imply, imitates both. We may never know exactly what fish make of this mutant hybrid species, but it fools them nonetheless, and it spares the indecisive fly angler from having to decide which crustacean fly to use.

5. **The Classic Hairwing:** The classic hairwing is one of the original saltwater flies, a crossover from a freshwater streamer most popularly fished for salmon and trout. Its beauty lies in its simplicity: As basic as any fly gets, the hairwing can be tied using different colors to imitate a vast array of different fish and eel species.

6. **The Seaducer:** Originally designed for tarpon on the flats, the seaducer (or sea ducer) has a proven track record up the US East Coast for bluefish, striped bass, and even tuna.

7. **The Whistler:** Dubbed "the whistler" for the sound that its bead chain eyes make as they're flung through the air, this fly gives off vibrations underwater and works well in deep, open water for pelagic species as well as murky, backcountry waters for snook, tarpon, or striped bass.

CLASSIC HAIRWING

WHISTLER

TYPES OF BAIT

Bait preference and technique vary by angler and type of catch. Most of all, keep hooks sharp and clean. Rust weakens hooks and can transmit tetanus. Barbed circle hooks minimize fish injury and keep bait secure.

Live Fish: If using minnows, use smaller hooks (~2/0). Lead the tip of the hook from the bottom of the mouth up through the top, between the jaw and the nose, so the fish can still swim. If using larger fish (menhaden, herring), use larger hooks (~4/0 to 9/0) and hook the fish's mouth or hook roughly halfway between the dorsal fin and the caudal (tail) fin, above the spine. Don't puncture the spine, or the baitfish will be paralyzed.

Cut Fish: With chunks of fish (chicken nugget–sized), hook in one side of the spine and out the other with smaller bait and hooks, or in and out the same side if using larger bait and hooks (~4/0+). Expose the tip for a clean hookset. Strips or long, thin fillets can be effective bait for flounder, striped bass, and grouper, especially when attached to a lure such as a jig. Fillet an isosceles triangle-shaped strip several inches long, sending the hook through the skin side and out the flesh.

Shrimp: Tricky to hook and keep alive, but many fish will happily eat a dead shrimp. Use a 1/0 to 3/0 hook. For drift fishing, hook shrimp up from the chin and out between the two dark patches in the carapace. For distance casting or bottom drift fishing, hook through last "joint" before the tail. In weed beds, use this method, but leave the hook buried to avoid snagging.

Crab: Use a 1/0 to a 6/0 hook. Dead or alive, insert the hook through one rear leg joint and out another, on the same side of the carapace. Remove the claws; wise fish consider them a threat.

Mollusks: Shuck mollusks before baiting. On clams, cut off most of the foot and hook as many times as possible, burying the final turn in the soft belly.

Fish make up three of the seven phyla of vertebrates on Earth: *Agnatha* (jawless, scaleless fish, such as lampreys and hagfishes), *Chondrichthyes* (cartilaginous fish, or sharks and rays), and *Osteichthyes* (bony fishes like tuna, salmon, and basses). How different are they from terrestrial creatures? Well, for one, they don't "sleep" the way mammals do. Most are believed to rest, either by slowing their metabolism and floating in "suspended animation" or by holing up in caves, nests, sand, or mud.

Most fish—sharks excluded—bear a protective slime that defends them from parasites, diseases, and various pathogens. Sharks have rough, sandpapery skin and, thanks to hundreds of millions of years of evolution, an ability to fend off cancers and many diseases. Fish, like birds, have sensory organs called lateral lines that alert them to movement. Sharks and rays have incredibly sensitive electroreceptors (known as Ampullae of Lorenzini). Meanwhile, bony fishes usually have two air-filled sacs called swim, air, or gas bladders that allow them to regulate buoyancy at depth.

Fish also possess the widest-ranging life-span of all vertebrates. The pygmy goby only lives about fifty-nine days. The average life-span of freshwater fish is one to three years, while marine fish average about twelve years. Alaskan rockfish and the equally popular orange roughy can reach centenarian age—maybe even 175 years. Then there's the ostensibly interminable Greenland shark, which can survive upwards of four centuries. But that still doesn't beat the North Atlantic quahog clam. The oldest on record is 507-year-old "Ming" (1499–2006), named for the Chinese dynasty during which it was born, and accidentally killed by scientists trying to determine its age. Still, that's just a hiccup for *Monorhaphis chuli*, a species of deep-sea sponge, and a living animal, that is believed to live upwards of 11,000 years.

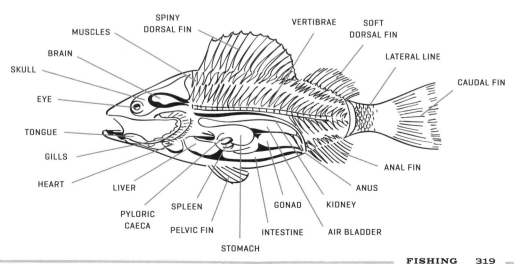

SPINY
DORSAL FIN · MUSCLES · BRAIN · SKULL · EYE · TONGUE · GILLS · HEART · LIVER · PYLORIC CAECA · SPLEEN · PELVIC FIN · STOMACH · INTESTINE · GONAD · KIDNEY · AIR BLADDER · ANUS · ANAL FIN · CAUDAL FIN · LATERAL LINE · SOFT DORSAL FIN · VERTEBRAE

WHAT'S THE BEST TIME TO FISH?

Tide is time in the ocean, and it means food for fish. Knowing when (as well as where) fish are eating is key to catching them, and—according to an extensive study in the 1930s by famed fishing author John Alden Knight—three factors help determine when fish are most active: the tide, the sun, and the moon. That said, weather and other local conditions also affect a fish's schedule.

GOING WITH THE TIDE

Twice per lunar day—with some exceptions—the sea swells and abates, or vice versa, flushing shorelines and coastal waterways with a fresh dose of oxygen- and nutrient-rich H_2O vital for fish (see "Sitting on the Dock of the Bay," page 172).

Tide factors heavily into feeding time for inshore fish, and different fish feed on different parts of the tide, so deciding the best time depends on the species you're after. Most ambush predators are active between tides, when they can let the running tidal current do the work while they lie in wait, behind structures to ambush weaker-swimming prey. Many scavengers and foragers, on the other hand, delay their quests for food until near dead high and low tides, when currents abate and prowling through weed beds and structures requires less energy.

Many fishermen prefer to fish during the first and last third of a tide (high or low), or the two hours on either side of a tide, when the water is moving, but not rushing. When fishing offshore where tidal variations aren't great, currents take precedent over tide, and fishing between two opposing currents is often the best bet.

THE RHYTHMS OF SUN AND MOON

Aside from seasonal spawning and migration, when fish gorge themselves as much as they can, dawn and dusk are almost always the best times to fish. Once the sun is high in the sky, many fish become lethargic or wary of predation, unless an easy opportunity like a large aggregation of baitfish presents itself.

Some hypothesize that fish behavior correlates with the moon phase. While "solunar theory," as it's called, is scientifically accepted, the debate over when fish are most active remains subjective, if not a complete mystery. The moon's phases are broken into quarters, with smaller "neap" tides during half-moons, when the sun, Earth, and moon are at a right angle, and bigger "spring" tides during new and full moons, when the Earth, sun, and moon are in line.

All manner of lunar variables can come into play, depending on seasons and the behavior patterns of predator and prey. In New England, for example, striped bass feed heavily on small worms that burrow into the mud and follow the moon phase to spawn. The worms seem most active in the dead of night, several days before or after a spring tide, and that's indeed a good time to catch a New England striper.

Other fish are said to be more active simply because of the increased flow of water from bigger lunar tides. More water flowing means more baitfish and other prey are at the tide's mercy, creating a veritable smorgasbord for predatory gamefish.

If you want a deeper dive into all this, pick up the Farmers' Almanac Fishing Calendar, whose predictions are based on lunar phases and historical catch records.

HOW TO CATCH A CRAB

As with fish, catch legalities vary with crabs, so know what's legal when it comes to crab size, sex, catch methods, and locations. Then, after catching, dump crabs into a slurry of ice-filled saltwater before killing humanely (page 323). Also keep the following in mind:

- A crab's left claw is the cutter and usually faster. The right one is the crusher—slower and stronger. Both hurt.

- Catch crabs ecologically with the remains of fish you've already caught to eat.

- If you catch a female with eggs, let her go to procreate, even when and where not legally required.

- To grab a crab, hold the crab down—claws pointing toward you—with a bucket and carefully slide the bucket forward until you can get a hand around each claw. Or, carefully shift to a one-handed hold by extending claws in front with tips close together and then grabbing both claws with one hand.

METHODS FOR CRABBING

Trotline: Cut 30 feet of long line (⅛-inch or thinner) and attach a series of 3-foot-long strings about 5 feet apart with a half-pound weight at the end of the line. Securely tie fish heads, fish entrails, tripe, or turkey/chicken necks to the attached strings, then heave it off a dock or a tidal creek beach in shallow water. Wait twenty minutes, or until the line is clearly twitching and tightening as crabs tear at the bait. Reel the line slowly to ensure feeding crabs remain feeding. Stealthily slide a net under crabs, scoop them off, and shake them into a saltwater-and-ice-filled cooler.

Single Line: Same as a trotline, only with one piece of bait at the end.

Traps: A crab trap or "crab pot" is the low-effort method. In the trap, fill the bait area, heave into the water with a line attached to your dock or boat, and haul in an hour or two later.

Caution: Never leave traps in the water overnight or unattended. First, countless terrapin turtles die annually by drowning in unchecked traps. Terrapins are ecologically vital for salt marsh health and range all along the US Atlantic and Gulf Coasts. Second, when tidal flats drain, they can expose and kill crabs in traps, and your bait will stink up the neighborhood. If you find abandoned "ghost traps," remove them so they won't keep killing creatures.

COMMON TYPES OF CRABS

Blue crabs: The most commonly caught and eaten crustaceans, blue crabs live in brackish to fully salty Atlantic tidal zones from Nova Scotia to Uruguay. With big, omnivorous appetites for nearly anything living or dead, and powerful cobalt-tinted pinchers, they're ornery and, if the water's warm, very agile.

Soft-Shell Blue Crabs: During spring and summer, blue crabs molt. Right after they shed their shells is when you can catch "soft-shell crabs." Oftentimes, female soft shells will seek protection beneath bigger male "Jimmy" crabs as their shells harden over two to four days. These are called "doublers." Females will follow Jimmies into traps to mate and for protection.

Stone Crabs: Only eat the claws of stone crabs. Grasp the crab from behind holding both claws. Firmly twist one claw down and away from the carapace, and the crab will likely release the claw on its own with a light "snap." Never take both claws or the crab can't defend itself. Toss the live crab back into the water to regrow another claw (in about a year).

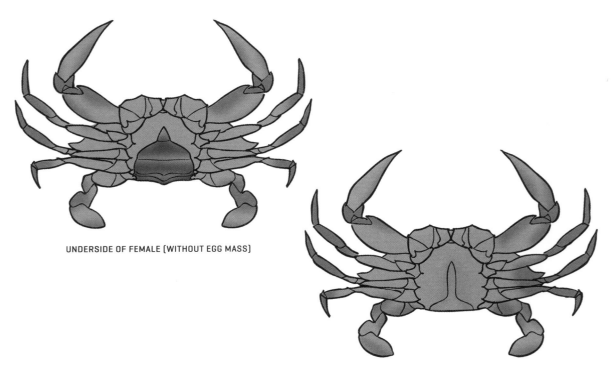

UNDERSIDE OF FEMALE (WITHOUT EGG MASS)

UNDERSIDE OF MALE

HOW TO KILL FISH AND CRUSTACEANS HUMANELY

Once you catch fish, shrimp, or crabs, what should you do with them? First of all, don't toss them on deck to let them writhe in agony. This not only fills them with pain; it flushes their flesh with stress-activated lactic acid and leaves a bad taste in the meat. If you aren't ready to kill your catch immediately, place it in aerated saltwater until you're ready, but don't wait too long.

- When live saltwater critters are put in freshwater, they suffer an awful death from osmotic shock.

- Keeping fish and crustaceans out of water suffocates them and can desiccate their meat.

- Saltwater without adequate aeration equals slow death.

Among the most humane courses of action is to ikijime, a technique of Japanese origin that literally means to "close the fish alive." The technique is to first stun and then spike the creature, and this varies by type of animal.

KILLING FISH HUMANELY

- First, sharply stun the fish with a blunt object to the head. Our expert Jimbo Meador calls this "a wood shampoo."

- Next, take a marlinspike, sharpened screwdriver, or a sharp, metal fish-killing tool of your choice, and drive it just behind and above the fish's eye. This will kill it.

- Next, make a "bleed cut." This starts at the heart, just behind the gills and in front of the pectoral fin, and finishes at the throat to hasten the outflow of blood and the toxins it carries.

- If you prefer, others argue that simply cutting the throat is the best way to dispatch a fish.

- After killing, immediately put fish in a slush of ice and saltwater to keep them fresh.

KILLING CRUSTACEANS HUMANELY

Never kill shellfish you plan to eat by simply dropping them alive into boiling water. As soon as possible after catching them (if not immediately), chill crustaceans in a saltwater-and-ice slurry (three parts ice to one part water) for at least twenty minutes to slow them to a torpor. Shrimp chilled in this way will eventually die. Large crustaceans like lobsters may need to go into a freezer until they are essentially immobile but not actually frozen.

To kill a lobster, flip the chilled lobster on its back. Using a large, very sharp knife, cut the lobster in half: Make the first cut from hind legs to head, and the second from abdomen to tail. Split the lobster and quickly remove the entire chain of nerves that run from antennae to tail.

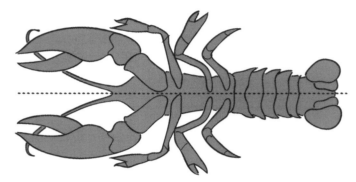

CUT ALONG CENTER BEFORE SPLITTING

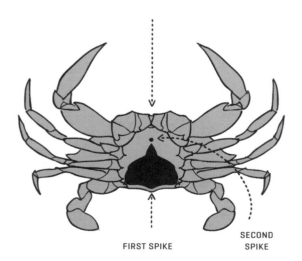

FIRST SPIKE

SECOND SPIKE

To kill a crab, flip the chilled crab on its back. Drive a sharp, heavy knife into the crab's head and abdomen (see diagram) to kill nerve ganglia. Spiking does not work on lobster because of their body-length nerves.

CATCH AND RELEASE AND CONTROVERSY: LETTING THEM GET AWAY

The goal of catch-and-release fishing is to allow fish to live while minimizing the suffering that fishing itself causes. This is, ostensibly, a humane approach, but opponents of the practice say that if you don't intend to catch and eat, then you shouldn't fish, since mortality rates are high for caught-and-released fish. For instance, Florida studies have shown that mouth-hooked fish have a 2 to 16 percent mortality rate, while gut-, gill-, and throat-hooked fish die at a 50 percent rate.

Follow these tips to release any caught fish for any reason. After all, you may unintentionally hook a protected fish or a roe-filled momma, and you'll want to set them free with the best chance of survival.

- Use appropriately sized hooks per species and size. We recommend using circle hooks, which hook fish in the lip rather than the gut.

- Best of all are barbless circle hooks, which dramatically reduce injury to fish (page 311).

- Work hooked fish to the boat as quickly as possible, so they're not exhausted and vulnerable to predators upon release.

- Wet your hands with saltwater before handling fish: Dry hands remove a fish's vital protective "slime layer," exposing them to parasites and infections.

- Keep fish in the water and remove the hook as delicately as possible—using a good set of hook-removing devices. If the fish swallows the hook, cut the line inside of the mouth and release the fish without removing the hook. If the fish is lucky, it will swallow the hook or the hook will rust away, allowing it to survive. If you suspect the fish is too injured, dispatch and eat it (provided it's of legal size and species).

- If you remove fish from the water (say, for a photo), do so as briefly as possible with a knot-free rubber net to protect the slime coat. Do not "lip" or grab fish by the lip, which can cause jaw damage.

- Revive exhausted fish, who sometimes can't even swim after being caught. Hold fish upstream or up current so that water flushes through the gills; if there's no current, push the fish back and forth through the water. Once it begins to thrash, let it go. If it doesn't swim after a few minutes, the fish will likely die, so consider keeping that fish to eat.

DEEPWATER FISH GET THE BENDS

Deepwater fish like grouper, snapper, and rockfish have an internal air bladder to maintain neutral buoyancy, but as they are reeled up, gases in their bodies can expand, and they may experience barotrauma—which is sort of like the bends that affects divers (page 280). A fish's stomach may balloon out of its mouth and the eyes bulge from the sockets. If handled properly, the fish can recover and be released. If not, it will likely float on the surface until it dies or another fish eats it.

To prevent this, the best approach is to slowly lower the fish in a "descending device" so it can recompress. There are hooks that do this, but the fish can still be eaten on the way down, so place the fish in a weighted upside-down milk crate or rubber basket to protect it. Lower it to the bottom. When the crate is raised, the fish swims free. Another technique, called "venting," uses a hypodermic needle to literally deflate the fish, but don't do this. Infection and death are likely results.

CLEAN, SCALE, AND **FILLET A FISH**

Most fish don't actually need to be filleted. If serving a fish whole, just scale it and remove the entrails. Even scaling isn't required for fish like salmon and trout, whose scales are tiny and easily digestible. The head should be savored—the cheek meat, which lies right behind the eye and the jaw's apex, is a delicacy. Then again, some fish are difficult or inconvenient to cook whole, such as dense-fleshed fish like grouper (which take expertise to cook evenly), while gurnard (aka "sea robin") and lionfish have spiny frames, bony heads, and nearly all the good meat is in the tail.

THE FIRST CUT: YOUR FILLET KNIFE

Fillet knives have long, thin blades, with a gentle curve from heel to tip. The pointed tip allows for the knife to cleanly puncture the fish's skin, while the gentle curvature of the blade allows for steady sweeping lateral cuts through soft flesh along the fish's spine.

Make sure your knife is very sharp. After use, clean, dry, and lightly brush the knife with vegetable oil to prevent corrosion, then keep the knife sheathed.

PREPARE THE FISH: SCALING AND GUTTING

Scaling can be performed with a scaler or a spoon. Scales dislodge faster when the fish is chilled. If you're preparing fresh-caught fish, and have killed them humanely (page 323), they should already be chilled. To scale, use a gentle scraping motion along the skin from the tail forward. It's tedious and messy, so do it outside.

Guts must be removed before cooking. Carefully cut into the vent, or the exit end of the fish, and cut toward the gills in a straight line. Be careful not to puncture any organs, since the release of fluids, especially urine, will tarnish the meat. Also, don't pop the membrane that separates the visceral cavity from the spinal cavity, which runs along the spine. Spinal fluids are pungent and can store toxins. Once the opening is large enough, grab the jaw, reach in, and yank everything out from the head toward the tail. Some organs will dislodge more easily than others, so gently sever holdouts with a knife, and then scrape the cavity gently with a spoon to fully clean. Next, behead the fish unless you're cooking it "head on." The organs and head make excellent garden compost.

Note that fish don't usually need to be gutted while you're still fishing so long as they are kept in icy saltwater. However, clean and gut fish before freezing or extended refrigeration. The exceptions are sharks and rays, which should be cleaned *immediately*. They literally pee inside themselves as they die, releasing ammonia into their flesh.

Once saltwater fish are scaled, gutted, and rinsed clean, soak them in lukewarm saltwater for about ten minutes, especially oily fish like bluefish or mackerel. Don't soak in freshwater (which can degrade the flesh). After soaking, pat the fish dry with a paper towel.

FILLET AND SKIN THE FISH

1. Place the fish on a flat, even surface, so that its back, or dorsal spines, are facing you.

2. Holding the knife horizontally, use the knife tip to pierce the skin just behind the head and along the spine, creating a single clean, head-to-tail cut. You can tell if you're running along the spine by the coarseness of the blade on vertebrae, but *don't cut the bones*, or you'll end up with rib bones in your fillets. Use a series of slow, gentle cuts, opening the fish a little more with each stroke.

3. Once you've cut deep enough to see the "frame" (or skeleton), make single-motion, sweeping cuts along the frame—near the fish's "shoulder," just behind its head. When you feel the knife come up against the rib bones, gently cut around them. Once you reach the end of the ribs, cut the fillet away from the ventral cavity. Gently scrape out any remaining gut material.

4. Keep making sweeping cuts from front to back, while leaving the fillet barely attached at the tail, which makes skinning the fillet easier.

5. Once the fillet is attached only to the tail, flip the fillet skin-side down. Starting from the tail, slide the knife between the meat and the skin. With a sharp knife, you can remove the skin with one single, slow motion. Run your fingers along the fillet: If you feel any bones, cut or pull them out. If you're unsure, alert dinner guests to watch for stray bones.

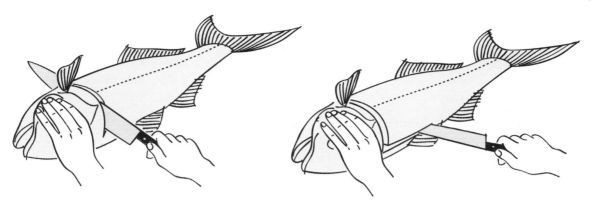

Pierce the skin behind the head.

Cut along the spine from head to tail.

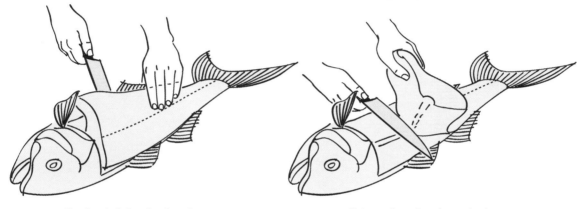

Cut along belly from head to tail.

Make small cuts from front to back to separate fillet from bones.

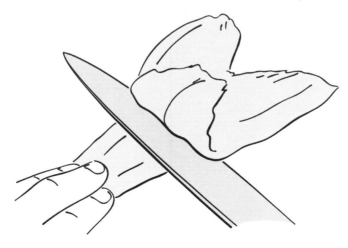

Remove the skin.

REMOVE THE BLOODLINE

Along their lateral lines, fish have a strip of dark meat often referred to as a "blood-line." Many people prefer to remove the bloodline in fillets, since bloodlines tend to give certain fish their undesirable "fishy" flavor. However, with oily fish like bluefish, mackerel, mahimahi, wahoo, and even tuna, removing the bloodline is necessary, since it's rich with mercury and other toxins, and it's the first part of the fish to spoil. It's also been linked to bacteria-borne scombroid poisoning.

To remove the bloodline, cut a triangular-shaped wedge into the dark meat that runs along the lateral lines, parallel to the spine. Depth and size differ in every fish; make slow cuts to ensure that you don't remove good flesh. Larger fish like tuna do tend to have very deep bloodlines.

FILLETING A FLATFISH

Flounder, fluke, sole, halibut, and others don't have rounded ribcages like sea bass and tuna, making them among the easiest fish to fillet. Using the knife tip, score the fish lengthwise down the back, along the center or spine line (there's actually a visible line). Score another two lines on either side of the head, forming a Y shape. Work the knife edgewise, parallel to the bones on one side of the scored line, and separate bones from meat. Repeat with the remaining meat on that side, flip fish over, and repeat, creating four fillets. Skin fillets if you like, but flounder and fluke skins have small scales, are full of vitamins, and are delightfully crispy when fried or broiled.

PREP WORK: COOK OR STORE FISH

What do you do if you mangle your fillet? Don't despair. Just adjust your preparation. Perhaps cut the fish into bite-size pieces, roll them in flour or douse them in batter, and pan fry. They'll make great fish tacos.

Once your fillets are trimmed up, pat them dry with a clean towel. Fresh fillets are good for about two days in the fridge; if they won't be eaten that soon, move to the freezer immediately. Freeze by either filling a Ziploc bag with freshwater and freezing the fish inside to prevent freezer burn, or just seal the bags tightly (ideally in a vacuum bag) and immediately freeze. Generally, fresh frozen fish will look and taste just as fresh a month later.

FISHING FROM A KAYAK OR S.U.P.

Fishing from a kayak or standup paddle-board (SUP) is arguably the most efficient way to fish in shallow water—especially in muddy areas. A SUP also allows "sight fishing," since you can see into the water. Just remember, fish can see you, too—especially if you're moving around.

There are dedicated fishing kayaks, but any sit-on-top kayak (10 to 12 feet long) will work. Choose a wide, stable, 11-foot-plus SUP for stability. A V-shaped nose will avoid slapping against waves and spooking fish (or point the board's tail into waves). Know how to operate your vehicle before fishing from it. Here's the essential gear:

- A clip or Velcro strap to attach the paddle to your waist. This allows sculling the SUP with one hand.

- A PFD.

- A surfboard leash around your ankle, in case you fall off. Wind can blow away boards and kayaks faster than you can swim.

- A basket of fishing gear and a cooler or basket for fish.

- A means of securing the rod to the board, like an attached tube or a clip.

- A small anchor, like a mushroom anchor or bag of lead shot. Hook to bow using a suction cup or attach to leash plug.

- Polarized sunglasses and a "longbill" cap to reduce glare and see better.

- A drogue—a small, submerged "parachute" or even a submerged bucket with handle—which drags behind to slow progress and orient bow into wind.

- Scoop net.

On a SUP, cast from the most comfortable, balanced position: seated, kneeling, or standing. If standing, keep feet wide apart and face forward or backward. If you hook a strong fish, sit with both legs over one side to keep from being dragged around. Watch out for sharks attracted to struggling fish.

Finally, be prepared to capsize. Outfitted with accouterments, fishing kayaks and SUPs can be ungainly to right, and you might get entangled in gear. Know how to release gear and let it go. Think twice about wearing waders. If they fill with water, you might go down without the ship.

POLE A BOAT AND GIG A FLOUNDER

Gigging means spearing fish—generally bottom fish. To gig flounder near shore requires a shallow-water skiff or Jon boat that can navigate "skinny water"—less than 2 feet deep. The right gig is also key. A mass-produced B&M gig has three steel prongs and a wooden handle. It resembles a long trident with barbs on the end to grip the fish.

Finally, daytime gigging is generally illegal because some bad apples will indiscriminately gig as they go, killing everything. Check local regulations. If illegal, fish at night, using copious artificial light (use generator-powered lights or hold 12-volt LED flashlights). Flounder usually move to shallower water during the night and it's easier to spot them in the dark anyway. Late spring to early fall (May-October) is your best bet.

POLING A BOAT

Poling is an essential skill. Learn the basics on a calm day with little current, always have a friend aboard, and wear PFDs. Flats poles are 12 to 20 feet long and have a broad, curved "foot" on one end for pushing through soft bottoms and a spike for control in rocky/hard bottoms.

1. Trim up the engine.

2. If the boat has a platform above the motor, stand atop it and lower the pole straight down. Push hand over hand slowly with the pole extending astern to propel the boat forward—like a Venetian gondolier. Keep the pole close to the stern while practicing to maintain balance. Lift the pole's "foot" and repeat. If the boat lacks a platform, lower the pole as close to the engine as possible on either side and slightly angle the pole to counter the boat's tendency to turn.

3. To turn, lower the pole and push more forcefully in the direction opposite your intended turn. The boat will pivot with the stern as fulcrum.

4. To stop, lower the pole from the stern, dig in the pole foot, and pull the boat back toward you—avoiding dragging to prevent seafloor damage. Or lower the pole well forward of the stern along starboard or port rail and carefully push against it. The boat will turn in the direction you're pushing.

GIGGING A FLOUNDER

Start on an outgoing to nearly dead low tide, since the rising tide will also unstick the boat if you become grounded. With gentle current or tide astern, cruise along the bank, poling to move or control the boat.

On the seafloor, flounder resemble a spade in a card deck. They will be camouflaged and perhaps semi-buried. Seek two beady eyes positioned on the same side of the head, rounding down to a triangular tail. They tend to leave a trail on the bottom that you can follow. Follow the line from a recently abandoned "flounder footprint."

As the pilot poles, the fisherman/navigator scans for fish. When a flounder is spotted, the fisherman shouts "watch out" to warn the pilot as they wield the gig. Ideally, try to measure the fish before you gig it, to abide by minimum-length regulations (14 inches is common).

Light refraction makes fish appear farther away, and the deeper the water, the greater the effect; the more "over the top" of the fish you are, the less refraction. General rule: Aim low.

The pivotal place to stab the fish is right through the gill plates, about 2 or 3 inches below the eyes. Jab hard. The platelets are hard and the barb will only stick if you puncture all the way through. Once the flounder is on the gig, pull up at a low angle and tilt the head of the fish toward the boat. If it's flopping wildly, move the fish over land and then into the boat. Dispatch the fish humanely with a quick "wood shampoo" (page 323).

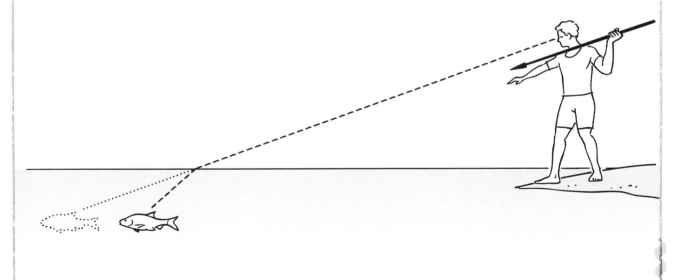

CATCH SHRIMP NEAR SHORE

Shrimp can be surprisingly easy to catch in near-shore waters, but offshore grounds are out of reach without a big deepwater trawler. As with crabbing, most regions strictly regulate time of year, method of catch, and quotas; get permits from your local fish and game department.

Fresh-caught live shrimp should be dumped immediately into an ice-and-saltwater slush. To store them, freeze in freshwater to prevent freezer burn. Cut the top off a gallon jug, fill it with water and unpeeled shrimp, and freeze. Ziploc bags can work, but sharp shrimp parts may puncture the plastic.

CAST NET AND SCOOP NET

The simplest method is to use a large scoop net wherever shrimp are running. One surefire place to find shrimp in season is around dock or pier pilings at night. Pole a boat or run a trolling motor against the current—moving slowly and using a light to see—and scoop.

Or, from a dock or beach, throw a ⅜-inch mesh cast net 6 to 8 feet long (which spreads to a 12-foot diameter); see "How to Throw a Cast Net" (page 336). From a dock, moving tidal water will carry shrimp into your zone. Along a beach, a slow, stealthy approach along a sandy shoreline and a bunch of casts might eventually net you a cooler full of dinner.

"Deep-hole casting" is a tried-and-true method in murky waters with estuarine tidal flows (common in the Southeastern United States), where deep spots are created by swirling currents at the junctions of tidal creeks. You must modify the net—so it holds open during deep descent—by "sandwiching" a line of duct tape around the full circumference at the base of the net a few inches above the weights. Don't tape the draw strings. Use a depth finder to discover the holes, cast the net, let it settle to the bottom, and haul it in.

POLING FOR SHRIMP

To pole for shrimp, you need a boat, a cast net, five to ten bamboo or PVC poles to mark your bait locations, and bait balls (or patties). You can deploy the poles anytime, but dusk is often best. To make bait balls, combine fish meal or fishy cat food with marsh mud; ideally, make them ahead and freeze, so they thaw and dissolve slowly in the water.

Along a shore swept by tidal currents, place the poles along a stream bank 15 to 20 feet apart (starting at a lower tide), then place two or three bait balls around 6 feet from the down-current side of each pole. As the balls break down, the scent attracts the shrimp. Be careful not to disturb bait balls.

After thirty minutes or so, return to the first pole, cast the net over the bait ball location, and repeat until you reach your last pole.

SEINE NETTING OR TRAWLING

Essentially, two people walk down a sandy shore during a moving tide with a rectangular seine net attached to two poles for handles. The seine net has small floats at the top and weights at the bottom. As you walk along the shore and against the tide, shrimp are swept into the net. Wear shoes and gloves to protect against sharp shells and jellyfish. White shrimp will jump over a seine net, so you'll need a taller net with a deeper, recessed bag. If there's a current of 2+ knots, just anchor the two net poles in the mud or sand for an hour and let the tidal current work for you. When the net fills, bring its poles ashore to trap your catch while leaving the center in the water. Keep the shrimp and release other critters.

HOW TO THROW A CAST NET

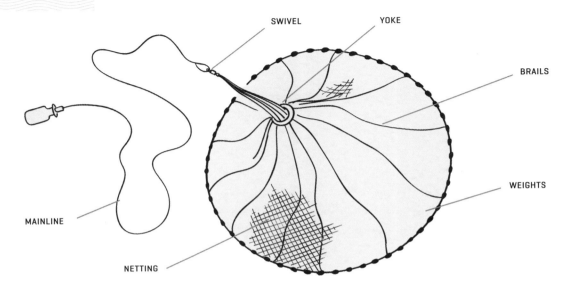

A cast net will catch you a cooler full of shrimp, a bucket of baitfish, or a nice supply of tasty crabs. There are many different throwing methods, but this one works well regardless of the radius of your net. Our expert, Jimbo Meador, has been slinging nets for seventy years. He suggests practicing on dry land for a while, since this time-honored skill, like casting a fly rod, doesn't come immediately. But don't be discouraged. As he says, "Your second hundred tosses will be better than your first hundred."

A net has the following parts:

- **Main rope or line:** Keeps the net attached to your body.

- **Swivel:** Attaches the main line to the brails, allows the net to spin.

- **Horn or yoke:** A loop of plastic or even bone that helps the net deploy and avoid tangles.

- **Brails:** Thicker monofilament lines that attach the main line to the net's monofilament.

- **Netting:** The woven monofilament that actually holds your catch.

- **Weights:** Lead or steel weights strung through the base of the net to enable it to be cast and sink over your quarry.

HOW TO CAST

For beginners, Jimbo Meador recommends using a 6- to 7-foot-radius cast net with a ¼-inch mesh size. Be sure you have the wind at your back, you're wearing something you don't mind getting wet and dirty, and you're clear of obstructions that could hang up the net.

PREPARING THE NET

- Loop the line around your wrist to prevent losing the net.

- Spool the main line into loose coils and hold in the same hand.

- Straighten the net so that the horn/yoke is at the top of the swivel.

- Gather the net, folding it over halfway, making a single loop slightly larger in diameter than the line coils. For longer nets, make more loops.

BITING AND HOLDING: PREPARING TO CAST

- Along the base of the net, gently bite a spot next to a weight.

- Shift the body of the net over the arm holding the line, so that roughly half of the weighted net is over your arm.

- In your other hand, grasp a segment of the net's base that's roughly an arm's length from your bite, and let about two feet of net hang below that hand.

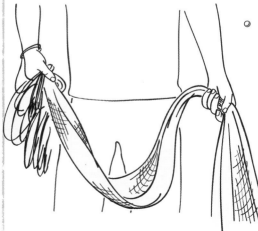

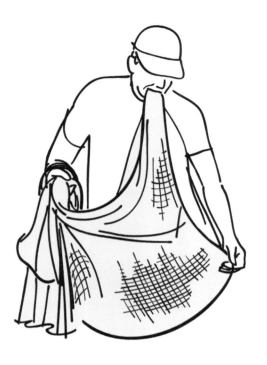

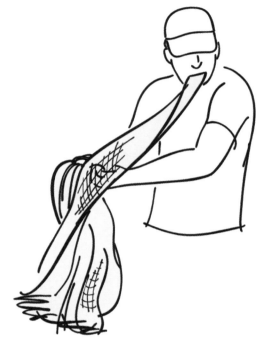

CASTING THE NET

- Twist your upper body backward, bringing the net back in preparation to throw.

- Twist forward, releasing the net in a circular motion, while keeping your feet planted; don't spin. You don't need to throw it very hard. It's more of a flipping-outward motion.

- At the top of the throw, open your mouth to release the base of the net.

- Follow this by releasing the forward hand holding the weighted base.

- As the net unfurls, release the net and the line in the other hand.

REELING IN YOUR CATCH

Before hauling in, let the net settle on the bottom if casting in shallow water, otherwise let it sink enough to surround the school.

- Take in the line, allowing the horn to slide down the brails until it bottoms out.

- Hold up the weighted end of net (higher than the catch) and place the weighted end inside a bucket or cooler. Otherwise, your catch will spill out and flop around the dock.

- Slide up the horn to loosen the weighted base and empty your catch.

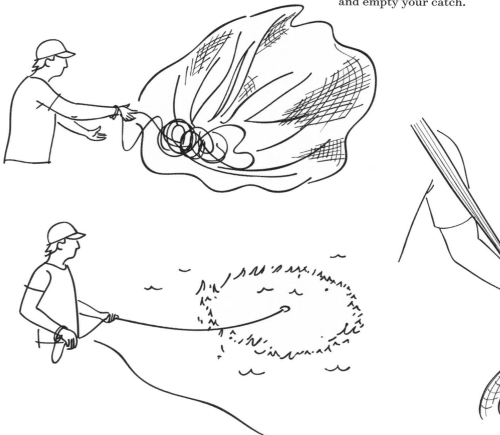

FISHING SPOTS AND TECHNIQUES

Every spot on and near the ocean has its own fishing techniques, but no location is foolproof. If the fish aren't biting, move on. That is, unless catching an actual fish would disrupt your meditative peacefulness.

Surf fishing: Fish around back eddies, jetties, and "sloughs." Deeper rip currents are conveyor belts for smaller prey and make a veritable buffet for predatory fish. Use longer fishing rods (9 feet and up) and reels equipped with extra line. Use pyramid sinkers heavy enough to keep your baited hook in place on the seafloor, and try casting and setting baits in different parts of a known deep hole. Finally, keep your eyes on the ocean for rogue waves (page 104).

Pier fishing: Piers offer some of the best opportunities for shore-bound anglers. Protruding beyond the waves, they extend the angler's reach. As you fish beyond the breakers and in and around pilings using larger bait, you have the potential for larger catches of pelagic fish. Use a flying gaff hook or scoop net to safely raise and land fish from a height. Also, be aware of neighboring anglers: Don't fish too close to others to avoid tangling with or hitting neighbors with your casts.

Marsh fishing: Marshes are best at low tide, when fish have no choice but to congregate in whatever water is left, often providing the angler their best advantage. Structures—anything from oyster beds to docks and shipwrecks—are aggregation sites (no matter the tide), along with drop-offs along banks and within deeper channels. To cover more ground, assess areas more easily, and approach fish without spooking them, fish shallow marshes from a kayak or SUP (page 331).

Mangrove fishing: Mangroves are nurseries of the sea. Inside their tangled jungle gym of roots lie juvenile schools of many tropical fishes and invertebrates, including snapper, spiny lobster, and sea snails. Meanwhile, along mangrove edges, predators lurk, seeking an easy meal. Since mangroves are delicate ecosystems and critical to many species, fish responsibly and conservatively. In fact, mangrove fish tend to be exceptionally wary. Fish similar to marshes, and use heavy monofilament or braided line that can withstand being wrapped around and pulled through roots and branches.

Deep-sea or bottom fishing: Successful bottom fishing requires knowledge of the geographical contours of the seafloor, either by way of GPS coordinates, dead reckoning from a chart, or your eyeballs. Fish as vertically as possible to ensure a good hook set and to prevent snagging. Use the least amount of weight possible, since fish can be suspicious of curiously heavy bait. Since snags are common, use a monofilament or fluorocarbon leader that will break off on the bottom. Be aware of, and be prepared to help, any caught fish suffering from barotrauma (page 326).

Pelagic fishing: Trolling for pelagic (open-ocean-swimming) fish is popular, especially when sailing. A short "boat pole" and a conventional reel spooled with thick or wire line is favored. Live-bait fishing around aggregation sites (like wrecks or seamounts) and "running and gunning"—that is, chasing surface-schooling fish and casting artificial lures—are other popular methods. That said, trolling can be tedious, since the open ocean is a vast desert. Look for any potential refuge fish might use, even random floating objects like derelict buoys. Converging currents are also places where life gathers.

EIGHT PLACES TO FISH
BEFORE YOU DIE

Cook Inlet, Kenai Peninsula, Alaska: The snow-capped mountains and taiga forests surrounding shimmering Cook Inlet create a superlative landscape. The summertime quarry is salmon, and your fishing partners are black or brown bears. Land the right outfitter, and you'll cast from a boat near mother bears teaching their cubs to fish. Don't argue if momma decides the sockeye you just hooked is hers.

Mayaguana, Bahamas: This easternmost Bahamian Island is a true outer Caribbean outpost—a sleepy paradise inhabited by around three hundred people. Access is via private boat, Bahamian mailboat, or small plane. Aside from mangroves, flocks of flamingos, and world-class diving, Mayaguana offers the best fly-casting for bonefish on Earth. Hire a guide to reach the "secret spots," but the miles-wide flats of gin-clear waters make excursions entirely doable. A patient, dawn patrol wading session might be rewarded by a tailing ten-pounder inhaling your shrimp or crab fly.

Cortes Bank, International Waters: A hundred miles due west of San Diego, Cortes Bank is an ancient seamount that holds the outermost kelp forest along the Pacific Coast. Winds this far out can blow hard for weeks; the best bet for calm is midfall to early winter, when massive high-pressure systems bring coastal heat waves. Cortes's shallow waters teem with massive schools of baitfish, which feed rockfish, lingcod, and huge schools of yellowtail, while bonito, bluefin tuna, and other pelagics cruise close by. Time your trip right, and you might see Cortes Bank's world-record wave break—a genuine wonder of the world.

Great Astrolabe Reef, Fiji: One of the world's largest barrier reefs, the 40-mile-long Great Astrolabe Reef (different from New Zealand's Astrolabe Reef) lines Fiji's Kadavu and Ono Islands. The depths outside the reef are a breeding ground for large pelagics and game fish, including marlin, tuna, and wahoo. As a result, certain sections, such as the Naiqoro Passage, are protected and require an entry fee. Inside the reef, anglers find a teaming cornucopia of gargantuan reef fish, including grouper and snapper.

COOK INLET

Ascension Bay, Mexico: Made famous by baseball legend Ted Williams, Mexico's Ascension Bay is an obligatory pilgrimage for avid fly anglers looking for the elusive grand slam—that is, to catch a bonefish, permit, tarpon, and snook all in the same day. Backing up into the Sian Ka'an Biosphere, Ascension Bay is a rugged middle-of-nowhere spot, so stock up in Cancun or Playa Del Carmen on your way from the airport. Apart from a few lodges and ma-and-pop restaurants, Punta Allen, the main outpost, is just a sleepy spit of sand with miles of golden sand flats, clusters of mangroves, and azure Caribbean waters.

Isla Mujeres, Mexico: Every winter from January through March, sailfish, along with occasional white marlin, gather in the Caribbean around Isla Mujeres off Cancun. Schools of sailfish congregate around "baitballs," or tightly formed schools of sardines. These congregations offer light tackle and fly anglers a unique chance at sight-fishing these vibrant, acrobatic billfish. Note that live-bait fishing is illegal here, as is casting gear (apart from fly rods), since both give the angler an unfair advantage.

Nantucket, Massachusetts: Between spring and fall along New England's coast, migrations of game fish like striped bass, bluefish, false albacore, and bluefin tuna all school en masse in pursuit of herring, menhaden, sand eels, and smaller prey. Along the sand flats of Nantucket Island, anglers can cast to striped bass and bluefish from shallow-draft skiffs, an experience not unlike bonefishing in the Bahamas. Since drastic tides can be dangerous, fish with a local or hire a guide.

Hervey Bay, Australia: Hervey Bay, along Australia's Northeast coast, is one of the few places where marlin and sailfish can be seen on the flats just yards from the beach. They're only juveniles, but still. Part of Fraser Island, a World Heritage Site, Hervey Bay also hosts an array of cold- and warm-water species, including longfin tuna, trevally, and grouper, which can all be caught on light tackle.

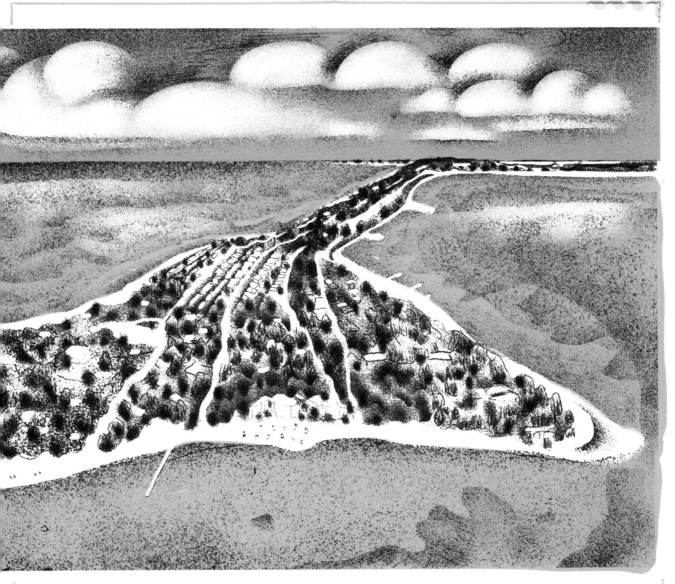

ISLA MUJERES

SELECTED EXPERTS AND SOURCES

In addition to the individuals whose names you've read throughout the chapters in this book, we're eternally grateful to the following for their facts, insights, and wisdom.

Alaska Marine Safety Association

Alaska Sea Grant, University of Alaska, Fairbanks

Shawn Alladio is a wonderwoman and the director of K38 Rescue.

American Academy of Family Physicians

American Museum of Natural History

American Red Cross

The American Sailing Association

Berkeley Wellness

The Boat Owners Association of the United States

Chris Brown is captain of the NOAA and South Carolina Department of Natural Resources vessel, R/V *Palmetto*, Charleston, SC.

Jenny Brown is Queen Wahine at the Shaka Surf School, Folly Beach, SC.

Steven Callahan is the author of *Adrift: 76 Days Lost at Sea*.

Centers for Disease Control and Prevention

Chapman School of Seamanship

Cleveland Clinic

Sean Collins is a late, great wave researcher and forecaster, and was the founder of Surfline.

Bill Dance is a master and commander Southern fisherman.

Dr. Alyssa DiRienzo, ND. North Bend, Washington State. www.drdirienzo.com.

Divers Alert Network

Clayton Everline is co-author of *Surf Survival: The Surfer's Health Handbook*.

Florida Fish and Wildlife Conservation Commission

Florida Keys National Marine Sanctuary

Florida's Poison Control Centers

The Get Bear Smart Society

John Gookin is a backcountry lightning-risk management expert at The National Outdoor Leadership School.

Tristan Gooley is the author of *How to Read Water*.

Bates Hagood is a journalist and the manager of the Ocean Surf Shop, Folly Beach, SC. www.oceansurfshop.com.

Joshua Hall is the outdoor program manager of Charleston County Parks and Recreation and an American Canoe Association Level 5 instructor.

Guy Harvey is a legendary fisherman, conservationist, and artist.

Shane Helm is the former director of Rip Curl and developer of the Rip Curl GPS surf watch.

Frances and Michael Howorth are the authors of *The Sea Survival Manual*.

John "Hub" Hubbard is chief wetsuit designer at Patagonia.

Captain Jim Hughes is a WWII-era Merchant Marine and mentor of Owen James Burke.

International Coral Reef Society

Richard "Buffalo" Keaulana is an iconic Hawaiian waterman and lifeguard descended directly from King Kamehameha.

Louisiana Sea Grant, Louisiana State University

Maryland Department of Natural Resources

Maryland School of Sailing

Mayo Clinic

Tim McConnell and Justin Torrance are boat whisperers at Cove 2 Coast Marine, Charleston, SC.

Dr. Pauline Meekins is an emergency room physician and a badass extraordinaire.

Captain Cargall Michael is the author of *The Captain's Guide to Liferaft Survival*.

Captain William Miller is the owner of the Charleston Sailing School in Charleston, SC.

Monterey Bay Aquarium Seafood Watch

Andrew Nathanson is co-author *Surf Survival: The Surfer's Health Handbook.*

National Ag Safety Database

The National Aquarium (U.S.)

The National Center for Biotechnical Information

National Oceanic and Atmospheric Administration Coral Health and Disease Program

National Weather Service National Oceanic and Atmospheric Administration

National Weather Service Southern Region Headquarters

Nature Foundation of St. Maarten

New Zealand Maritime Museum

NOAA's Atlantic Oceanographic and Meteorological Laboratory

North Carolina State University Extension

Israel Paskowitz is a surf teacher and the director of Surfers Healing.

Arnold Postell is a shark expert and a senior biologist and dive safety officer at the South Carolina Aquarium.

Mark Renneker is co-author *Surf Survival: The Surfer's Health Handbook.*

Charles Ricks was a lifelong fisherman and is the venerable late grandfather of author Chris Dixon.

Dougal Robertson is the author of *Sea Survival: A Manual.*

Royal Society for the Prevention of Cruelty to Animals

San Francisco Maritime National Park Association

SHARKPROJECT International

Tim Sherer is the stoke broker at the Goofy Foot Surf School, Maui, Hawaii.

South Carolina Department of Natural Resources

Surfline.com

Tsunami.gov

Tsunamizone.org

UCLA Center for East-West Medicine

United Kingdom National Health Service

United States Coast Guard

United States Environmental Protection Agency

University of Florida Wildlife Ecology and Conservation Department

University of Maryland Medical Center

The U.S. Environmental Protection Agency

The U.S. Food and Drug Administration

The U.S. Geological Survey

The U.S. National Institutes of Health

The U.S. National Parks Service

Robert "Wingnut" Weaver is the author of *Wingnut's Complete Surfing.*

Sterling and Wayland Windham are flounder gigging and flatwater poling authorities.

Jonathan White is a sailor and conservationist, and is the author of *Tides: The Science and Spirit of the Ocean.*

Dr. Christy Wilcox is the author of *Venomous: How Earth's Deadliest Creatures Mastered Biochemistry.*

Miranda Wilson is a wetsuit repair specialist at Patagonia.

Rick Wilson is a senior staff scientist at The Surfrider Foundation.

John "Lofty" Wiseman is the author of *SAS Survival Handbook.*

Roger Wood is director of research at the Wetlands Institute.

Dr. Angel Yanagihara is a jellyfish expert and faculty member at the University of Hawaii at Manoa.

5 Gyres Institute

ABOUT THE ARTISTS

Frida Clements is a Seattle-based illustrator known for her nature-inspired screen-printed music posters and art prints. More of her work can be found at www.fridaclements.com.
Pages 147–149, 151, 163–165, 171, 177, 189, 205, 207, 209

Francisco Fonseca, also known as Francis.co, is an illustrator and street artist based in Porto, Portugal. His artwork is strongly inspired by his surroundings, and exploring outside is the most important part of his creation. Having recently completed his master's degree in drawing and printmaking at the Fine Arts University of Porto, Francisco has now embarked on a full-time illustration career.
Pages iii, 1, 87, 141, 191, 259, 297

AJ Hansen is a San Francisco native practicing graphic design in New York. Her work bridges novel production methods, unique material experiences, and narrative fiction.
Pages 13, 27, 62, 76–78, 154, 159, 172–183, 194, 239, 240, 262–263, 313

Ricardo Hernandez is a Miami-born illustrator currently living in Austin, TX. He attended Pratt Institute in Brooklyn, NY, and has work spanning an array of mediums, including children's books, editorial illustration, event merchandise, and film posters. www.ricardodiseno.com.
Pages 5, 7, 12, 15, 19, 34, 37, 41, 53, 61, 67, 96, 108–109, 111, 155, 227, 242, 249–251, 265–268, 270, 292–293, 295, 307–309, 311, 316–317, 335, 342, 345

Arthur Mount is an artist and illustrator. Since 1995, he has illustrated more than thirty-five books. His editorial clients include the *New York Times*, *GQ*, *Wired*, and *Dwell*. He recently completed building his house on the Central California Coast. www.arthurmount.com.
Pages 25, 28–31, 38, 43–47, 49, 52, 64–65, 79, 82–83, 105, 114–117, 119–120, 135, 153, 180, 182, 196–200, 204, 210, 212, 235, 264, 274–277, 314–315, 319, 322–324, 329, 333, 336–339

Christina Sun is an artist who has always lived by water and worked on small boats. She draws ships, sea creatures, sailors, and teapots. Passionate about open-water swimming, she teaches swimming (when possible) in Long Island Sound and the waters of the North Fork of Long Island, NY, where she lives.
Pages 84–85

Kat Yao is a Taiwanese-American illustrator and designer living in the Bay Area. She creates drawings that tell stories. See more of her work at www.katyao.com.
Pages 9, 14, 26, 58–59, 68, 69–74, 124–128, 216–218, 221, 246, 271, 300–306, 312

OUR CONTRIBUTORS

Carolyn Sotka is a marine biologist, ocean policy expert, science communicator, writer, and photographer  driven to share stories about the intersection of culture, society, science, and ocean conservation. This passion has led her and her family to remote islands and wild coasts around the world, and more than forty countries. She is co-author of *The Death and Life of Monterey Bay: A Story of Revival*, a nonfiction bestseller that continues to inspire positive conservation action throughout the Monterey Bay. Carolyn has helped build conservation programs for the New England Aquarium and COMPASS (Communication Partnership for Science and the Sea); for Duke University, Stanford University, and the College of Charleston; and in government with the National Oceanic and Atmospheric Administration (NOAA). Carolyn leads science communication classes and training workshops at professional, graduate, and undergraduate levels. She lives in Charleston, South Carolina. Visit www.carolynsotka.com to learn more.

Surfer, free diver, spearfisherman, and aquatic entrepreneur **Brian Lam** was a key inspiration for this book. Before founding the titanic website Wirecutter,  Brian did time in the digital trenches at *Wired* and *Gizmodo* as an editor. He also founded the blog The Scuttlefish, whose motto was "Love the Ocean, Wish You Were Here." He's fielded angry phone calls from Steve Jobs and did time beneath the sea with Sylvia Earle in *Aquarius*, the last remaining undersea research lab. "Diving down to it is like falling slowly into another world," he wrote. "I wish I could live there. The fish would be my neighbors. The sky would always be blue—if a little wet. And, instead of a stroll, I'd just go for a swim."

Owen James Burke grew up on, in, and around the murky brown waters of Long Island Sound, where he  worked on fishing boats and spent any free time he had aboard his fishing skiff, *Blues Dory*. A founding writer for Wirecutter and The Scuttlefish, he has searched for waves in and guided surfers and fishermen from Myanmar to Morocco to Fiji. Burke currently, and perhaps bafflingly, resides in New York City, where he is a freelance writer, fleeing at every opportunity to spend time in, on, under, and around the sea chasing fish, waves, and stories.

Captain Jimbo Meador is a certified Master  Naturalist. Hailing from Mobile Bay, Alabama, he has nearly eighty years of experience fishing, hunting, shrimping, and guiding along the waters of Mobile Bay, the Caribbean, and the Gulf of Mexico. He has run tug boats, shrimp boats, and commercial fishing boats, and has worked as a fly-casting master instructor for the Orvis Company. In the early 1990s, Meador's voice was recorded by a dialect coach for Paramount Pictures and used to develop Tom Hanks's southern accent for the film *Forrest Gump*. He counts the likes of Tom McGuane, Jimmy Buffett, and the late, great Winston Groom as good friends (some even posit that his maverick life on Mobile Bay was an inspiration for Groom's *Forrest Gump*). His writing and musings have been published in *Garden & Gun*, *Sports Afield*, and the *New York Times*. Take a watery tour with this legendary waterman through Jimbo's Delta Excursions.

To our wives, Quinn Dixon and Carla Spencer, without whose sweet support and forbearance this book would not exist. To all of our beloved kids—may your adventures always be amazing. And to Mr. Herman Melville, in token of our admiration for his genius.

Chris Dixon and Jimmy Buffett, Montauk, NY

ACKNOWLEDGEMENTS

The authors would above all like to thank their parents, who took them on their first nautical adventures. We're also extremely grateful to agent Meg Thompson and Chronicle Books editors Steve Mockus, Juliette Capra, Jeff Campbell, and Sarah Malarkey, along with Brooke Johnson, Jon Glick, Tera Killip, and Steve Kim, all of whom helped us realize our creative vision. Chris's mother, Gloria Ricks Taylor, pitched in whenever we needed it, and brainstorms with Jimmy Buffett helped shape this book and determine the experts with whom we collaborated. Our sincerest thanks to you all.

ABOUT THE AUTHORS

Chris with his wife, Quinn, and their kids, Lucy and Fritz

CHRIS DIXON is the author of *Ghost Wave* and a contributing author of *Surfing: 1778–Today*, *The Big Juice*, and *New York Times* best seller *The Southerner's Handbook*. His writing has appeared in *The New York Times*, *The Washington Post*, *Outside*, *Popular Mechanics*, *Garden & Gun*, and *Men's Health*, among others. The founding online editor of *Surfer*, he once spent a year documenting the life of singer-songwriter Jimmy Buffett. He lives in Charleston, South Carolina, with his family.

Jeremy with one of his three daughters, Daphne (photo by Carla Spencer)

JEREMY K. SPENCER is an award-winning writer and editor whose work has appeared in publications such as *Men's Journal*, *Wired*, *Vice*, *The Millions*, and *Outside*, where he was a longtime senior editor. He has edited multiple *New York Times* best sellers and, as a creative director, has helped dozens of top global brands tell their stories. A native of Memphis, Tennessee, he now lives with his family in Portland, Oregon.